The Roots of Sorrow

The Roots of Sorrow
Reflections on Depression and Hope

Richard Winter

CROSSWAY BOOKS • WESTCHESTER, ILLINOIS
A DIVISION OF GOOD NEWS PUBLISHERS

For Jane, Johanna, Matthew
Rebecca and Triona
who give me great joy
—that they may have hope
in a world where
there is much sorrow

First printing USA edition, 1986.

Cover Revision by K. L. Mulder.

Printed in the United States of America.

Library of Congress Catalog Card Number 85-72916

ISBN 0-89107-383-3

'Cans't thou not minister to a mind diseas'd,
Pluck from the memory a rooted sorrow,
Raze out the written troubles of the brain,
And with some sweet oblivious antidote
Cleanse the stuff'd bosom of that perilous stuff
Which weighs upon the heart?'
Macbeth Act V. iii.

'I will make the Valley of Trouble a door of hope,
Then she will sing as in the days of her youth.'
Hosea 2. 15.

'Sorrowful, yet always rejoicing.'
2 Corinthians 6. 10

Acknowledgements

This book could not have been written without the constant encouragement, patience and help of my wife and children. It would also not have been written without the initial encouragement and constructive criticism of a friend and neighbour, David Porter. As it grew, at first in my mind, and then on paper, many others have contributed ideas and criticism. My thanks to Dr. Monty Barker who initially encouraged me into psychiatry and taught me well. Thanks too to Dr. Francis Schaeffer who prepared me for the battle of ideas and world-views that I encountered in the arena of psychiatry and who also gave me a deep respect for the relevance, authority and trustworthiness of Scripture in relation to the whole of life. I am indebted to the Christian psychiatrists group in Bristol, the Care and Counsel Study and Research group and to my dear friends and colleagues at the English L'Abri with whom I have shared and explored these ideas. Thanks also to Adrienne, Marion, Monty, Daphne, Birdie and Mary for their helpful criticism of the manuscript. And those who have bravely and kindly given me permission to share their pain with others may never know how much it means to readers to know that others have been that way before. I am deeply grateful to Christine and especially Pam Hendry who have spent many long hours patiently typing and correcting the manuscript. And finally I know that my parents have contributed much to this book through their love and encouragement in my early years and in their faithful example of living out the truth of the Christian hope in a broken world.

Richard Winter
January 1985
All quotations and references used with kind permission from the publishers.

Contents

PREFACE

Talking with a friend the other day about his feelings of depression and despair, we found that after an hour we had crossed the boundaries of many disciplines – medicine, psychiatry, psychology, counselling, sociology, philosophy and theology. We talked about his father's and grandfather's history of depression and their need for treatment in hospital, his reaction to the loss of his mother when he was ten years old, his ways of expressing his anger towards his father, his responsibility for his moods, and his questions about the purpose of life and why God allows such suffering. In the experience of depression these questions are no longer academic. They are grounded in the reality of day to day life.

One of my greatest concerns in the last ten years has been to understand the relevance of these disciplines and the wealth of information that comes from them. From a Christian perspective many psychological systems (such as Freudianism, or Behaviourism) can be seen to be partial truths which have been accepted by many as the whole truth about man. It is only with a clear understanding of the Christian framework that we can separate what is true from what is false. I have tried, as far as possible, to translate some of the jargon of the specialists into everyday language and to bring together some of the insights of science and psychotherapy within a biblical framework. For some there are chapters that will be too complicated, for others chapters that are too simple.

In Part I, Chapters 1-5, I have explored different factors that make some people more vulnerable to depression than others. For example, loss of parents or rejection in childhood, an inherited biological tendency, a lack of purpose in life, and involvement in the occult. On their own these factors may give the impression that anyone who is depressed is a victim of circumstances and without any responsibility for their own state of mind, but the final chapter in Part I explores the importance of our inner attitudes and values and how they shape our response to the things that happen to us. In Part II, Chapter 7 looks at some of the ways in which psychiatrists and counsellors have begun to attempt to deal with psychological problems. It also demonstrates some of the common ground that exists between Christians and non-Christians in counselling and psychotherapy – as well as some of the differences. Chapters 8, 9 and 10 deal with the question of determinism and freedom. How much are we victims of circumstances? How do we come to terms with bad things that have happened in childhood? How much can we change? In Part III, Chapter 11-13 looks at four specific areas commonly associated with depression; anger, guilt, low self esteem, and bereavement, and begins to explore the factors that bring about healing of depression which are taken up more fully and practically in Part IV. The final chapter shows how a biblical perspective on life is important in reducing vulnerability to depression and giving a basis for hope.

You may attempt to read this book, or give it to a friend, thinking that it will solve the problems of deep depression. You (or they), if in such a state, would probably only manage a few chapters. It is written primarily for those who are slipping down into depression or for those who are climbing out the other side. I hope it will also be a help to prevent some from going beyond the usual 'ups and downs' of life, and others who have experienced deeper depression, to resist its advances. It is for those (probably most of us) who find themselves vulnerable to depression and want to find ways of resisting the slippery slopes and vicious circles of confused emotions. For those who offer comfort and counsel to the depressed it should help to provide a framework and perspective within which to evaluate the causes of depression and then bring healing and hope.

The reader will find that I have frequently referred to 'counselling and psychotherapy' together under the general heading of 'talking treatments'. Although there is considerable overlap between the two I would see them on a continuum from simple supportive counselling (just listening to someone's trouble over a cup of tea) to in-depth psychotherapy which has the aim of major personality change and reconstruction.

Some of the personal examples I have used are based on real situations but names and some details have been changed. Other letters and stories have been used with permission.

All Biblical quotations are from the New International Version unless otherwise indicated.

PART I

CHAPTER ONE

'That perilous stuff which weighs upon the heart'

The experience of depression

Julia sat opposite me, staring at the floor. She spoke in a quiet monotone, but only when I asked her a question. Occasionally she smiled, but it was an empty expression for her eyes betrayed a deep sadness and perplexity. She could dimly remember times when life had seemed different, when life seemed to have some colour. Now she pushed herself from one day to the next. The office work was the one thing that kept her going and provided a temporary relief from the negative thoughts of the lonely hours before dawn or the long evenings wandering listlessly around the house, or sitting blankly in front of the television. What was wrong with her, she wondered? What had gone wrong? Surely no one else was as hopeless or incompetent as she was.

Julia did not realise that she was in good company with Isaac Newton, Beethoven, Darwin, Van Gogh, Tolstoy, Spurgeon and many others who suffered from severe depression at some time in their lives. Yet, among most people, the subject is often veiled in silence, disapproval or suspicion. Many, like Tony Lewis, speak of their shame at being depressed:

> Until I became ill I had neither experienced mental illness nor observed it in others. I knew of a few

people who had mental breakdowns but the term meant nothing to me. If anything I looked down on 'them' as being weak, spineless people society would do well rid of. When a psychiatrist told me I was mentally ill, I was horrified. I felt ashamed of being ill – guilty, even. I told a constant stream of lies to cover up my visits to psychiatrists, my hospital attendances and my reasons for not being a student or holding down a proper job . . . To feel a slow poison paralyse every faculty, to become gradually more and more helpless, and not to know how or why . . . My own depressive illness grew from something mild and infrequent into a brutal scourge I believed I could escape only through death.[1]

One in every seven people, and three times as many women as men, will at some time in their lives have such an experience. Severe depression is being recognised as one of the major health concerns of this century, affecting somewhere between one and two million people in the world. The World Health Organization is giving the subject top priority in the 1980's. In terms of lost production, it is estimated that it costs the world fifty billion pounds every year.

Each year, one adult in 250 attempts suicide and about one in 10,000 succeeds. In more than two out of three suicides, depression that could have been helped by some sort of treatment may have been a contributing factor. In this country and in the U.S.A. and Canada suicide is now the second most common cause of death after accidents in the 15 to 34 year old group.

Depression is common in every culture and many of the expressions used throughout the world describe it in similar graphic terms. The Dutch talk about being 'fed up,' 'beaten down,' or 'sitting down with the luggage.' In Ghana, 'the heart is hidden in a case.' In Arabic, the 'heart is closed.' We talk about 'the blues,' being 'down in the dumps,' 'fed up,' and 'lifeless.'

The word 'depression' is used to cover a whole range of feelings, from a fleeting sense of unhappiness to profound, enduring, suicidal hopelessness. The ups and downs of each day are usually related to the frustrations or disappointments of normal life. Sometimes a sense of dejection colours our thoughts and activities for hours, or even days, as we come to terms with the loss of a job, a broken relationship, disappointment at lack of promotion at work, a failed exam, or the frustration of plans foiled by unexpected circumstances. For some, moods change with dramatic speed and intensity for all to see! Others, more placid by temperament, experience little variation in mood. Most of us live behind a mask. Only our closest friends know how we really feel.

Severe depression

Because the word depression is used in so many different ways, it is important to distinguish between passing moods of sadness or frustration and a permanent depressive attitude to life, or serious depression, both of which needs some sort of help or treatment. Aaron Beck, a famous psychiatrist, writes of the 'central core' of severe depression as being a state of mind where 'the self seems worthless, the outer world meaningless and the future hopeless.' A friend described it as 'the past is terrible, the future worse!' There is 'a loss of interest in things and people normally dear and exciting,'[2] – an inability to enjoy anything. Sylvia Plath describes this in her book *The Bell Jar*. Esther, a young journalist has just won a fashion magazine contest:

> . . . I wasn't steering anything, not even myself. I just bumped from my hotel to work and to parties and from parties to my hotel and back to work like a numb

trolley bus. I guess I should have been excited the way most of the other girls were, but I couldn't get myself to react. I felt very still and very empty, the way the eye of a tornado must feel, moving dully along in the midst of a surrounding hullabaloo.[3]

Or William Cowper, the poet and hymn writer of the 18th century, writing to his cousin:

You describe scenes delightful, but you describe them to one who, if he even saw them, could receive no delight from them, who has a faint recollection, and so faint as to be like an almost forgotten dream, that once he was susceptible of pleasure from such causes . . . Why is the scenery like this, I had almost said, why is every scene, which many years since I could not contemplate without rapture, now become, at the best, an insipid wilderness to me?[4]

Or Hamlet's famous words:

I have of late – but wherefore I know not – lost all my mirth, foregone all custom of exercises; and – indeed – it goes so heavily with my disposition that this goodly frame, the earth, seems to me a sterile promontory.[5]

In severe depression, the person involved feels persistently sad and is often moved to tears at the most trivial events, sometimes crying excessively without good reason, or they may long to cry, but be unable to do so. It seems as if all emotion has been drained dry. Concentration is difficult so that settling down to anything or making even small decisions becomes an enormous burden. Constant feelings of inadequacy, failure, worthlessness, and guilt plague the mind, and it seems as though others are watching and critical of every action. Fears and anxieties, which are normally trivial, become greatly exaggerated. Life has no purpose. Simple tasks become enormous obstacles. Sylvia Plath describes Esther's thoughts as she sits in the waiting room of the psychiatrists's office:

> I was still wearing Betsy's white blouse and skirt.
> They drooped a bit now, as I hadn't washed them in my three weeks at home. The sweaty cotton gave off a sour but friendly smell.
> I hadn't washed my hair for three weeks, either.
> I saw the days of the year stretching ahead like a series of bright, white boxes, and separating one box from another was sleep, like a black shade. Only for me, the long perspective of shades that set off one box from the next had suddenly snapped up, and I could see day after day glaring ahead of me like a white, broad, infinitely desolate avenue. It seemed silly to wash one day when I would only have to wash again the next.
> It made me tired just to think of it.
> I wanted to do everything once and for all and be through with it.[6]

There may be constant irritability with occasional outbursts of frustration or rage. Some people become restless, agitated, irritable and demanding – easily offended and difficult to please. Others may withdraw, become very slow in their reactions to people and events, and show little emotion. They may even appear quite normal because they can still cover their inner confusion with a smile and a joke. Constant tiredness is common and sleep patterns are usually interrupted so that waking at two or three in the morning is not unusual. Cowper describes his churning thoughts and exaggerated fears at such times. 'The terrors that I have spoken of would appear ridiculous to most . . . I am hunted by spiritual hounds in the night season.'[7] For some, with the day too painful to face, there is a longing to sleep forever. In younger people the sleep problem in depression may be an inability to get off to sleep at night and a tendency to sleep on long into the next day.

Nearly two hundred years ago John Colquhoun vividly described the symptoms of severe depression in 'The Nature and Signs of Melancholy in a True Christian' in his *Treatise on Spiritual Conflict*:

> A man so depressed is utterly unable to exercise joy or to take comfort in anything . . . He is always displeased and discontented with himself . . . His thoughts for the most part are turned in upon himself . . . He commonly gives himself up to idleness; either lying in bed, or sitting unprofitably by himself . . . daily harassed with fears of want, poverty and misery, to himself and to his family . . . He is weary of company, and is much addicted to solitude . . . His thoughts are commonly all perplexed, like those of a man who is in a labyrinth, or pathless wilderness . . . He has lost the power of governing his thoughts by reason . . . He can no more cease to muse on that which is already the subject of his thoughts, than a man, afflicted with a violent toothache, can forbear, at the time, to think of his pain.

And as the depression becomes deeper he may believe people are watching him or are even intent on killing him (paranoid delusions).

> If he but perceives anyone whispering to another, or winking with the eye, he presently suspects they are plotting to take away his life.

and

If his melancholy becomes very deep, the dejected believer often imagines that he hears voices and sees lights and apparitions. (visual hallucinations).

For someone with Christian belief there are particular problems.

The Bible often seems irrelevant, prayer a pointless exercise, forgiveness impossible, and God seems far away—if He exists at all.

Through his imagination he is disposed to aggravate his sin, or misery, or anger . . . He thinks his days of grace are past and that now it is too late for him to believe, to repent or to expect mercy. He is perpetually apprehensive that he is forsaken by God and always prone to despair . . . He is incapable to engage in secret prayer and meditation . . . He dares not hope, and therefore dares not pray . . . and feels an uncommon degree of averseness from religious exercises. He is constantly troubled with hideous and blasphemous temptations against God.[8]

And then the despair may become so deep that thoughts of suicide begin to invade the mind. At first it is an occasional thought but may become an insistent pressure as if someone were driving them to self-destruction. Judy had told me of her feelings of depression but I did not realise how serious it was until one day she handed me a poem describing how much of a burden she felt to everyone.

I'm going off to die now, goodbye.
Goodbye my dear loved ones.
Shall I spend 2 years hugging each of you goodbye?
No it suffocates and stunts and binds
And anyway, I must go.

I must go.
I cannot stay now.
I am empty, ashamed, hollow, and dead already.
The death in me already smells.
I can see your noses wrinkling at the stink and I love
you all too much
to cause you such discomfort.

Do not shake your heads and say too bad.
This is best.
Those of us who do this really understand how broken
we are; menaces.
This is my public duty.
It's a favour to you all.

Exhale relief: one less broken life to cope with.
Lift your hands and praise your Lord who has given
you all life.
I will bow before Him and beg – my eyes down.
Should He lend me His hand to stand I will sing
a new song.
If not I will crawl ever downward from His
presence understanding why.[9]

Many of these experiences David vividly describes in
the Psalms. 'My tears have been my food day and night.'
His soul is downcast and disturbed within him; his body
is wracked with weariness and pain and seems to be
wasting away; he feels like a worm; all who see him mock
him, and God seems far away. He feels utterly
overwhelmed, 'all your waves and breakers have swept
over me.' David was a man of strong emotions, of
powerful joy as he danced before the Lord, and yet at
times, he, too, descended into the depths of depression
(Psalm 31.9-13 and 42).

The writer of Lamentations describes his own vivid
experience of depression as he meditates on the sins of
his people and the destruction of Jerusalem:

I am the man who has seen affliction by the rod of His wrath. He has driven me away and made me walk in darkness rather than light; . . . He has made my skin and my flesh grow old and has broken my bones. He has besieged me and surrounded me with bitterness and hardship. He has made me dwell in darkness like those long dead. He has walled me in so that I cannot escape; He has weighted me down with chains. Even when I call out or cry for help, He shuts out my prayer. He has barred my way with blocks of stone; He has made my paths crooked . . . I became the laughing-stock of all my people; they mock me in song all day long . . . He has broken my teeth with gravel; He has trampled me in the dust. I have been deprived of peace; I have fogotten what prosperity is. So I say, 'my splendour is gone and all that I had hoped from the Lord' (Lamentations 3.1-18).

William Cowper

William Cowper, whom I have already quoted, is a classic example of a man besieged by severe depression. He was a child of nervous temperament and tragically, his mother, who was everything to him, died when he was six years old. It seems that he never really recovered from this shattering of his world. He was sent away to boarding school and there cruelly bullied by an older boy. After some apparently happy years at Westminster School, he studied law in order to please his father. His years studying and then practising law were accompanied by a growing sense of futility. He became increasingly depressed and was thrown into an agitated state when he was offered a very responsible job at the House of Lords, because of his fear of not doing well in the job. Several times he attempted to kill himself, by poisoning, with a knife, and then by hanging. He was taken to a home for the insane under the care of a Christian doctor. A few months later, he was delivered from the depths of the pit of depression as he meditated on Romans 3.25:

> In a moment I believed and received the gospel. . .
> Unless the Almighty arm had been under me, I think I should have died of gratitude and joy.[10]

Although he improved rapidly from that time, he was never completely free of depression for long.

Soon after his conversion, Cowper went to live with the Unwin family and entered the happiest six years of his life. He established a very close friendship with John Newton, the converted slave trader. John Newton encouraged Cowper in his poetry, and together they wrote many hymns. His experience of feeling abandoned by God in the middle of depression is expressed in some of his hymns.

Two years after his brother's tragic death, Cowper's depression began to return. Newton wrote in his diary, 'Mr. Cowper is down in the depths.' He became increasingly agitated with thoughts of suicide and eventually went to stay with John and Mary Newton for almost a year. Several times he tried to kill himself. He thought that John Newton was an impersonator, his food was poisoned; and worst of all, God had rejected him for ever! After two years in this terrible state, Cowper began to improve, but the marks of depression remained with him. 'I am like a slug or snail, that has fallen into a deep well: slug as he is, he performs his descent with an alacrity proportioned to his weight: but he does not crawl up again quite so fast. Mine was a rapid plunge; but my return to daylight, if I am indeed returning, is leisurely enough.'[11] Over the next 26 years, he wrote his best poetry and hymns. He became a distinguished name and to casual visitors, he appeared quite happy.

Fourteen years before he died in 1800, he had another six-month bout of desperate suicidal depression, and, sadly, he remained depressed for the rest of his days. His friend John Newton never doubted his salvation and wrote to a friend after Cowper's death:

> What a glorious surprise must it be to find himself released from all his chains in a moment, and in the presence of the Lord whom he loved and whom he served![12]

Nowadays few people will reach the extremes of Cowper, or the melancholy described by John Colquhoun, without seeking help from a doctor or counsellor. Fortunately, help can be given to prevent most depressions reaching such severity.

Signs of severe depression

Scientific studies of depression have linked together severely depressed mood, lack of interest in the normal routine of life, strong feelings of self-reproach and depressive delusions (e.g. belief that one is bankrupt or has committed some terrible crime – when neither are true!) as indicating a major 'depressive illness.' Many counsellors and psychiatrists would agree that if, in addition to feelings of depression and crying, at least four of the following eight symptoms are present for more than a short period of time, then professional help should be sought: loss of appetite or weight loss, sleep difficulties (early morning waking, sleeping too much), fatigue, agitation (being overactive and restless) or retardation (being generally slowed up), loss of interest, difficulty in concentration, feelings of guilt and thoughts of suicide or wishing to be dead.

The swing of the pendulum – manic depression

Some people who are vulnerable to severe depression also experience times of being unusually happy and carefree, even euphoric. It was only after he was admitted to a psychiatric hospital that we were able to piece together Colin's story. The day before, he had felt 'on top of the world.' In fact he had never felt better. As he walked, or rather ran down the street, he sang the few lines he could remember from an old Beatle's song, mixed with some of his own. The baker whose last conversation with Colin two weeks previously was monosyllabic and gloomy, was amazed at the change. It was difficult to follow what he said because he seemed to flit from subject to subject, often throwing in a pun or a rhyme. He seemed almost larger than life:

> ' "Beautiful day" . . . the race begins at two-thirty on Leading Lady . . . O Grady says, "run" . . . yes I'll have one bun . . . no half a dozen, Mr. Glacey, please . . . how are you I'm fine . . . right on the line . . . they'll be off soon . . . I'll win a thousand grand . . . I must fly – goodbye . . . bye . . . bye.'

It was when he started giving away five pound notes in the street and walking out in front of the traffic that the police interfered. As he was detained at the 'station' while someone called a doctor, he amused everyone with a cossack dance, a song and a bout of anger and irritability at being so misunderstood by the law. After all, he said, he had a right to entertain the public in the streets.

For three months prior to this episode, Colin had been severely depressed. He had now swung up into what doctors call a 'manic' phase. Besides the euphoria described above, there may, in such a phase, be moments of depression, transient tearfulness, irritability and anger. Mild over-confidence may later become a strong belief in being a messenger of God or a member of the royal family. Thought and conversation seems to be non-stop, often changing from one subject to another in midsentence especially if distracted. Little sleep is needed and sexual promiscuity or suggestiveness may give rise to considerable concern in relatives and friends.

Intense religious experiences of 'conversion', 'baptism of the Spirit,' mystical rapture or messages from God or Satan may confuse the situation. Jo was normally a quiet, gentle soul often thought of by others in the church as a very sensitive, spiritual person. After the breakup of a relationship with a boyfriend she seemed to be taking it very well and was full of praise to God. Her friends began to get a little worried when they heard her singing in her room at four in the morning. Next day she stood up in the middle of the church with a message of gloom and judgement from God. In the early hours of Monday morning several people in the church received phone calls from her with sermons about the sexual immorality in the church and some rather suggestive comments. Finally she was arrested by the police for preaching incoherently on street corners in the city and was admitted to a psychiatric hospital. This same pattern of reaction to stress occurred several times over the next few years. Each time she needed medication and help to come to terms with the difficulties in her life and relationships.

One of the most difficult problems in trying to help such a person is that they feel perfectly well and lack insight that anything is wrong. Years ago, before the discovery of modern tranquillizers, some patients with untreated mania would have died from exhaustion because of their ceaseless activity, just as some people with untreated depression would have starved themselves to death if they did not kill themselves more actively.

This tendency to swing between extremes of mood, often staying 'depressed' or 'high' for weeks or months at a time, is called 'manic depression'. It must be distinguished from the daily ups and downs of the 'temperamental' person. Whether 'high' with an apparent absence of any problems or cares in life, or 'low' with the weight of the world on one's shoulders, both states of mind involve a distorted view of reality and are extreme ways of reacting to stress. Considerable help may be needed to begin to get things in perspective again and these extreme states of 'mania' or deep depression should be urgently treated by a psychiatrist.

Depression in disguise

Depression is often disguised and may appear in the form of marriage conflicts, sexual problems, drug or alcohol dependence, chronic pain, aggression and violence, and so called 'personality problems'. Children and adolescents may become withdrawn or emotionally unstable, aggressive, phobic and generally antisocial without obvious sadness. Adolescents who are unhappy or have physical symptoms such as migraine or stomach ulcers may be living in fear of not living up to unreasonable parental expectations of academic achievement. Old people may have multiple physical symptoms, and become convinced that they have cancer or some other fatal illness. Only on questioning does one discover that with many of these problems there are also all the symptoms of severe depression.

I have described the two ends of the spectrum – of severe depression and mania – in some detail – and most people's experiences fall somewhere in between the two. Being aware of the extremes gives some idea about how seriously to be concerned about milder forms of depression. On the depressive side of the spectrum it is important to ask a few simple questions. Is it a passing mood due to criticism from a friend? Is it a regular black day or two before a menstrual period – predictable but sure to pass? Is it a complete change of character for someone who is normally coping well but over several weeks becomes increasingly irritable, tired and pessimistic? Or is it a longstanding gloomy view of life which at intervals becomes worse and shows all the signs of severe depression? Obviously if it is more than just a passing phase help will often be needed.

Depression – a symptom of deeper problems

In attempting to help someone who is 'feeling low' or 'depressed', the first question we usually ask is, 'What's happened?' 'What's gone wrong?' There is a widespread belief that sadness, misery and depression are caused by adverse circumstances. For the vast majority of people, this is true. Just as stomach pains may be due to simple indigestion, appendicitis or occasionally cancer, so depression may be a symptom of a variety of problems in life.

But we recognise that some people are, for a variety of reasons, more vulnerable to depression than others. A wide range of influences affect our moods, ranging through early childhood events, repressed anger, guilt, genes, hormones, brain chemistry, season of the year, climatic conditions, loss of a loved one, and frustrations in life. Each of us is vulnerable to depression in different ways in different circumstances. Two people, because of different temperament and life experiences, will react to exactly the same adverse circumstances in completely different ways. One may become very depressed while the other remains calm and confident. In the following chapters we will consider a number of different influences that are involved in causing depression.

References

1 Tony Lewis, *The Guardian*, May 5th, 1982.
2 Aaron Beck, quoted by G. W. Brown and T. Harris *Social Origins of Depression* (Tavistock Pub. 1978).
3 Sylvia Plath, *The Bell Jar* (Faber & Faber 1963) p. 2-3.
4 William Cowper, Letter to Lady Hesketh Oct. 1978. *Letters of William Cowper* selected by William Hadley (Everyman Library J.M. Dent & Sons Ltd. 1925).
5 William Shakespeare, *Hamlet*, Act II.
6 Plath, op. cit. p. 134.
7 William Cowper Letter to William Hayley, *William Cowper's Letters* Ed. E.V. Lucas (Oxford Univ. Press 1908).
8 John Colquhoun, 'The Nature and Signs of Melancholy in a True Christian' from *Treatise on Spiritual Comfort* 1814 Extract published in *The Banner of Truth*, Issue 96, Sept 1971 p. 33.
9 Personal communication – used with permission.
10 William Cowper, quoted in *William Cowper and His Affliction*. The editor, *The Banner of Truth*, Issue 96, Sept 1971, p. 16.
11 Ibid. p.23
12 John Newton, ibid p. 32.

CHAPTER TWO

Some rooted sorrows

Causes of depression – psychological and social factors

When I was ill the physicians made me take as much
medicine as if I had been a great bull. Alack for him
that depends on the aid of physic. I do not deny that
medicine is a gift of God nor do I refuse to
acknowledge science in the skill of many physicians
but take the best of them how far they are from
perfection. When I feel indisposed, by observing a
strict diet and going to bed early I generally manage to
get round again, that is if I can keep my mind
tolerably at rest. I have no objection to the doctor
acting upon certain theories but they must not expect
us to be slaves of their fancies.[1]

So wrote Martin Luther, a man troubled with many
aches and pains of body and mind, and a man who was
acutely aware of the many different explanations of
illness in his own day.

Causes, cures . . . and confusion?

Amongst Greek philosophers and physicians there
was conflict over whether the cause of depression was
biological (excess black bile) or emotional. Evil spirits or
the influence of the planets were often blamed as well.
John Cassian, a monk of the first century, understood
the psychological causes of depression in much the same
way as we do today.

'Of dejection there are two kinds; one, that which
springs up when anger has died down, or as the result
of some loss we have incurred or of some purpose
which has been hindered or interfered with: the other,
which comes from unreasonable anxiety of mind or
despair.'[2]

Don Duarte, King of Portugal in 1435 'lists six causes
of depression: fear of death, dishonour and pain, anger,
unfulfilled desire, dishonour and death of others. . . '[3]

Towards the end of the eighteenth century interest in
depression among the clergy waned, and under the
influence of the rising faith in science, the biological
explanations became more fashionable.

So, today, some say that depression is caused by
abnormalities of the chemicals in the brain. Others say it
is due to conflicting emotions; perhaps anger, guilt or
frustration repressed since early childhood. Some go
even further back and blame pre-birth experiences
within the womb. Some blame bad habits of thinking,
feeling and behaving learned in childhood. Others say it
is due to vitamin deficiency or allergies of one sort or
another. And there are those who find the cause in faulty
family relationships or in wider social problems such as
inadequate housing and unemployment.

Amongst Christians we find a similar diversity of
views. Depression, we are told, may be caused by a
'spirit of depression' and, therefore, needs binding or
exorcism; it may come as a result of sin and be cured by
repentance, right biblical attitudes and right behaviour;
it may be that we have not received a 'second blessing' or
have not been sufficiently broken before God in
repentance. We need to learn, it is said, what it means to
live 'the victorious Christian life', or the 'secret of the
happy Christian life'. Or perhaps we need 'inner healing'
or 'healing of the memories' to deal with the roots of

problems in childhood. Maybe the cause is further back than childhood or even before birth. Some Christians would say the problems arise in the first three months of life when a mother's depression is 'transfused' to her child in the womb. We need to go back to re-experience the pain of that time in order to know release from it.

We would all love to have some simple solution, but there are few easy answers when facing the complexity of our life in this world. Through the centuries, there have always been many schools of thought and as many different therapies. This is because biological, psychological, social and spiritual factors usually all weave together and several of the possible causes may be relevant at different times in different individuals. Sometimes it is relatively easy to see the cause; at other times so many factors are involved that it is difficult to know where to begin.

A number of scientific studies throw light on the subject. It has been shown for example that in severe depression there are changes in the chemicals in the brain, and medicines which work by restoring the chemical balance help to relieve depression. This discovery has certainly brought help and hope to those who suffer from severe depression, but it has unfortunately led thousands of other unhappy people to believe that there is an easy chemical answer to life's problems and pains. The theory which claims that depression is a disease which needs to be diagnosed and treated with drugs like any other illness is called the 'medical model'.

It has also been shown that difficulties in infancy and childhood can lead to later emotional problems and that counselling and psychotherapy ('talking treatments') may help to overcome the early psychological damage. This theory, in contrast to the medical model is often known as the 'psychological model'. There are a number of other theories such as the 'behavioural model' which finds the cause of depression in faulty habits of emotions and behaviour. Old habits need to be replaced with new ones. The 'social model' focuses on the difficulties in relationships as the cause of depression. These so called 'models' are all attempts to build theories to explain the cause of psychological problems. There are still some psychiatrists who will believe in one theory to the exclusion of others, but most take what they like or what they think is true from each theory and produce their own mixture! Each psychiatrist or counsellor will have a slightly different emphasis. Even the different out-patient clinics and wards in one psychiatric hospital may offer different treatment 'packages' based on different theories. For example, one may focus on 'physical treatments' like drugs and electroconvulsive therapy, while another may focus on 'talking treatments' such as psychotherapy and group therapy. As we shall see later, there is in fact *some* truth in all these views.

Although there is a danger of being slaves of the current scientific theories, we can try to develop a framework which will give some guidelines to the importance of the many factors which make one person more vulnerable to depression than another. Both 'scientific' and 'spiritual' schools of thought tend to hold onto one explanation at the expense of another. Each one is a partial truth and in reality, as we shall see, the 'scientific' and 'spiritual' cannot be separated from each other.

Causes of depression – psychological and social factors

Most reasonably mature and stable people have a deep inner sense of their significance, worth and value. They are neither over-inflated with pride nor so self-demeaning that they feel that they are hopeless failures. The most important fact that emerges from the many psychological and sociological studies of depression is that anything which undermines a person's awareness of their significance and security will tend to reduce their sense of self-esteem and thus make them prone to depression. Conversely, anything which raises a person's awareness of significance and security will tend to increase their sense of self-esteem and make them less prone to depression.

Loss and separation

It has been shown that loss of a parent in childhood may impair a person's basic sense of security. A study in Canada, found that men were more vulnerable to depression in later life if they had lost a parent, particularly father, before the age of 17.[4] A study in London found a link in women, with the loss of a parent before 17 and especially mother before the age of 11. 'Loss of mother before 11 may have an enduring influence on a woman's sense of self-esteem giving her an ongoing sense of insecurity and feeling of incompetence in dealing with the good things of the world.'[5] Another study demonstrated that separations between the ages of 5 and 10, caused by parental illness or marital discord, were associated with depressive problems in later life.[6] So it is not only loss by death; other studies have shown the link to be stronger if the loss is by separation caused, for example, by parent's divorce. This may have something to do with the fact that separation is much less easily resolved in a child's mind than death. With separation, there is always a glimmer of hope that the person will return. It usually means that the person is away from home completely, but it may also apply for example, to a woman who is severely depressed and may be so emotionally withdrawn from her children that they experience a sense of emptiness in the relationship. Early loss or separation from parents may produce an attitude to life which is less resistant to later loss or disappointment and, therefore, is more vulnerable to later crises.

William Cowper's mother died when he was just six. His whole sense of security rested in her presence and when she was gone, it was as if his whole world was shattered. He never really got over this loss, for she was like 'an omnipotent goddess' of that golden age when he was absolutely happy. Forty-seven years later he wrote, 'I can truly say that not a week passes, perhaps I might with equal veracity say a day, in which I do not think of her.'[7] Cowper's grief was compounded by the lack of a close relationship with his father and by being sent off to a boarding school shortly after his mother's death.

It is difficult for a child, with a sensitive temperament, who is so devastated, to develop an optimistic approach to life, or to feel in control of anything. Aaron Beck, who had done much research on depression, is a strong advocate of the view that depression arises from ideas and beliefs about life and relationships that we develop at an early age. In his book on depression, he discusses what he calls the vulnerability of the depression-prone person as due to a set of 'enduring negative attitudes about himself, about the world, and about his future'. Even though these attitudes are not obvious most of the time, they lie in wait 'like an explosive charge ready to be detonated' by appropriate circumstances.[8] Once the negative attitudes have been activated they 'dominate the person's thinking' and usually lead to a typical state of depression. Although a child usually shuts away painful memories in the unconscious, the memory may continue to influence both what he thinks and how he feels. Where there has been separation or loss, it is the child's private feelings of sorrow, anger and loneliness which often have to be repressed.

This is illustrated by my interview with Mr. Colson, where it emerged that his depression was related to his problems in his marriage. His wife, several years older than himself, had become bored with his obsessive addiction to work and was threatening to leave him. I could not understand why this apparently capable man was so utterly child-like in his depression. As we talked about his parents, it soon became clear that he had probably been made more sensitive to the present crisis by losing his mother in the war. He was four at the time and his father was away in the Army. He was sent to live with his grandmother, but it was not many years before she, too, died of a stroke. As soon as his wife used the word "separation" all the memories of the earlier separation and the fears of the war years were jolted into activity and he was pushed into a desperate depression. So, early loss and separation may, (though not inevitably) produce a vulnerability to later loss by undermining one's sense of self worth. If others are there in the family such as grandparents, aunts or uncles to make up for the loss, this will help to reduce later vulnerability.

It is, of course, not only loss by death or separation which may affect a child's sense of security. The atmosphere in the house before and after the loss is also important. Long term tension in the home may make the reaction to the loss more complicated. A negative, rejecting attitude from the parents to the child may cause just as much difficulty as an actual loss or separation. This is, of course, far more difficult to measure than a clear event like a death of a parent, but I am convinced it is probably more important.

The early years

Soon after conception, at only a few weeks old, a baby within its mother's womb will respond to sound, light, and painful stimuli. It is probable that in some way it can pick up the mother's emotional state so that the baby may sense depression, anxiety, rejection, or anger as well as feelings of calm, joy, and happiness while in the womb. There is a growing amount of fascinating research which suggests that children can remember events in the first year or two of life and that babies may in some way register some of the experiences in the womb. This is very difficult to prove scientifically but it does strengthen the biblical view that an unborn baby is a person from conception onwards. I believe that we must assume that each baby *is* a sensitive, living, feeling person within the womb and so we should value, love and pray for each unborn child. The relationship begins to be made (or broken!) in those nine months before birth and should continue to grow and develop after the baby is born.

And as children grow they need not only food but warmth, acceptance and love. Many studies have demonstrated that babies given only food and deprived of touch and eye contact fail to develop naturally and many even die. The work of John Bowlby on 'attachment and loss' has demonstrated the crucial importance of the 'bonding' between mother and child.[9] A simple example of the effect of this research is in the change in medical policy so that parents are now allowed to stay with their children in hospital when previously they would have been allowed only brief visits during the day. Many people can remember terrifying experiences of being alone, in hospital in pain, with desperate longing for their parents to comfort them. Similarly, mothers (and fathers) are encouraged to hold their newborn babies immediately after birth, when previously the baby would have been whisked away to the nursery!

Our children are so dependent on our approval for their sense of achievement and self worth. It is strange and sad that we are so quick to criticize and condemn and so slow to affirm and approve. If approval is consistently given then there will be a growing inner core of a sense of self worth and significance which is less and less dependent upon external events or relationships. A sense of self esteem becomes built into the personality. If however, a child has grown up in an atmosphere of being constantly undermined and criticized and perhaps accepted only when he performs well, he will probably become self critical, frustrated, and easily prone to depression. Firm, consistent and loving discipline is also necessary for the development of a right sense of self worth.

Particular incidents in a child's life may deeply affect their view of themselves. Many people have speculated about the cause of Van Gogh's depressive tendency. It is interesting to note that although Vincent was the eldest child he was not in fact the first. Exactly one year before his birth, to the day, the first child was stillborn. That child was called Vincent too, and was often mentioned in discussion in the family. Every Sunday the young artist-to-be would have to walk past the grave of his dead brother. Perhaps, he felt that he could never live up to his parent's expectations of the real Vincent because we know that he often wrestled with guilt and the feeling of being an 'inadequate usurper'.

For as long as she can remember, Barbara's parents had argued and fought. In her teens, each would pour out their problems to her with little awareness of the burden of care they were placing on her young shoulders. Somehow she had to keep the peace. Any needs of her own had to be forgotten because her mother's needs seemed so much greater. Mother often retired to bed with headaches and father would usually be drinking too much to take his daughter's troubles seriously. She tried to be perfect to please them, but always failed, and now, in her mid-twenties, she found herself caught in a trap. She longed to leave home and live a life of her own, but felt very guilty because her parents needed her to be at home to make them happy. Not surprisingly, in her turmoil and depression, some of the memories of childhood began to flood back:

There are so many fears that haven't been voiced,
that I've not allowed to surface – just try to ignore the
gnawing feelings. Growing up wondering if there
wasn't something dreadfully wrong with me and what
if everyone else already knew it or discovered it?
Always feeling that it wasn't enough or okay to just be
me – whoever that is – I won't be liked, approved of,
loved. How can I be? A definite lack of trust in
people, insecurity. . .
It's scared me to look at a lot of this. I look back and
'see' this little girl who covers up and hides what's
happening and any pain from EVERYONE! What a
task! And off to school goes this quiet, lonely little girl
– wanting approval, to be liked . . . but so insecure
and it really showed. So much fear holding her back,
cruelty of kids and sometimes rejection. And I hurt
for her, but it's still for 'her' – not for me as if they're
two separate people. I'm really trying to keep this
distant! Lots of pretending that everything was okay,
the fighting at home was okay, lack of confidence and
security was okay, but I'm seeing that it wasn't!
'Don't let yourself FEEL any of this.' But I'm starting
to, and that frightens me, too. The courage to face it
all is fleeting and feeble.[10]

A feeling of being unlovable and unloved is very
common in people who are prone to depression.
Because they lack a deep sense of value and significance
they feel they always have to be earning other people's
approval. Early childhood experiences colour our
reactions to people we meet as we grow up. The child in
us lives on. For example, someone whose father has
always criticised him may tend to be over-sensitive to
any hint of disapproval from any older man who is in a
position of authority.

A study from Australia demonstrated that depressive
suicidal thoughts were more common in people whose
parents were separated or if the parents were rejecting,

unaffectionate and punitive and showed more interest in other brothers or sisters. The recurring theme predisposing to depression is rejection and lack of self-esteem.[11] Freud saw depression as caused by anger, due to the loss of a loved person, turned back on oneself. Children, unable to know who is responsible for the pain and anger they feel, often blame themselves and this sets up a habit of repression of anger. We will return to the subject of anger in a later chapter.

Automatic thoughts

Aaron Beck speaks of 'automatic thoughts' which are rather like tape recordings which switch on as a reflex response to certain situations. They are unhelpful habits of thinking which deeply affect our moods and behaviour. Beck believes that the self-defeating character of the depressed person is due to the illogical reasoning that he uses when faced with a difficult sitution. He twists the evidence so that he produces an unduly gloomy view of himself and his worth. Beck describes some of the 'primary assumptions' which predispose people to depression:

1 To be happy I must be accepted by all people at all times.
2 If I make a mistake it means that I am inept.
3 If someone disagrees with me, it means he does not like me.
4 My value as a person depends on what others think of me.[12]

Because of the absence of an inner sense of worth such a person is dependent on the approval of others. Just as he needs food for physical survival, so, for psychological survival, he desperately needs repeated assurances from others and enough success experiences to defend himself against the inner feeling of failure and uselessness. He is usually profoundly sensitive to things that might please or upset those around him, and may react in two different ways. In attempting always to please he may never assert his own views or personality, and this may lead to inner frustration and anger at being so dependent upon other people. Alternatively, because of his fragile sense of self esteem he may over-react to any criticism or disagreement with dogmatism and aggression.

Perfectionism

Those who are very self-critical often set very high standards for themselves and for others, and this may be seen in their perfectionist approach to life. Perfectionism is sometimes inherited, sometimes learned from parents, and is sometimes a way of coping with insecurity from a difficult childhood. Or it may be a result of all these factors.

Like other aspects of our temperament, it is at times an asset, and at times a great hindrance. All of us lie somewhere on a scale of, at one end, being able to tolerate chaos around us, to those at the other end who require everything to be perfectly neat, orderly, and clean before they can have any peace of mind. Some are perfectionists in just a few areas of life while able to tolerate disorder in other areas. The London study of depression already quoted found that women with three or more children under the age of 14 at home were more prone to depression. It is not difficult to see why! Life is always on the edge of chaos – at least, that is the way it feels to me with our own four children! Constant demands for attention and help echo around the house. Nothing stays in one place for long. It is difficult for a woman looking after children at home to feel that she is doing a good job. And she probably won't know for 15 or maybe 20 years, if she has made a good job of it! Married women, particularly those with young children have four times as much depression as single women.

The emotional and physical demands of bringing up a family are enormous. For a woman who is anxious to be in control of things, who has a particlarly perfectionist attitude to life, this is going to be more difficult than for others who can live with a measure of chaos.

Jean was a very capable school teacher. She was much respected by her colleagues and pupils for her abilities. Her life was disciplined and very efficient, and she always appeared to be happy and 'on top of things'. When the first baby was born, she gave up work and devoted herself to her new daughter and to the home. Unfortunately, babies do not always fit in with the routine and often create quite a mess. Dirty nappies, food on the floor, crying, sleepless nights, and a sense of imminent chaos and loss of control produced a sense of hopelessness and depression. Her perfectionist tendencies which had once been such a asset now became a definite hindrance!

David Burns in an article in *Psychology Today* aptly entitled, 'The Perfectionist's Script for Self Defeat' outlined a number of problems in the perfectionist's way of approaching the world. They tend to be all-or-nothing thinkers. They see themselves as either a brilliant success or a total failure. It is hardly surprising that they fear mistakes and over-react to failure. They tend to jump to the dogmatic conclusion that a negative event will be repeated endlessly. When they make mistakes, they tell themselves, 'I'm always making mistakes, I'll *never* get this right.' They tend to be ruled by an over-critical conscience, the tyranny of the 'should'. This inevitably leads to enormous guilt, and terrible fears of failure. Their whole sense of self-esteem depends on achieving a perfect performance. 'I did perfectly on this. This shows I'm okay; I deserve to feel good.' Because perfectionists see themselves as inefficient and are likely to fall short of their unreachable aims, they are plagued by a sense of helplessness to achieve desired goals. This may lead to extreme lack of motivation in periods of depression.

> Perfectionists fear and anticipate rejection when they are judged as imperfect, they tend to react defensively to criticism. Their response usually frustrates and alienates others and may bring about the very disapproval perfectionists most fear. This reinforces their irrational belief that they must be perfect to be accepted.[13]

One root of perfectionism lies in attempts to be perfect in order to earn the acceptance and love of parents (especially if the parents' sense of self-worth depends on the child's success), and in attempts to control a chaotic world of conflicting emotions and insecurity. ('If there's no security out there, I'll build my own little security system in here.') So we can see why many people who have unreasonably high standards, and struggle to reach impossible goals, are more vulnerable to depression and self-defeat.

Lack of a caring, confiding relationship

Another factor found to be associated with depression in women is a lack of a close relationship in marriage. Studies have shown that a 'non-confiding' relationship predisposes to depression. Sociologists Brown and Harris wrote in their London study:

> The risk of depression was greatest among working class women with children at home for whom a sense of achievement would be most closely related to their roles as mother and wife. She needs to be 'told' she is doing well to refurbish her sense of self worth.[14]

Mary Boulton in a study of women in 50 London families has described:

the extensive influence a husband can have on a
woman's experience as a mother. A husband's
appreciation is a reward in itself as well as supporting
a sense of accomplishment in the way she deals with
day to day problems of child care. His acceptance that
there are difficulties and frustrations legitimizes the
experiences of pervasive irritation and unhappiness
felt by many women about the routine care of
children and helps them to accept that this does not
reflect on themselves. In general his support helps a
woman to create a rewarding idea of herself . . . many
men see their wife's jobs as 'easy' and 'cushy' thereby
trivialising their work and lowering their wife's sense
of self worth.[15]

Many studies have shown how important support and
friendship is as a protection against depression. When
someone experiences serious losses in their life, such as
death of a close relative or being made redundant, they
are much less likely to become severely depressed if they
have a caring husband or wife with whom they can share
their anxiety, frustration and depression. For many
women, a good marriage is enough to cancel out the
effects of an unhappy childhood and thus reduce their
vulnerability to depression. It is not just in marriage that
a caring, confiding relationship is important. Whether it
be a parent, brother, sister, uncle, aunt, husband, wife,
or friend, we all need someone in whom to confide and
with whom to share our struggles, pains, successes and
joys. Without it, we are more vulnerable to depression.
It is sad to see many people in the world today whose
relationships are so superficial that they have to pay to
relate to somebody at a deeper level whether it be
psychiatrist, counsellor or therapy group. On the other
hand it is encouraging to see that many churches are
taking up the challenge to provide a caring community of

people in a world where, especially in the big cities, so many people are lonely and unfulfilled. Many people searching for their identity within themselves do not realise that they will discover themselves only in relating deeply to others.

Unemployment

There is a strong association between depression and unemployment. This is obviously a very important factor in the current economic situation. Studies have shown that many people who lose their jobs pass through a number of stages of adjustment. Almost all go through a period of depression. Some get into a vicious circle of declining self-respect, money worries and boredom and become chronically depressed and pessimistic. We will see in a later chapter how reaction to loss of a job is similar to reactions to other major losses in life such as loss of a limb by amputation or the death of a loved one.

Learned responses

Other factors that may increase vulnerability to depression are the behaviour and emotional responses we learn by example from our parents and family. One can often trace particular styles of coping or collapsing through several generations of a family. Some, when under pressure, always withdraw into a silent world of their own. Others, when angry and frustrated set the whole atmosphere ablaze with their derisive, critical comments, and often do considerable damage to any furniture, dogs, or cats in the vicinity. But learning may also work in a positive direction as we are taught by example and discussion not to deny anger or distress, but to deal with it constructively and with a measure of self-control.

Another less commonsense aspect of learning is the concept of 'learned helplessness,' propounded by a psychologist called Seligman. He put dogs in one half of a room with a barrier down the middle of the room over which the dog could jump. It was possible to give the dog an electric shock through a grid in the floor of the first side of the room. When the shock was applied, the dogs would leap to safety. If, however, the dogs were repeatedly shocked, but unable to escape because restrained in a harness, when released from the harness, they did not jump to freedom from the shocks, but endured the shocks while cowering in the corner. If they were then lifted over the barrier each time a shock was passed, they slowly but surely re-learnt the escape route and became more confident and healthy again.[16] Now there are some reservations about applying animal experiments to human beings, but perhaps children or adults who are continually frustrated in their attemps to escape difficult situations eventually give up in the same way and become hopeless and helpless. This is seen dramatically in the response of young children to prolonged separation. There is at first much crying in protest, but this eventually gives way to hopelessness and despair.

The rewards of depression

There is another side of the 'learned helplessness' picture. Depression does sometimes have considerable rewards! After someone has been depressed for a while, they begin to appreciate (albeit subconsciously – sometimes consciously!) the secondary benefits of the sympathy and attention of others who had previously ignored them. It may also be a convenient escape from the responsibility of living in a hard and difficult world. For a few people, being 'depressed' is the only thing they know how to do well. There is a certain status and identity in the depressive lifestyle. It would be too big a risk to 'get better' and take on the responsibilities of life and relationships again!

References

1   Martin Luther, *Table Talk* (Ed. W. Hazlett, G. Bell & Sons 1909) p. 317.

2   John Cassian, Conferences in *Nicene and Post-Nicene Fathers* J. L. Gibson (Ed. H. Wace and P. Schaff. Series 2. Vol XI Oxf. 1894) p. 343-344.

3   Don Duarte, Leal Consulheiro p. 22 Quoted in *Depression: A linguistic, historical and philosophical exploration* F. J. Roberts. (M.D. thesis Univ. of Bristol 1973) p. 57

4   Alec Roy, Vulnerability Factors and Depression in Men *British Journal of Psychology* Jan 1981 Vol 138 p. 75-77.

5   George W. Brown and Tirril Harris, *Social Origins of Depression – A Study of Psychiatric Disorder in Women* (Tavistock Pub. 1979).

6   C. Tennant et al., The relationship of childhood separation experiences to adult depressive and anxiety states *British Journal of Psychiatry* 1982, Vol 141, p. 475.

7   William Cowper, *The Stricken Deer* Lord David Cecil. (Constable & Co London 1929) p. 172.

8   Aaron Beck, *Depression: Clinical Experimental and Theoretical Aspects.* (London: Staples Press 1967) p. 277.

9   John Bowlby, *Attachment and Loss* (Harmondsworth: Pelican Books 1971).

10 Personal communication & used with permission.

11 Family Systems of Suicidal Children *American Journal of Psychotherapy* 1981 Vol 35. No. 3.

12 Aaron Beck, *Cognitive Therapy and the Emotional Disorders.* (Meridian 1976) p. 29ff.

13 David Burns, The Perfectionists Script for Self Defeat. *Psychology Today* November 1980 p. 34.

14 Brown and Harris, op. cit., p. 287.

15 Quoted in Brown and Harris, op. cit., p. 287.

16 M. E. P. Seligman, *Helplessness: On Depression, Development and Death* (San Francisco: W. H. Freeman 1975).

CHAPTER THREE

'A mind diseased'

Genes, chemicals and other mysteries – The Biological Factor

John was found unconscious in his bedroom. A note on a chair left no doubt that this was a very deliberate attempt to end his life. He had swallowed a whole bottle of sleeping tablets. Fortunately, he recovered from the overdose and was admitted to a psychiatric hospital. Over the following day or two, his story emerged. His wife had left him for another man. His normally successful business was declining under the pressure of the recession. When his wife was contacted, she described how, over the previous six months, he had become more and more difficult to live with, was occasionally very violent and seemed to have lost interest in everything. He did not talk much to her, and she thought from the number of cigarette ends that she found in the ashtray that he had been getting up very early in the morning and sitting alone in the living room. His father had been a manic depressive, but apart from a few ups and downs in adolescence, John had never been seriously depressed before. In hospital, he remained very low, believing he was a total failure in life and convinced that his business was bankrupt. He was so preoccupied with these negative themes that it was impossible to help him to change his view of the situation. He was eventually given a course of six electroconvulsive therapy (ECT) treatments. After the third treatment, he began to see a glimmer of hope, and after the sixth, he had dramatically improved and was able to talk rationally about his business and his marriage. His wife, fortunately, became much more sympathetic to his situation and, after marriage counselling she returned to him, and he returned to work with a much more realistic attitude to his business.

It appears that John had inherited a vulnerability to become depressed. His life was relatively unstressful until his business began to decline and under pressure he began to slide down into a vicious circle of deep depression. Fortunately he responded well to ECT and medication and was soon able to get a better perspective on his situation.

Our bodies and minds are so closely interwoven that we do not have a clear idea of how much is due to biology and how much is due to psychology, but biological and genetic factors *do* have considerable influence on our temperament and personality.

Temperament and personality

Those of us who have children are only too well aware that temperament is to a large extent 'given' – it is the basic inherited building block of personality which is then shaped and moulded in childhood and adolescence. Some are very sensitive both physically and emotionally to the world around them. They may have a more acute awareness of colours, textures, smells, tastes and sounds. There is an obvious difference between children in what is called their 'pain threshold' – some feel the pain of a cut or bruise more than others. They may also have a higher anxiety response under stress. Some children are much more fearful than others. They may be also more sensitive to rebuke or encouragement and to the atmosphere of the relationships around them, especially to what is going on between their parents. This sensitivity is in one way a great gift and may, for instance be cultivated by someone with an interest in the arts. It enables you to glory in the beauty of spring flowers breaking through the ground or in the joy of a close relationship. But it also leaves you more vulnerable to ugliness, pain and broken relationships.

Another child may be less sensitive and able to ride the inevitable ups and downs of life more easily. An easy-going temperament is in some ways a great asset, but such a person may miss out on the experiences of the extremes of pleasure and pain. Many children are sensitive in some areas and not in others. Very often one sees the more sensitive and 'difficult' child falling into a negative vicious circle of criticism from parents and low self esteem. The more easy going child tends to produce more positive responses from parents and thus easily slips into an upward spiral of affirmation from others and high self esteem. But the tender plant usually needs more affirmation and help than the tougher one.

One of the hardest tasks for parents is to help the more sensitive child to be tough enough to cope with the real world and yet not lose their sensitivity completely. Sadly, many sensitive children are forced to retreat into themselves either becoming very shy and withdrawn or developing a 'couldn't care less' attitude to life. Some will build a tough aggressive exterior to protect the sensitive person inside. This interaction of a child's temperament and their relationship with parents, teachers and friends is obviously complex and it is often difficult to sort out cause and effect.

If some people inherit a vulnerability to depression, is it a particular temperament which makes them more sensitive to rejection, loss or other difficulties in life? Or, do they inherit particular chemicals deficiencies in the brain which give them a lower threshold to stress and make them more prone to depression? The answer is that it is probably both and different for each person.

Brain chemistry

We know that we can inherit a tendency to develop other obviously physical diseases like diabetes, so there is a possibility of inheriting a chemical vulnerability to depression. There is a large amount of research showing that there is a biological component to depression, particularly in its more severe forms. Somtimes our bodies seem to dominate our minds. An example of this would become apparent if you were to slip some LSD into my tea! For a while I would be almost a different person, controlled by the chemicals in my body. I well remember being called to see Mrs. Gray. She had just had a major operation and the nurses on the ward were very distressed because she believed that they were putting poison in the injections they were giving her. When we did some tests we found that a number of the chemicals in her body (electrolytes) were seriously abnormal and once the balance was restored she was once more in her right mind.

A letter from a friend described his struggle with depression. There were many factors involved in his family and business, but his doctors had done a five hour glucose tolerance test and discovered that he suffered from hypo-glycemia (low blood sugar). He was aware that this is a very fashionable diagnosis at the moment, particularly in America, but as he says, 'the proof of the pudding is in the eating!' He wrote, 'all the sugar and tea and coffee I have been drinking has been giving me severe problems with 'sugar blues'. He (the doctor) has put me on a sugar free diet, healthy unrefined fresh food, gobs of vitamins for an 8 week program, and I can't believe I am the same person. All the anxious fearful feelings, the constant headache, the night sweating, the packed up over-stuffed feelings are all gone . . . I feel well again at last. I have even been able to get up in the morning and do exercises! I will soon be off all medication (vitamins) and I haven't had to take any uppers or downers, thank God, in weeks and months.'[1] The excess sugar he had been eating had produced excess amounts of insulin which caused his blood sugar to drop dramatically.

A more extreme example of the way our brains may be affected by disease is seen in the process of senile dementia. My grandmother, a dear Christian woman, declined in her old age into a state of confusion and disorientation, thinking that she was back in her early life in India, as the process of senile dementia destroyed her brain. The person that was my grandmother, still visible for brief moments, was apparently caged in by a failing body and brain. She was finally released by death and will, thankfully, when Christ returns again, be given a new body which will be the perfect vehicle through which a completely renewed mind will be expressed.

So if we are thus limited by our bodies and brains, it is important when considering depression to have some idea about how big a factor the physical or biochemical structure of the brain really is. There are numerous genetic and biochemical studies in the medical literature and I will attempt to summarise them without becoming too technical.

Genetic studies

It has been found that anxiety, and to a lesser extent depression, is more common in the relatives of those with anxiety and depression than in the general population. This means that either a genetic factor is at work or that particular styles of dealing with stress are learned from other family members. Both are probably true, our temperament is partly inherited and partly learned. Studies of twins brought up in the same family and twins brought up in different families are helpful in sorting out what is commonly called the 'nature–

nurture' debate, the question of what is inherited and what is learned. Identical twins, who carry identical genes, brought up in the same home, or adopted at birth and brought up in different homes, are more likely to suffer from the same emotional problems (69% risk) than non-identical twins, who carry different genes, brought up apart or together (13% risk). For example, say Bob and David were identical twins: Chris and John were non-identical twins and both pairs were adopted at birth. Each child was brought up in a very different home in different parts of the country. When interviewed later in life, Bob and David would be much more likely to experience the same emotional problems even though they had been raised in very different homes than Chris and John. And this experiment could be repeated with many other twin pairs. Almost all studies have agreed that close relatives of those with severe depression have a 10-15% risk of having the same problem compared with 2-3% in the general population (i.e. five times the risk of the general population). For example, if my father has suffered from severe depression then there is a 1 in 10 chance that I will do the same. If no relative has suffered from depression the chances improve to 1 in 50. These statistics sound ominous but of course there is nothing inevitable about it, because many other factors are involved besides genes.[2]

The risk appears to be greater in female than in male relatives and in relatives of those who become severely depressed at a younger age. The risks are also higher for relatives of those with what is called bipolar depression as opposed to unipolar depression. Bipolar depression is another term for what is commonly known as manic depression, which was described in the first chapter. Unipolar depression is when the mood changes are always depressive and never swing up into periods of prolonged euphoria. So the evidence for a genetic factor is certainly present, though variable from person to person and family to family. It appears that the more severe the depression, especially if associated with manic episodes, the stronger the genetic factor.

Biochemical studies

If we accept that there is, in some people, a genetic vulnerability which may affect their temperament so that they are predisposed to depression, we must assume that some of its influence is on the chemicals in the body, particularly the brain. The function of the brain depends on the transmission of tiny electrical impulses along millions of chains of nerve cells. The transfer of electrical energy between the ends of the nerve cells (neurones) is done by substances called transmitter enzymes. Many studies have demonstrated that the level of these enzymes is lower in depression and tends to rise as the depression lifts, thus suggesting a reduction of the transmission of electrical energy in the brain in depression.

A recent study of sixty physically and mentally healthy volunteers showed a significant relationship between abnormal amounts of some of the transmitters and a family history of psychiatric illness. In fact, those who had low concentrations of one enzyme were 2.7 times more likely to have a family member with psychiatric illness.[3] This certainly suggests a family predisposition to breakdown under stress, because of lower enzyme levels in the brain. The chicken or egg question is: does the chemical change in the brain come before the stressful event and make that person more vulnerable to depression or does the stressful event produce the biochemical change? The answer seems to be that both happen at once. In one individual a genetic predisposition may be a strong factor but then their reaction to stress produces further chemical changes and thus a biological vicious circle is set up. In others, in whom there is no genetic predisposition, a prolonged depressive reaction to stress is the main trigger mechanism for the chemical change.

Another piece of evidence is the simple fact that antidepressant drugs work, in most people, better than placebos. Placebos are tablets that look and taste the same as the real tablets, but have no active chemical in them. In other words, it is not just the effect of taking a pill and believing it will work. The antidepressant chemical does do some good. One drug which has changed the lives of many people with severe and extreme swings of mood (manic depression) is lithium, a basic salt compound. It helps to reduce the number and the strength of the swings of mood thus decreasing vulnerability to depression. Various tests are being developed to ascertain which patients will respond to which treatment, and to distinguish those in whom there is a large biological component of the depression.

Electroconvulsive Therapy (ECT)

The advantages and disadvantages of ECT have been debated fiercely in recent years. We have to admit that we do not know exactly how it works, but it does have a very dramatic effect in the type of severe depression where thought processes are so disturbed that the person may suffer from delusions and suicidal ideas. In the past, it was much over-used by psychiatrists and was given to many patients who did not benefit from it. Nowadays we have a much clearer idea of the types of depression it will probably relieve.

Recent studies have shown that the majority of subjects when questioned did not find ECT a painful or unpleasant experience. After the initial apprehension they were surprised to find it was no more upsetting than a visit to the dentist. Most thought that ECT had helped them.[4] Unwanted effects of ECT are largely confined to an effect on memory which is troublesome in approximately half the patients. There is difficulty in remembering recent events and sometimes new information. This problem does not usually last more than a few days but may occasionally persist for a few months. This persistent loss of memory is thought to be due to continuing depression or perhaps too much medication.[5]

Before the days of antidepressant medication, a trial of ECT dramatically demonstrated its effectiveness, at least in saving lives. The death rate amongst the severely depressed patients in a large psychiatric hospital between the years 1900-1939 was found to be 16% in men and 14% in women. In the years 1940-1948, it was found that while the death rate remained as high in untreated patients, in the patients treated by ECT, it fell to 2% or less.[6]

Many people still believe that ECT is given as it was shown in the film *One Flew Over the Cuckoo's Nest* – the patient being held down and electrodes being applied to his head while he is still conscious. Nowadays when ECT is given, the patient is given a brief anaesthetic and a muscle relaxant to reduce muscle spasm to a minimum. One recent study showed that ECT worked better than the anaesthesia and a muscle relaxant alone, though the anaesthesia did appear to have some placebo value. In another study, however, ECT was no better than anaesthesia – both groups of patients improved.[7] The question remains as to whether the patients improved because they thought they had had ECT, or did the anaesthesia, in fact, have some real helpful chemical affect on the brain? Further research is being done to elucidate some of these mysteries.

The important thing is that all recent studies have shown ECT to be a remarkably effective treatment in severe depression and it works more quickly than antidepressants which is important when helping someone who is very disturbed and suicidally depressed. But ECT is not particularly good at preventing further episodes of depression. Anti-depressant medication with psycho-therapy are necessary as well.

Antidepressants (drug treatment) and psychotherapy (talking treatment) will be adequate for many forms of depression, but ECT may sometimes be necessary. It is interesting that we find much evidence to suggest that antidepressant medication and psychotherapy are more effective in reducing symptoms than either treatment alone.[8] The less severe the depression, the more one can rely on talking treatments alone.

There is much research being done on pain-relieving chemicals that have been found in the brain. These 'endorphins' are released in the body during exercise and some doctors recommend running as a cure for depression! It is interesting that many long distance runners report that they experience a 'high' feeling after they have been running for some time. Certainly exercise is beneficial for improving one's self-image. This is due to a sense of gaining control over oneself, increased fitness, and also probably to the release of endorphins in the brain.

Finally, we find that some physical illnesses (e.g., thyroid disease, hepatitis, glandular fever, low blood sugar, and viral pneumonia), some drugs (e.g., for blood pressure, chemotherapy for cancer), electrolyte disturbances (e.g., after major operations), vitamin B12 deficiency, and hormonal changes (e.g. after childbirth) may precipitate depression.

When depression occurs after a physical illness or operation there are usually a number of other factors that have made that person more vulnerable to it. For example, for one woman who has a difficult marriage and problems of low self esteem, to have her womb removed may seem like the final statement that she is not really much of a woman. Yet for another woman who has had a happy marriage, several children and then develops very heavy bleeding it may be a great relief to have a hysterectomy. So for each individual a severe illness or operation will have a particular significance and meaning which will affect their reaction to it.

It is rare for the biological factors to be the sole cause of depression. There is usually an interaction of many different influences.

Premenstrual tension

Many women find themselves more vulnerable in the five to ten days before their period, describing a variety of physical and psychological symptoms. These may be headaches, craving for food, thirst, nausea, dizziness, fatigue, breast tenderness and swelling, and abdominal cramps and bloating. It seems that the physiological changes are due to hormonal changes (although no consistent changes have been found) and these also affect the chemicals in the brain. The emotional symptoms were described by Frank in 1931 as 'a feeling of indescribable tension,' and 'a desire to find relief by foolish and illconsidered actions!'[9] There may also be irritability, sensitivity to criticism, guilt, a desire to be alone, lack of concentration and depression sometimes with suicidal ideas. If there is much external stress then these symptoms will be worse. One woman described to me her desperate feelings of hopelessness and her strong desire to escape to bed just before her periods. She was struggling with conflicts in her marriage and difficulties in her work. When the marriage and work problems were sorted out her premenstrual tension was much less noticeable.

Many extravagant claims have been made for different treatments for premenstrual tension but few have stood the test of time and experimental research.

Recognition that the condition has a partial physical basis is often helpful in learning to live with it. With mild symptoms adequate exercise, reduction of salt intake, and elimination of coffee, tea and chocolate from the diet have been found to be helpful. Vitamin B6 and evening primrose oil which can be obtained from health food stores or chemists without prescription have both been shown to relieve some of the symptoms.[10] Katherine Dalton has popularised the use of Progesterone,[11] and this is helpful in some cases, but recent research has not supported her impressive claims.[12] There are a number of other remedies which can be tried and it is worth consulting a doctor who should be able to help each person to find the most helpful treatment.

Post-partum depression

I gazed out of the window. The trees were black and bare in the little square outside Paris, round which the hospital buildings were clustered.
The pale sun had stopped trying to break through and a grey dullness surrounded everything, including me. Tears began to creep slowly down my face, and I didn't know why there was such a blankness, a heaviness inside me, like the weather outside.
I couldn't understand it. Christopher was a beautiful nine pound baby. We all wanted him and already loved him. And yet inside me there was this blackness, this hopelessness, this unwillingness to face the future.
The day dragged on and just when the hospital was settling down to its evening routine the sister came in. 'We'd like you to see one of the doctors before you go home,' she began.
'But I see them every day,' I answered.
'Not this one,' she continued, taking a deep breath. 'I think he'll be able to help you.' . . .

'I'll be all right once I'm home,' I answered.

'We want to make sure of that,' she ended. 'I've asked Doctor Dufour to pop in.'

'But why?' I enquired. 'Who is he?'

The sister took another deep breath. 'A psychiatrist.'

I looked at her in alarm. 'I don't need a psychiatrist. I'm just a bit tired, that's all.'

'It's more than that,' she said quietly.

I'd heard about 'baby blues' – an understatement to say the least. I'd experienced them first when Yves was born, and I took it that they must be a normal part of childbirth which I had to accept.

But with Christopher the depression was deeper and darker. I was mentally ill and needed help.[13]

The interaction of physical, psychological, and social factors is clearly seen in depression after childbirth – post-natal or puerperal depression. Many women are much more vulnerable to depression in the months after childbirth because of the hormonal changes in the body and all the adjustments to the arrival of a new person in the family. At least 10% of women giving birth are troubled by post-partum depression of some sort. Approximately half of all women will experience weepiness on the fifth day after childbirth – the so-called maternity blues. The mood seems to vary from hour to hour and there is often a feeling of despondency and inadequacy and some difficulty in concentration. This usually disappears within a few days.

In a few cases, women who have usually been well during pregnancy and had a normal delivery, suddenly within a week or two of childbirth, become very confused, restless and sleepless, and may become severely depressed, with thoughts of harming themselves and the baby, and intense guilt and despair. Sometimes they may become euphoric and overactive and may appear to be hearing voices and seeing visions (hallucinating). Sometimes the mood varies from day to day with both depression and anxiety. There is often overwhelming tiredness and a feeling of inability to cope with anything. Although tired, there is great difficulty getting off to sleep and the rest of the family may be met with irrational bouts of frustration and anger. This form of illness is called puerperal psychosis and it is believed to have a biochemical cause. Admission to hospital for treatment with antidepressants and often ECT usually produces a complete cure within a few weeks.

There are two other forms of post-partum depression which are not usually so severe as puerperal psychosis. One, like the other forms of depression we have discussed in Chapter 2 is associated with such factors as loss of mother before the age of 11, an unsupportive husband, poor housing and few friends. The other is more specifically associated with forming a close relationship with the new baby. For most women the natural 'bonding' between mother and child seems to happen naturally and easily, but for a few women it does not happen so quickly, and they may become quite depressed. These mothers may need to be taught how to relate to the baby – how to handle it, to smile at it and to talk to it so that the relationship can develop. Because the relationship of 'bonding' has not developed spontaneously it does not mean that it cannot do so – but help is needed. Fortunately, in this country, many psychiatric hospitals have 'mother and baby units' to which they can be admitted and the appropriate treatment and help given. The combination of biological treatments, support for the family (especially the husband who is often bewildered by what is happening) and help with practical details of caring for a new baby are usually enough to get rid of the feelings of depression.

Climate and season

Other influences, as yet little understood, include the effects of climate and season. One striking example is the effect of the hot wind from the desert as it blows across other countries. These winds have been given various names like Santa Anna and Chinook and appear to have marked effects on behaviour and mood. Instability, accident proneness, loss of self-control, depression, and suicide are all found to be more common at such times.

There is also some evidence that sunspots affect mood and behaviour. Suicide rates in England, Wales, Australia, and Japan have been found to be higher from spring to mid-summer. Because there is also an increase in conception over the same period, it is suggested that there is a seasonal increase in 'drive' so that those who are already depressed are driven further into despair and suicide, while those who are healthy tend to reproduce!

From the evidence that we have considered, we can, without doubt, say that there is a biological element in depression and that sometimes antidepressants and even ECT are necessary to break a chemical vicious circle. Some forms of depression seem to have a large biological element and some individuals are particularly vulnerable in this way. In others social and psychological factors play a large part in causing depression and the biological vulnerability is a very small factor. So the treatment for depression will vary enormously according to the person and the situation.

References

1 Personal communication – used with permission.
2 Robin Murray, Adrianne Reverley, *British Journal of Hospital Medicine* Feb. 1981, p. 185 and Aug. 1980 p. 166.
3 G. Sedvall et al., *British Journal of Psychiatry* 136 April 1980 p. 366-374.
4 C. P. L. Freeman, R. E. Kendell. ECT: Patients' Experiences and Attitudes. *British Journal of Psychiatry* 137 July 1980 p. 8-16.
5 L. R. Squire, P. C. Slater, P. L. Miller. *Arch. Gen. Psychiatry* 1981, 38. p. 89-95.
6 E. Slater, *Journal Mental Science* 1951, 97. p. 567.
7 E. C. Johnstone, J. F. W. Deakin, P. Lawler et al., *Lancet* 1980. 2. p. 1317-20.
8 M. M. Weissman, G. Klerman et al. *Arch. Gen. Psychiatry* 1981, 38. p. 51-55.
9 R. T. Frank, 'The hormonal causes of premenstrual tension.' *Arch. Gen. Psychiatry* 1931, 26. p. 1053.
10 Symposium on Premenstrual Tension, *The Journal of Reproductive Medicine* 1981 Vol 28. No. 7.
11 K. Dalton. *The Premenstrual Syndrome and Progesterone Therapy.* (London, William Heinemann 1977).
12 Gwyneth Sampson. Premenstrual Syndrome: A double-blind controlled trial of Progesterone and placebo *British Journal of Psychiatry* 1979 135, p. 209-215.
13 Noreen Riols, *The Eye of The Storm* (Hodder and Stoughton) used with permission.

CHAPTER FOUR

'Chasing after the wind!'

'The Meaning of Life' – The existential factor

Overwhelmed with the absurdity and pointlessness of life, Bill set out to kill himself. A lonely copse in the country, a bottle of sleeping tablets . . . nobody would even notice his absence for a few days. For many months his mind had been in a turmoil of questions but now he knew it was a waste of time to even ask them. He had expected to find the answers in the great halls of learning at University, but was amazed and disappointed that most of the other students and even his teachers did not want to take his questions seriously. His childhood in a country village had been very happy but now, at 19, he was facing a much bigger and more complicated world. After school, he had worked for a year as a gardener. It was there, working alone for many hours that he began to think about the purpose of life. Is there a God? Why is there so much suffering and evil? What does love mean? How do we know life is not just a bad dream?

After a few months at University he became progressively more disillusioned. To fill his spare time and to distract himself from his own thoughts he spent hours in the cinema. But, far from an escape, many of the films only highlighted his dilemma, as they vividly portrayed the pain and meaninglessness of life. The books he read and even the music he listened to, only served to exaggerate his pessimistic mood. As he set out to put an end to his struggle, it was a clear, crisp January day. The sun was shining and fortunately he was not past

noticing the beauty of the fields and trees around him.
His purposeful step did not falter for some time but after
a while he hesitated. A flicker of doubt crept into his
mind. This world is not completely without beauty, he
thought – maybe I should try just one more time before
giving up completely. Feeling rather cowardly he
retraced his steps, not knowing where to look next.

He remained confused and depressed over the
following weeks until he was invited by a friend to meet
some people who took his questions seriously and
seemed to understand his need for answers. They were
discussing a book in which the writer seemed preoccupied with the same theme that had haunted him for the
past few months. 'Everything is meaningless, a chasing
after the wind' (Ecclesiastes 2. 11).

What is the point of it all? Why do I exist? Where did I
come from? Where am I going to? Viktor Frankl, an
Austrian psychiatrist, wrote 'more and more patients
are crowding out clinics and consulting rooms complaining of an inner emptiness, a sense of the total and
ultimate meaninglessness of their lives.'[1]

In Shakespeare's Macbeth we hear an echo of the
same theme:

Tomorrow, and tomorrow, and tomorrow,
Creeps in this petty pace from day to day
To the last syllable of recorded time,
And all our yesterdays have lighted fools
The way to dusty death. Out, out, brief candle!
Life's but a walking shadow, a poor player
That struts and frets his hour upon the stage
And then is heard no more: it is a tale
Told by an idiot, full of sound and fury,
Signifying nothing.[2]

Cause or effect?

In deep depression there is often a strong sense of the futility of life. Some psychiatrists believe that questions about the purpose of life are part of the neurotic ramblings of depression. Freud wrote in a letter to his friend Marie Bonaparte, 'The moment a man raises the question of the meaning of life he is sick.'[3] Certainly, some people who normally have a deep sense of purpose in life may express hopelessness when depressed because their perception of the world is so distorted. But loss of meaning is not only produced by depression, it may also be the primary reason for depression.

Carl Jung, in contrast to Freud, recognised the validity of the search for meaning. 'Among all my patients in the second half of life – that is to say over 35 – there has not been one whose problem in the last resort was not that of finding a religious outlook to life.'[4] Most people go through life avoiding such major questions about the ultimate purpose of existence, because they believe that there are no real answers. Only at times of major crisis in their lives might they face them for a moment. When the crisis is passed, the questions are usually forgotten. Some philosophers of the late nineteenth and early twentieth century (the existentialists) have been acutely aware of the way most people avoid facing the big questions about the purpose of life and the reality of their own death. Ernest Becker highlights man's dilemma in his book *The Denial of Death*:

> Man is literally split in two; he has an awareness of his own splendid uniqueness in that he sticks out of nature with a towering majesty, and yet he goes back into the ground a few feet in order blindly and dumbly to rot and disappear forever. It is a terrifying dilemma to be in and to have to live with.[5]

Becker sees many of life's activities as distractions from facing the reality of the ultimate meaningless of life. We cannot live for long with a conscious awareness of our situation, so we repress it and distract ourselves by endless activity:

> Modern man is drinking and drugging himself out of awareness, or he spends his time shopping which is the same thing . . . or alternatively he buries himself in psychology in the belief that awareness all by itself will be some kind of magical cure for his problems.[6]

Viktor Frankl writes of the existential vacuum of the 20th century. He believes that it is vitally important for man to have a sense of meaning in his life. Man's search for meaning is a primary force in his life. It is not, as Freud believed, merely a product of instinctual drives and defence mechanisms.

> A man's concern, even in his despair, over the worthwhileness of life is spiritual distress but by no means a mental disease. It may well be that interpreting the first in terms of the latter motivates a doctor to bring his patient's existential despair under a heap of tranquillizing drugs. It is his task, rather, to pilot the patient through his existential crisis of growth and development.[7]

Frankl describes in his very moving book, *Man's Search for Meaning*, how, in the Nazi Concentration Camp of Auschwitch, it was those who had some sense of meaning and purpose who survived. Those who had lost a sense of purpose soon gave up and succumbed to illness.

The prisoner who had lost faith in the future – his
future – was doomed. With his loss of belief in the
future, he also lost his spiritual hold; he let himself
decline and became subject to mental and physical
decay. Usually this happened quite suddenly, in the
form of a crisis, the symptoms of which were familiar
to the experienced camp inmate. We all feared this
moment – not for ourselves, which would have been
pointless, but for our friends. Usually it began with
the prisoner refusing one morning to get dressed and
washed or to go out on the parade grounds. No
entreaties, no blows, no threats had any effect. He
just lay there, hardly moving. If this crisis was brought
about by an illness, he refused to be taken to the
sick-bay or to do anything to help himself. He simply
gave up. There he remained, lying in his own excreta,
and nothing bothered him any more.

I once had a dramatic demonstration of the close link
between the loss of faith in the future and this
dangerous giving up. F-, my senior block warden, a
fairly well-known composer and librettist, confided in
me one day: 'I would like to tell you something,
Doctor. I have had a strange dream. A voice told me
that I could wish for something – that I should only say
what I wanted to know, and all my questions would be
answered. What do you think I asked? That I would
like to know when the war would be over for me. You
know what I mean, Doctor – for me! I wanted to know
when we, when our camp, would be liberated and our
sufferings come to an end.'

'And when did you have this dream?' I asked.

'In February, 1945,' he answered.

It was then the beginning of March.

'What did your dream voice answer?'

Furtively he whispered to me, 'March thirtieth.'

When F- told me about his dream, he was still full of

hope and convinced that the voice of his dream would be right. But as the promised day drew nearer, the war news which reached our camp made it appear very unlikely that we would be free on the promised date. On March 29th, F- suddenly became ill and ran a high temperature. On March 30th, the day his prophecy had told him that the war and suffering would be over for him, he became delirious and lost consciousness. On March 31st, he was dead. To all outward appearances, he had died of typhus.[8]

But Frankl did not mean that people needed a sense of overall meaning, but that they need to discover a purpose such as writing a book, escaping from prison, or returning to loved ones . . . those who lost even this sense of day to day purpose gave up and died. There is of course some truth in this. Most of us live for particular relationships, for a career, for some ambition, or for the next holiday. This is a sense of purpose on a day to day level. But I do not agree with what Frankl wrote at that time. 'The meaning of life differs from man to man, from day to day, hour to hour . . . one should not search for an abstract meaning to life.'[9] In his later writings he does stress the importance of religion and some sense of ultimate meaning.[10] There are differences in day to day meaning, but it would demand a considerable amount of irrational optimism and courage to face a future with no *ultimate* meaning. And this predicament is at the heart of existential philosophy, which has deeply affected the world of contemporary counselling and psychotherapy. Sartre, one of the fathers of existential philosophy sums it up;

If I've excluded God the Father, there has to be someone to invent values . . . To say that we invent values means nothing more nor less than this; that there is no sense in life *a priori* . . . It's yours to make sense of, and the value of it is nothing else but the sense that you choose.[11]

Many young people who do not even know the word existentialism, let alone how to spell it, are absorbing it all day long as they listen to the radio and to their records. Songs of cynical despair are mixed with songs of irrational optimism that love will conquer and everything will be all right in the end. The writer of the following song, sung by the Buzzcocks in 1981, was suicidal at the time, and he brilliantly expresses the cynicism of many young people who have everything, and yet nothing to believe in. The despairing cry, 'there is no love in this world anymore' occurs 20 times in the song.

> In these times of contention
> It's not my intention to make things plain
> I'm looking through mirrors to catch a
>   reflection that can't be mine,
> I'm losing control now, I'll just have to slow down
>   a thought or two.
> I can't feel the future and I'm not even certain that
>   there is a past.
> I believe in the workers' revolution
> And I believe in the final solution
> I believe in . . . I believe in . . .
>
> I haven't an idea of what to do
> I'm painting by numbers
> But can't find the colours that fill you in.
> I'm not even knowing if I'm coming or going to
>   end or begin.
> I believe in the immaculate conception
> And I believe in the resurrection
> And I believe in . . . I believe in . . .

There is no love in this world any more.

I've fallen from favour while trying to savour
   experience,
I'm seeing things clearly but it has quite nearly
   blown my mind.
It's the aim of existence to offer resistance to the
   flow of time
Everything is and that is why it is will be
   in the line.

I believe in the web of fate
And I believe I'm going to be late
So I'll be leaving what I believe in
There is no love in this world any more. [12]

So for those who dare to face these questions about the reality of the world we live in, and questions of where our values come from, there may be a major crisis in their lives. If the normal distractions of job, family, and friends, do not prove enough, panic and despair may lead to deep depression. However, a courageous search for answers may lead through the valley of depression to a time of great growth and development.

Karen's search

Karen had coped pretty well with life until this year; after breaking up with her boyfriend she had become preoccupied with the futility of life. She had always accepted what she had learned at school. It all came back to her now as if she was seeing it for the first time. Man, she had been taught, is just the product of millions of years of chance speeding through space on a microscopic planet in one of millions of galaxies in the universe. She wondered if we are really so utterly insignificant? Her mind was full of questions. Is there anything beyond death? Is there a God? How do I know I'm not just dreaming – perhaps its all a terrible nightmare? How do I know what's right and wrong? What's the point of it all? As she walked out of the Monty Python film *The Meaning of Life* she found herself in tears, humming the song:

> Is life just a game where we make up the rules
> While we're searching for something to say
> Or are we just simply spiralling coils
> Of self-replicating DNA?
> What is life? What is our fate?
> Is there Heaven or Hell? Do we reincarnate?
> Is mankind evolving or is it too late?
> Well tonight here's the Meaning of Life.'[13]

But there was nothing there except obscenity and satire. Her friends told her not to be so neurotic. 'Enjoy yourself', they said, 'none of us knows the answers to those questions. Nobody really does.' But Karen was too desperate to be able to switch off the incessant searching of her mind. She turned to transcendental meditation to try to relax and was told that she was thinking too much. She had to learn to see reality differently, they said. Really there are no problems, it is just our minds that think there are. While meditating she had some experiences of real peace and the questions became less insistent. Other friends had joined the Divine Light Mission or were into Zen Buddhism and they seemed to know the answers to her questions. But did they? As she tried to talk to them she realised that they didn't have any reasonable answers. They believed they were experiencing God, the oneness of all things, and they didn't need answers anymore.

Eventually her depression overwhelmed her and she was admitted to a psychiatric hospital. There the doctors gave her anti-depressants, which certainly helped her to think a bit more clearly and rationally. They talked about her problems with her family and with her boyfriend, but seemed to ignore the other bigger questions buzzing in her mind. One doctor even told her that those questions about the meaning of life wouldn't worry her so much once she was better. The hospital chaplain was sympathetic but implied that he too was struggling to find answers to those questions. 'Your search is very important, my dear, it gives life meaning!'

After she left hospital she continued her search. She met some friends who were Christians and spent many hours talking with them. Gradually she began to see that if there really was a God who had created her and now loved her and wanted to have a relationship with her, then it made sense of her deep longings for meaning, for love and for a sense of what was ultimately right or wrong – because God had made her that way 'in His image'. Somehow it took less 'faith' to believe in that – it seemed more reasonable – than in the idea that there is no God and that we are no more than highly evolved animals who have no sure idea of why we are here or where we are going. It explained the amazing beauty, design and variety in the world around her. And it did not ignore the ugliness and suffering in the world but recognised that it was a result of man trying to live without God. She began to see that however anti or irreligious people claim to be, they normally have to put their faith in something, whether it is evolution, science or an optimism that says 'it will all work out alright in the end', or even some sort of mystical belief in the oneness of everything. It seemed to her to take more faith to believe in the atheistic prophets of the twentieth century – Freud, Marx and Darwin, who had their own explanations of man's nature and purpose, than it did to believe Jesus' view of the situation. She had to come to terms with all that *he* did and said. Was he crazy, power hungry, out to deceive people, or was he speaking the truth? He claimed to be the Son of God – God come in human form, to make it possible for men who had tried to live without him, to come back into a relationship with their Creator. And then the evidence for his death and resurrection was pretty overwhelming.

Who should she believe? Should she remain on the fence, agnostic, finding ultimate meaning in the search itself? Should she become a cynic – not believing there are any answers? Should she join her friends and hide her head in the sand? It became increasingly clear that Christianity was not just a prop to help her whistle in the dark, but a way of seeing things which really made sense of the world we live in – it was the truth about reality. And it involved not just a belief that the Christian understanding of the world is true, but it took her into a relationship with the living personal God where she found a deep sense of forgiveness, purpose, significance and value.

Meaning stimulates the will

Like Victor Frankl, Colin Wilson writes, 'the deeper my sense of the meaningfulness of the world, the fiercer and more persistent my will.'[14] If we have a deep conviction that we are here for a purpose, and are not just the products of time and chance – if we know that we have been created by a God who loves us, and is working in us to restore us to the perfection of the way we were originally created – if we are sure that death is not the end, then the daily events of life, relationships, gardening, working, washing-up, take on a new significance. There is an upward spiral of increasing awareness of meaning leading to increasing stimulation of the will. Conversely a downward spiral of despair and hopelessness and meaninglessness paralyses the will. 'Boredom cripples the will, meaning stimulates it.'[15] 'If you allow the will to remain passive for long periods, it has the same effect as leaving your car in the garage for the winter. The batteries go flat. When the batteries go flat, life fails.'[16] So with the little will that someone who is depressed seems to have, they need to reach out, search for and grasp meaning. It takes a willingness to commit oneself to some belief about the purpose of existence. Many people, as I have said, avoid questions of ultimate meaning and manage to keep going by finding a purpose in their job, their family, their next holiday or a relationship, and these are important things. At one level as I stir myself up to plan a holiday, I have a temporary sense of meaning, something for which to live. At another level as I affirm my belief in a Creator God and His purpose for me a deeper meaning infuses my will and gives me energy to get up and go on. It also gives me a framework of truth to understand what is going on in the world. Nietzsche, although himself unable to find any ultimate meaning 'for' or 'in' his life wrote 'he who has a *why* to live can bear with almost any *how*.'[17]

So, for many people these questions about life will certainly be one of the reasons for their vulnerability to depression. For some it will be the most important factor.

References

1   Victor Frankl in, A Conversation with Victor Frankl of Vienna *Psychology Today*, Feb. 1968.
2   William Shakespeare, Macbeth, Act V. iv.
3   Sigmund Freud, quoted by Victor Frankl. Op. cit.
4   C. G. Jung, *Modern Man in Search of a Soul* (New York: Harcourt, Bruce, 1933) p.229.
5   Ernest Becker, *The Denial of Death* (Free Press. Macmillian Pub. Co. Inc. 1973). p. 26.

6 Ibid., p. 284.
7 Victor Frankl, *Man's Search for Meaning* (Hodder & Stoughton 1974) p. 104-105.
8 Ibid., p. 74-75.
9 Ibid., p. 110. Frankl describes three ways of discovering meaning (1) by doing a deed (2) by experiencing a value (3) by suffering (p. 113).
10 Victor Frankl *The Will & Meaning* (Souvenir Press. 1969) p. 146. The existentialists may be divided into two groups – those who believe in God (like Frankl), but who say we cannot talk meaningfully about God, we can only experience him, and those who do not believe in God or any ultimate purpose (like Sartre), for whom facing an absurd universe with courage is all that they can do.
11 J. P. Sartre, *Existentialism and Humanism* (Eyre Methuen Ltd. 1973) p. 54.
12 Buzzcocks.
13 Monty Python, *The Meaning of Life*.
14 Colin Wilson, *New Pathways in Psychology: Maslow and the Post Freudian Revolution* (Taplinger Pub. Co. New York 1972) p. 31.
15 Ibid., p. 26.
16 Ibid., p. 28.
17 Nietzche quoted by Victor Frankl in *Man's Search for Meaning* op. cit. p. 106.

CHAPTER FIVE

The devil and all his works

Depress, deceive and destroy – the demonic factor

Margaret came from a churchgoing family. But the Sunday formality had little relationship to the rest of life. In her mid-teens she rebelled against anything to do with the church and later became involved with friends who regularly smoked marijuana and occasionally used LSD. Gradually she became fascinated with the occult world of mediums and seances and finally decided to become an active member of a Satanist Church. Soon after this she began to be haunted by deep fears – becoming increasingly depressed and suicidal. She felt trapped and unable to extricate herself from her decision. Finally she left the country to get away from her 'friends' but the torment continued and she eventually sought help from Christians. The urge to commit suicide or run away increased but finally after a great struggle she was able to confess to God what she had done and pray for deliverance from Satanic influence.

In a similar way Fiona, the only child of middle class non-Christian parents, drifted into the drug culture. Often on her drug trips she saw a figure in white who kept turning towards her but she never saw a face. She presumed it was God and felt encouraged to continue these trips. However she became increasingly haunted by fears, depression and an urge to destroy herself – by jumping from a high window or throwing herself in front of a car. On one occasion she asked the figure to turn around and she said, 'I saw it was Satan and was terrified'. She phoned the only Christian she knew who had previously been involved with drugs, tarot cards and seances. She took her to a Christian counsellor and in the context of dealing with a number of problems in her life she prayed for forgiveness and protection from the evil one. As she moved into her new life as a Christian she was increasingly free from fear and depression.

Scientific sceptics or a surfeit of spirits?

Most psychiatrists would not take the reality of a demonic influence seriously. Because it cannot be proved 'scientifically' and perhaps more importantly because it is too unbelievable, it is not even worth considering. Freud explained what men once called 'demonic' or 'evil spirits' to be 'base and evil wishes' deriving from 'impulses which have been rejected and repressed' in one's personality. Carl Jung implied that the demonic is the area of 'autonomous complexes', the parts of our personality that we have difficulty in admitting to ourselves. For those who have abandoned the supernatural reality of God and Satan, explanations for disturbed behaviour have now to be found only within nature itself, without our genes, our bio-chemistry, and our childhood. Neurosis, schizophrenia, and hysteria are the common labels used to identify what once might have been described as 'demon possession'.

Christians have a different set of difficulties in this area and there are many who believe that all psychological problems are caused by demons. There have been times in history when this belief has given rise to 'witch hunts'. Spirits of depression, anxiety, loneliness, lust and alcohol may need to be exorcised or bound. People are seen as a battle ground of divine and satanic forces with little significance being given to their own good or bad choices, and little emphasis placed on the fact that

Satan's destructive influence in the world is far wider than just the area of his effect on individual people.

So, on the one hand there are those who put all their faith in science, and do not believe in a supernatural world. For them, only that which can be observed and measured is real. On the other hand there are growing numbers of people who recognise that there is more to the universe than meets the eye, and set out to explore the supernatural and spiritual realm. Within the church there has been an increasing concern to go beyond the formalities of doctrine and belief to experience God's power at work in our lives today. At the same time, in the last few decades we have seen an extraordinary resurgence of interest in the mystical, occult and supernatural amongst non-Christians.

All the major bookstores have large sections on the occult often bigger than the sections on Christianity. Many novels and especially young peoples' comic books feature stories about astrologers, mediums, and occult powers. It is a commonplace leisure activity to dabble in astrology, seances, spiritual healing, para-psychology and black magic. And Colin Wilson in his book *The Occult* says:

> It would probably be safe to say that there are now more witches in England and America than at any time since the Reformation.[1]

The dangers of dabbling

Many people are totally unaware of the dangers of such involvement. Dennis Wheatley in an interview for his book, *Man, Myth and Magic?* said, 'I do not approve of mediums attempting to contact the dead . . . mediums who get in touch with occult forces are laying themselves open to serious danger. The powers that mediums contact are not the dead, but evil entities, and they are very dangerous indeed.' John Richards comments, 'how ironic that such authorities on the occult are more biblical in their approach than some authorities in the church.'[2]

In his book *Modern Witchcraft*, Frank Smyth writes, 'despite the fact that superstition has always been with us, the last few years of the 1960s saw a flowering of interest in occult matters which would have been inexplicable to an earlier generation . . . Now . . . it seems scarcely possible to pick up a newspaper or turn on a television set without some reference being made to ghosts, demons, magicians, or witches. The occult, which lay dormant for so many years, is once again up and thriving all around us.'[3]

In psychology, many have turned from the hope that their problems will be solved by self-awareness and traditional psychotherapy, to commitment to eastern philosophy and meditation, which frequently leads on into the development of various psychic powers, often called 'powers of the mind.' There appears to be a vortex effect so that a person dabbling in such fringe activities as astrology, telepathy, and ESP, can be sucked into deeper things. The attraction has been the same since Satan first tempted Adam and Eve. 'You shall be as gods', – the temptation of power and knowledge independent of God.

While there is obviously a vast revival of interest in the occult both among non-Christians and Christians, C. S. Lewis's oft quoted comment is a timely reminder in an age when we so easily swing to extremes. 'There are two equal and opposite errors into which our race can fall about the devils. One is to disbelieve in their existence. And the other is to believe, and to feel an excessive and unhealthy interest in them. They themselves are equally pleased by both errors . . . '[4]

The wiles of the devil

When we turn to the Bible to discover who Satan really is we find that he was once an angel who rebelled against God and later tempted Adam and Eve. In *The Silmarillion* Tolkien describes the creation of the world and the origin of Satan in a wonderful imaginative picture based on the true Scriptural account. Iluvatar (God) made Ainur (the angels) who 'were with him before ought was made . . . and they sang before him, and he was glad . . .'

> And it came to pass that Iluvatar called together all the Ainur and declared to them a mighty theme, unfolding to them things greater and more wonderful than he had yet revealed; and the glory of its beginning and the splendour of its end amazed the Ainur, so that they bowed before Iluvatar and were silent.
>
> The Iluvatar said to them: 'Of the theme that I have declared to you, I will now that ye make in harmony together a Great Music. And since I have kindled you with the Flame Imperishable, ye shall show forth your powers in adorning this theme, each with his own thoughts and devices, if he will. But I will sit and hearken, and be glad that through you great beauty has been wakened into song.'
>
> Then the voices of the Ainur, like unto harps and lutes, and pipes and trumpets, and viols and organs, and like unto countless choirs singing with words, began to fashion the theme of Iluvatar to a great music; and a sound arose of endless interchanging melodies woven in harmony that passed beyond hearing into the depths and into the heights, and the places of the dwelling of Iluvatar were filled to overflowing, and the music and the echo of the music went out into the Void.

But now Iluvatar sat and hearkened, and for a great
while it seemed good to him, for in the music there
were no flaws. But as the theme progressed, it came
into the heart of Melkor to interweave matters of his
own imagining that were not in accord with the theme
of Iluvatar; for he sought therein to increase the
power and glory of the part assigned to himself. To
Melkor among the Ainur had been given the greatest
gift of power and knowledge, and he had a share in all
the gifts of his brethren. He had gone often alone into
the void places seeking the Imperishable Flame; for
desire grew hot within him to bring into being things
of his own, and it seemed to him that Iluvatar took no
thought for the Void, and he was impatient of its
emptiness. Yet he found not the Fire, for it is with
Iluvatar. But being alone he had begun to conceive
thoughts of his own unlike those of his brethren.
Some of these thoughts he now wove into his music,
and straightway discord arose about him, and many
that sang nigh him grew despondent, and their
thought was disturbed and their music faltered; but
some began to attune their music to his rather than to
the thought which they had at first. Then the discord
of Melkor spread ever wider, and the melodies which
had been heard before foundered in a sea of turbulent
sound.[5]

The Bible does not define in precise detail how the
devil influences the world but gives a number of principles which help us to understand something of his
activity in relation to psychological problems. Firstly, in
the New Testament, in many places, illness is clearly
distinguished from demon possession. (Matthew 4.24,
Mark 6.13, Luke 6.17-19, Acts 19.11-12). Those who
were not demon-possessed were not healed by exorcism
or binding of spirits. The Bible makes a clear distinction
between natural and supernatural causes of disease.

Ultimately, in tempting Adam and Eve to disobey God, Satan is partly responsible for the entry of disease, disharmony and death in the world. But this is not the same as direct possession by an evil spirit. Secondly, man can sin without Satan's assistance. 'Each person is tempted when by his own evil desire, he is dragged away and enticed.' James 1.14 (see also Mark 7.20-21 and Jeremiah 17.9). It is our sinful nature which leads us to sin. While acknowledging the reality of Satan's activity and power there is I believe a great danger in many churches today of explaining too much abnormal behaviour in terms of demonic forces. This immediately removes our responsibility for recognising and confessing our own sinfulness. Paul describes the acts of the sinful nature–'sexual immorality, impurity . . . jealousy, rage, selfish ambition . . .' He exhorts the Christians 'not to indulge the sinful nature'. (Galatians 5.13-21). Satan is not mentioned here. Montgomery writes 'the devil made me do it' is not an acceptable theological stance but rather a demonic form of escapism to avoid confrontation with the 'personal sin within'. If we see ourselves as passive victims caught up in a battle between the forces of good and evil, there is little incentive to make any change in our lives because our own actions have little significance. We are but pawns in the cosmic drama of spiritual warfare. Paul gives a good example of the usual relationship between our sinful nature and Satan when talking about anger. He does not say 'cast out a spirit of anger' but he talks of the acts of the sinful nature as hatred and fits of rage. We are responsible for our actions, but he warns, 'do not give the devil a foothold'!

And so we see that, thirdly, Satan does tempt us directly. Christ was tempted by Satan (Matthew 4.1) and there are other references to this in Scripture. We are told that Satan has considerable freedom now but will one day be completely destroyed (Revelation 20.10).

For the moment he is active in trying to destroy our faith and hope, and in taking advantage of our points of vulnerability and weakness. We must constantly pray for protection from the evil one as he 'goes about as a roaring lion seeking whom he may devour'. (1 Peter 5.8). He will accuse and deceive us and sometimes he will disguise himself as 'an angel of light' (2 Corinthians 11) to beguile us. Paul reminds us of the spiritual battle in which we are involved and the need for protection from the evil one as he seeks to deceive, to depress and to destroy.

> Finally be strong in the Lord and in his mighty power. Put on the full armour of God so that you can take your stand against the devil's schemes. For our struggle is not against flesh and blood, but against the rulers, against the authorities, against the powers of this dark world and against the spiritual forces of evil in the heavenly realms. (Ephesians 6.10-12).

Oppression, possession or depression?

The concept of 'oppression' which is commonly used amongst Christians is not a biblical one, but seems to be a reasonable description of the fact that Satan does seem to be more active at certain times in some lives than in others. The Greek word for possession simply means 'demonised'. From the experience of many Christians has arisen the simple division into two sorts of particular Satanic influences, apart from his general destructive influence in the world. Firstly there are those who are oppressed or attacked involuntarily, without knowingly inviting it. And secondly those who are possessed voluntarily. They have openly sold themselves to Satan and willingly been involved in occult activity. I do not believe that the Bible suggests that a Christian can be possessed by the devil or evil spirits, but it seems that Christians who have been involved in some way with the occult are particularly sensitive to Satan's activity, and may be more vulnerable to oppression. Someone who has a family history of involvement in the occult (for example a mother or grandmother who was a medium or witch) or has been involved in activities such as astrology, seances or spiritualism, should be careful to renounce very specifically all connections and claims of Satan over their life. It is wise to destroy any charms, amulets, tarot cards, letters, or books which have any association with such activity. They should also ask forgiveness for their own dabbling in such things and renew their commitment to Jesus Christ asking for His protection in the future.

Peter came for counselling because he was in constant torment – depressed, withdrawn and often thinking of suicide and terrified that he would murder someone. From time to time he would have 'this red flash in my head' which was accompanied by an obsessive drive to kill someone or something. As he talked, it emerged that he had an extraordinary family history. His great grandmother had been hanged as a witch in Spain. His grandmother and mother were active mediums and several members of the family had shown signs of pathological depression and violence, while some had committed suicide.

After renouncing his own dabbling with occult things and praying for deliverance and protection from any satanic influence from his ancestors and relatives he gradually began to lose his fears of the 'red flash' returning and so was freed from depression. He needed help too in sorting out his relationship with his parents and found his sense of self-worth increasing as he realised that God loved him, and found that other Christians accepted him as he was. He is not studying for the ministry.

I do not believe that the three people I have described were possessed but they were certainly, amongst other problems in their lives, 'oppressed'.

Possession of non-Christians is, I believe, still rare in this country but it is probably increasingly common as more people become actively involved in occult activity and the worship of Satan. Os Guiness in his book *The Dust of Death* writes of the 'encircling eyes' of the wild beasts, the demonic forces, closing in around the fire as the flames of Christianity die down in the western world.[6] There are probably more cases of possession in countries where satanic forces are openly embraced, and where Christianity has not had its historic restraining influence, as it has in Europe and America.

In my own experience I have only ever met one person whom I seriously thought might be possessed. He was a young man of West Indian origin whose parents had been very heavily involved in voodoo. Much of his strange behaviour could however be explained on the basis of the extraordinary relationships within his family. How can one tell? So often the psychological, physical and spiritual factors are woven together. Usually those who are psychologically disturbed are attracted by the occult so that it is difficult to tell which is cause and which is effect.

John Richards in his book *But Deliver Us From Evil – an introduction to the demonic dimension in pastoral care* summarises the findings of those Christians who have written about the diagnosis of demon possession.[7] He says that there may be a change of personality with variable character, intelligence, demeanor or appearance. There may be physical symptoms such as extraordinary strength, epileptiform seizures, catatonic postures, falling, clouding of consciousness, anaesthesia to pain and changed voice. Mental changes may occur such as speaking in tongues, understanding unknown languages, or experiencing psychic powers such as telepathy and clairvoyance. There is usually a reaction of fear or blasphemy to the name of Christ and deliverance may be performed in the name of Jesus. Many of these symptoms and signs may occur for other reasons and it is certainly rare to see them all together in one person so that a diagnosis of possession is not easy.

However if demonic possession is not common in this country at the moment, that does not mean that Satan is asleep; on the contrary, he is always at work trying to lead Christians astray, to destroy the work of God in their lives and to wreak confusion and havoc in society. One factor that we seriously underestimate is the power of suggestion in our lives. Hypnotism and much so-called spiritual healing demonstrate that the human mind will believe what is suggested to it by a person who wields power and authority. Any system of explanation is willingly accepted to make sense of inner confusion. A person in distress, seeking relief, if told that they are possessed, will increasingly behave as if this is in fact the case and may show all the signs of relief and healing when it is suggested that the spirit is gone. We need great discernment in this area where there is such confusion.

Disease or demon?

We must return now to our particular theme and ask how all this relates to those who are depressed. There are some Christian counsellors who would say that because a depressed person finds it hard to pray and read the Bible, and because he doubts his own salvation and feels his heart is hard towards God, even to the point of being tempted with blasphemous thoughts, then these must be signs of demonic activity. The poor person who is so depressed may actually believe that he is possessed by the devil. But these morbid thoughts are characteristic of severe depression which may have been caused by any of the other factors we have mentioned in earlier chapters. Often people with morbid delusional beliefs have other false ideas as well – for example, that they are suffering from cancer, are completely poverty stricken, are being persecuted by the police or foreign powers or that they have committed the unforgiveable sin. Difficulty with sleeping, weight loss, tearfulness, agitation or retardation are also usually present in depression. Suicidal thoughts may result from the belief that they are a burden to everyone and have committed terrible sins. Doctor Alfred Lechler, writing on the need to distinguish between disease and the demonic, writes 'one can therefore establish the rule that if blasphemous thoughts arise within a person's heart and are consciously expressed without the slightest remorse, they will in almost every case have been prompted by the devil. On the other hand, if the thoughts force themselves upon the person, and instead of being expressed are abhorred and genuinely repented of, they will most likely be of a pathological nature'.[8] John Bunyan describes such compulsive blasphemous thoughts in *Grace Abounding to the Chief of Sinners* and his terrible fear that he had committed the unpardonable sin against theHoly Spirit.[9] Dr. Lechler continues, 'A demonically affected person will care little about his blasphemous thoughts, but the mental depressive will lament the fact that he is capable of thinking such things.' And in relation to suicidal ideas he writes 'there is a distinct difference between this (severe depressive) condition and the mental pressure experienced by a demonically depressed person. In such a case the pressure results from either some gross sin committed by the person himself, or from his own or his ancestors' involvement in occultism. The depressions experienced by a person in this condition will be marked by a terrible feeling of fear and unrest, accompanied by fits of anger and a defiance and aversion of everything to do with God and the Christian faith.'[10]

It is cruel and very harmful to tell someone in the depths of depression that they are spirit possessed unless there is a *very* clear evidence of such activity. There appears to be an increasing use of such simple minded formulations in the church today. This is probably the result of several factors. Firstly there is the temptation to dismiss anything 'psychological' which is not understood as 'demonic'. Then there is the desire for simple answers to complex problems and an inadequate understanding of the radical nature of 'the Fall' and its repercussions in every area of life. Finally, fear of feeling helpless and useless in the face of obvious suffering is also common amongst those dealing with the psychologically disturbed, and there is a strong temptation to be seen to have power and authority as a Christian healer and leader.

Wanted – a spirit of discernment

In this area, where it is so easy to underestimate or overestimate the devil's influence, we must pray for protection, discernment and wisdom. There are no easy answers. Satan is anxious that we remain confused and lays false trails in every direction. His most common way of working with us as individuals is described by C. S. Lewis in *The Screwtape Letters* when Uncle Screwtape, the senior devil, gives his young pupil Wormwood very practical advice about exploiting times of depression in the 'trough periods' of life:

My Dear Wormwood,

I hope that my last letter has convinced you that the trough of dullness or 'dryness' through which your patient is going at present, will not, of itself, give you his soul, but needs to be properly exploited. What

forms the exploitation should take I will now
consider.

In the first place I have always found that trough
periods of the human undulation provide excellent
opportunity for all sensual temptations, particularly
those of sex. This may surprise you, because, of
course, there is more physical energy, and therefore
more potential appetite at the peak periods; but you
must remember that the powers of resistance are then
also at their highest. Their health and spirits which
you want to use in producing lust can also, alas, be
very easily used for work or play or thought or
innocuous merriment. The attack has a much better
chance of success when the man's whole inner world is
drab and cold and empty. And it is also to be noted
that the trough of sexuality is subtly different from
that of the peak – much less likely to lead to the milk
and water phenomenon which the human calls 'being
in love', much more easily drawn into perversions,
much less contaminated by those generous and
imaginative and even spiritual conglomerates which
often render humans' sexuality so disappointing. It is
the same with the desires of the flesh . . . another
possibility is that of direct attack on his faith. When
you have caused him to presume that trough is
permanent, can you not persuade him that 'his
religious faith' is just going to die away like all his
previous phases? Of course there is no conceivable
way of getting by reason from the proposition 'I am
losing interest in this' to the proposition 'this is false'.
But, as I said before, it is jargon not reason you must
rely on. The mere word 'phase' will very likely do the
trick . . . You see the idea? Keep his mind off the
antithesis between true and false. Nice shadowy
expression – 'it was a phase' – I've been through all
that' – and don't forget the blessed word 'adolescent',
Your affectionate Uncle Screwtape.[11]

References

1 Colin Wilson, *The Occult* (Panther 1979).
2 John Richards, *But Deliver Us From Evil* (Darton Longman & Todd Ltd. 1984) p.77.
3 Frank Smyth, *Modern Witchcraft* (Macdonald Unit 75 1970) quoted in J. Richards op. cit., p.20.
4 C. S. Lewis, *The Screwtape Letters* (Fount Paperbacks – Collins 1977) p. 9.
5 J. R. R. Tolkien, *The Silmarillion* (Unwin Paperbacks 1979) p.15-16.
6 Os Guiness, *The Dust of Death* (IVP 1973) p. 277.
7 J. Richards op. cit., Chapter 6.
8 Dr. Alfred Lechler in Part II Dr. Kurt Koch *Occult Bondage and Deliverance* (Evangelization Pub. W. Germany) p.168.
9 John Bunyan, *Grace Abounding to the Chief of Sinners* (Oxford Univ. Press 1966.)
10 A. Lechler op. cit., p.173.
11 C. S. Lewis op. cit., p.48-52.

CHAPTER SIX

A way of seeing

The inner world of attitudes and values – the perspective factor

Martin was a successful doctor and a respected member of the local anglican evangelical church. He had risen rapidly in the ranks of the medical profession and was regarded as a possible candidate for the post of Professor in a few years time. He had married in his final year as a medical student and his wife soon conceived their first child. She had to give up her last year in university when the baby was born. She was a rather insecure person and when her mother, a dominating critical woman, came to live nearby, her confidence was continually undermined. Martin, impatient with her apparent weakness, had little time to listen. He had enough on his plate writing up his M.D. thesis, keeping up with the long hours in the hospital, and trying to attend the monthly church council meetings. In fact, he became so frustrated with the situation at home, the unmade beds, and the dust on the cupboards, . . . that in order to avoid losing his temper again he began to stay later and later at the hospital. By the time their third child was born he was a consultant. One day he came home to be greeted by a letter telling him that his wife had gone away for the weekend. The children were with her mother. She would be staying at their friend John's house. She reassured him that there was no adultery involved but that John had been such a support to her in this last year that she might well leave Martin if he would not spend more time with her. As the seriousness of the situation sank in over the next few weeks his concentration began to fade, and he slept badly. He felt trapped. There were enormous expectations from the patients and staff at the hospital, and his wife wanted more time from him at home. They tried to talk things out but always ended with her in tears and him frustrated, guilty and angry. He kept a good face on it for a while but one day, driving home in the car, after realising that he had just driven through a red light and narrowly missed an accident, he burst into uncontrollable sobs. He lay in bed all the next day and could not move. The G.P. called a psychiatrist to come and see him and he was admitted to the hospital with a diagnosis of severe depression.

Life events

It is not just being vulnerable in the many ways that I have described that brings about a state of depression, but there is usually some event such as the letter left by Martin's wife, coming on top of the other circumstances, which causes the change of mood. In Brown and Harris' London study, many of the women who were depressed had experienced what was called a 'major life event' in the six months before the onset of the depression. The 'life event' usually involved serious long-term threat to the woman or her family. (Short-term threats produced only temporary changes of mood.) The long-term threats were those which involved loss, threat of loss, or grave disappointment, where there was little chance of controlling the consequences. For example:

> Separation or threat of it . . . the death of a parent, a
> husband saying he is going to leave home, the
> break-up of any close relationship or threat of that
> break-up, an unpleasant revelation about someone
> close that forces a major re-assessment of the person

and the relationship, such as the loss of one's
conception of a relationship after finding out about a
husband's unfaithfulness, life threatening illness to
someone else, a major material loss or disappointment or threat of this, such as a couple living in bad
housing learning that their chances of being re-
housed were minimal, an enforced change of
residence or the threat of it. . . [1]

One can think of many other crises involving some
element of loss such as being made redundant or failing
an exam.

So if one woman who is vulnerable to depression
because of a genetic tendency, a number of losses in
childhood, and a poor relationship with her husband,
then discovers that her father has cancer, she may well
become depressed. But if the same event were to happen
to another woman, who also has a depressive tendency
in her genes, but who has not experienced major losses
or separations in childhood, and has a good relationship
with her husband, then she probably will not become
seriously depressed. But there is another factor, perhaps
the most important of all that will effect these women's
response to their circumstances and that is their inner
attitude towards them and the meaning that the events
have in their lives.

The meaning of the event

The event which has such consequences is usually an
experience which may produce emotions of anger,
frustration, guilt, anxiety, or grief, all of which, if not
dealt with in a constructive way, can be channelled into
the helplessness of severe depression. For example, the
loss of a close relationship, or the loss of a dream or
ambition in life, such as a thirtieth birthday which brings
home to a single person the fact that marriage and

having children is an even more remote possibility. An athlete may build his whole life around his physical abilities and have his identity crushed by a serious back injury. An illness may prevent a singer from performing any more. A couple making ambitious plans for their lives and their careers suddenly discover that the wife is pregnant. In a moment, all their plans are dashed! An elderly person's retirement from a job which had been the only thing which gave meaning in life may precipitate a major depression.

So it is not so much the actual event itself, but rather the meaning of the event to the person who has experienced it and their attitude to it, that is so important. Brown and Harris comment:

> Crises may raise fundamental questions about our
> lives. They focus our attention on the present and
> since this is the visible outcome of our past, our
> choices, commitments and mistakes, we may come to
> question what our life might have been, what it is
> about and what it will become. A son leaving home
> may produce for his mother alarming thoughts about
> the hollowness of her marriage and how she is to cope
> with it without him. Indeed anticipation of change
> may be enough, simply news that her son is proposing
> to emigrate.[2]

It is, therefore, not just the event of loss, disappointment, or frustration on its own, but it is our attitude to these situations that is so important. Crises may bring about a re-assessment of values, life goals, attitudes to death, possessions, career, and relationships. What we think about these things will deeply affect what we feel about them and how they influence our lives. We cannot blame the past or the difficulties in our lives for all our problems. It is how we react to them that matters. In a later chapter on freedom and determinism we will return to this theme in more detail.

Crises of values

Arieti, one of the most prominent writers on depression, points out that episodes of depression result from a person relying to a dangerous extent on external supports, such as a particular relationship or career, to maintain a sense of self-esteem. He calls these supports the 'dominant other' and the 'dominant goal'. What he means by these rather technical expressions is that some people live almost completely for another person and have little sense of their own separate identity. Life is lived to please the 'other'. All sense of security and value comes from the relationship with the 'other'. An independent existence is given up for the sake of the continued approval and support of the esteemed other. Loss of the 'dominant other' relationship may cause depression.[3] Others invest their self-esteem in the attainment of wealth, or achievement of some other major ambition. If the possibility of working towards or achieving the goal is taken away then they are likely to become depressed. Often those who rely so heavily on such a person or goal are not consciously aware of it because it is the only way they know how to survive in life.

Arieti has described something in psychological terms which the Bible often describes as idolatry. Without the knowledge that God loves us and values us for who we are, not just for what we achieve, as the core of our sense of self-esteem, we tend to rely on other things, on a dominant goal, or a dominant other person, to give a sense of self-worth. It is not wrong to get *some* of our sense of value from what we do or from the relationships that we have, but if these are the foundation stones of our self-esteem, then we are very vulnerable to loss and failure. We all build idols in our minds of the things that we think will bring us happiness and contentment, whether it be career, ambition, marriage, possessions, or good physical health. In the book *A Severe Mercy* Sheldon Vanauken tells how he discovered, through the death of his wife, that he had in fact loved her more than he loved God. Her death came to him as a 'severe mercy' because his wife and their romantic love had been a barrier which had prevented him from reaching a true relationship with God. So, through this terrible crisis, he had come to understand where his values and priorities had been wrong.[4]

The Old Testament is full of warnings and commands to Israel to destroy the idols they have set up in their lives, the false images that drew them away from their relationship with God. Job had everything taken from him and he was forced, in no uncertain terms, to evaluate his relationship with God and his attitudes to his possessions, his relationships and his family. That was a major crisis in his life! Sometimes it takes crises in our own lives to force us to re-evaluate and to understand what the Bible really says about the way we should be living and the way we should be thinking. We too often live in a fantasy world, looking to the future rather than living in the present. 'When I get married, when we have children, when we get a bigger house, when our financial problems are resolved, when we . . .' There is always a secret to happiness just around the corner and we never face up to the reality of our inner selves. We blame something or someone outside ourselves which needs to change, never our own attitude.

It is of course not wrong to want enough money to survive, a family, or a roof over our heads but when these become the central preoccupation of our hearts and minds from day to day then *something* is wrong! The syndrome of 'if only I had . . .' or 'when I get . . .' is basically breaking the tenth commandment 'you shall not covet . . .' And this is not easy because the whole advertising industry is out to make us covet; they use all the sophisticated psychological techniques of the 20th century to do so. We need to learn the secret of being content with what we have – something I struggle with every day. Paul writes to Timothy, 'godliness with contentment is great gain', (1 Timothy 6.6 A.V.) and Jesus taught us to seek first his kingdom and his righteousness and all these things would be added to us.(Matthew 6.33) It is a matter of priorities, and this is the focus of Jesus's teaching in the Sermon on the Mount – the inner world of attitudes and values.

It is important to recognise firstly that our attitudes and values affect our vulnerability to depression and secondly that depression, before it reaches the state of near paralysis, can be a positive experience, in that it drives us to look for the cause and deal with it. Pain, although uncomfortable, alerts us to the fact that something is wrong and leads us to the source of the disease. We are forced to face up to the fact that our thoughts, values, attitudes and actions may be wrong and need changing. We are forced to take stock and re-evaluate our lives in the face of a crisis.

So, just as crises of priorities and values may make us depressed, as we face them and work through the changes that need to be made, we also experience crises of expectations.

Crises of expectations

At a point of crises in our lives we may become aware of being under pressure from many different expecta-tions. Parents may be advising one course of action, the church another, and then friends both Christian and non-Christian have different views. And on top of that I have my own ideas of what I think God wants me to do.

In this situation, we can be paralysed into immobility or we can daily make choices to allow God's expectations to be the touch-stone by which all the other expectations are evaluated. Jesus gives a vivid example, 'if anyone does not hate father and mother . . . he cannot be my disciples.' (Luke 14.26) He did not mean that we should actually hate our parents, because this is in direct opposition to other commands in the Bible, but in comparison to our love for God, our love for our parents may appear very small. Although we must listen to and respect their opinions, we may have to do some things that they do not like if their values are very different from God's view of the situation.

As we talk of Christian values and God's expectations it becomes clear that Christian teaching is a crucial factor. False teaching can lead to wrong attitudes and unhelpful expectations, both of which can precipitate depression. Some examples may clarify this point.

Alice had had back trouble for several years. She had been to see several doctors but no-one seemed able to help. Her church had become progressively more charismatic and one member seemed to have a gift of healing. Alice became convinced by the teaching in the church that illness was not part of God's plan for her and that she should have enough faith to be healed. Hands were laid on her several times and many people were praying. But her back was no better. She struggled to have enough faith but she could not honestly join the others praising God for the way He had healed them. She tried to believe that she was healed but nothing happened. Not surprisingly she became increasingly depressed with terrible feelings of failure as a Christian. A theology of healing was not balanced here with an adequate theology of illness and suffering.

Robert had had sixteen spirits of various sins such as lust, envy, anger . . . cast out of him, or so the elders of his church thought. Sometimes he would writhe on the floor and shout when he was exorcised but still he remained unhappy, sullen and sometimes aggressive. No-one had taken the time to talk to him about the difficult relationship with his parents and the anger he felt towards them. In the teaching of that particular church any psychological problem was immediately interpreted as possession with an evil spirit.

Ruth was converted through a big evangelstic organisation. They encouraged her to give up her training in the theatre and music to work for them. She was taught that the most important thing in life was evangelism. As a Christian, apart from using her gifts in evangelistic crusades and rallies she should not continue her music and theatre. For three years she worked hard but found herself slipping into an apathetic irritable state of mind that rebelled against the restrictions of the life of the organisation. Surely there was more to life than this – mechanically but efficiently spreading the gospel. She was no longer the vibrant person she used to be. After much heart-searching she decided to leave the organisation. There was considerable resistance to her leaving, so much so that she began to feel terribly guilty and wondered if she was really stepping outside God's purpose for her and would make a terrible mess of her life. But other Christians encouraged her to leave. They encouraged her to see that evangelism, although one very important part of the Christian life, is not the only thing. As she studied the Bible it was almost as if she read it with new eyes. She saw that God wants us to use every part of our being, including the gifts of music and drama, to his glory. He wants us to enjoy the world he has given and to demonstrate the life of his kingdom here and now.

These examples demonstrate the importance of good teaching and also the awesome responsibility of teachers within the church.

No-one's perfect!

Expectations are also a problem at the heart of perfectionism. A certain amount of perfectionism is a great asset, and leads to an efficient, productive life-style. In no way do I disparage the desire to do well and to achieve high standards. But, at different points for each individual, these standards and expectations become a definite hindrance because they produce almost certain failure. Often people with perfectionist tendencies have a very low opinion of themselves. But this low self esteem may arise because they have a too high a view of what they can or should be. Their 'ideal self' is much bigger than their 'real self'. On one side of the coin is self-effacement, on the other there may in fact be pride.

Unfortunately many Christians who are also perfectionist tend to gravitate towards churches which reinforce rather than challenge their beliefs about themselves. Churches which emphasise 'perfectionism' and give more weight to the teaching of law rather than grace only compound the problem. The hope of complete healing that is given in many charismatic churches also attracts the person with perfectionist tendencies. As they have difficulty in accepting anything between categories of 'healthy' and 'sick' churches that promise complete health and wholeness in this life appear to offer a solution to all their problems. Slowly but surely, over perhaps many years, the person with a tendency to perfectionism needs to learn from the truths of Scripture, from the Holy Spirit, from the fellowship of believers, and ideally, if married, from their husband or wife that he (or she) is loved for who he is, not for what he does – loved 'warts and all'. He needs to learn that, although we are commanded to be perfect, the disciples knew we would not be so until we were with the Lord. We live in a fallen, imperfect world where 'if anybody does sin, we have one who speaks to the Father in our defense . . .' (1 John 2:1). Above all he needs to know that he is accepted by God with all his imperfections. He needs to know what it means to live under grace, not law, in this fallen and imperfect world. For many Christians this is a very painful thorn in the flesh which they may have to work against for many years, little by little, until they are made perfect by the One who accepts their imperfection. I will return to the theme of thorns in the flesh in a later chapter.

We have seen how our expectations and values deeply affect the way in which we react to crises in our lives. We have also seen how many other factors influence us and make us vulnerable to depression. In the following chapters we will begin to see how we can help ourselves to cope with depression when it threatens to overwhelm us. A breakdown need not be a total disaster, it can be a 'breakthrough'. Dr. Frederick Flach has written a helpful little book called 'The Secret Strength of Depression' in which he elaborates on this theme.[5] As one friend said a few years after his own breakdown 'Depression can be the best thing that happens to you.' It had forced him to re-evaluate his whole life.

First signs of sanity

One of the best places to begin is to learn to understand our gut responses to difficult situations in our lives. We need to learn to talk to ourselves. This is not necessarily the first sign of madness but may rather be the first sign of sanity! David cried out in the middle of his depression, 'my tears have been my food day and night' and then 'why are you cast down O my soul, why are disquieted within me?' (Psalm 42) He began to ask himself questions. We need to talk to ourselves rather than let our feelings talk to us and rule our minds. In our concern to know the truth about the world we live in and about ourselves we should ask questions of ourselves. Why am I angry? Why am I feeling guilty? Why am I withdrawing? What am I trying to hide? Am I hurt, rejected, guilty? Where are my attitudes wrong? Do I need to change? In order to change and be changed there has to be a healthy degree of self-awareness.

This is part of the process of becoming aware of and resisting what I think of as the grooves in which we normally run. We have been conditioned by our past, by our biochemistry, and by the attitudes of our parents and society to run in particular grooves – ways of thinking and feeling and behaving. Some of these will be good and some bad. Part of the process of sanctification is to get out of the bad grooves and to move into new ones (godly grooves!), so that we can live in the pattern in which we were intended to live. This can be a long and painful process. It is through crises and through times of depression, that we understand the sort of grooves that we live in, the habitual patterns which have been drilled into our being from the moment that we were conceived. Paul talks about struggling against his sinful nature. Another analogy is that of replacing old repetitive tapes in our minds with new ones. Introspection is not always bad. There are times in our lives when we need to look within and examine ourselves, not wallowing in self-pity, but deciding what action we need to take in dealing with wrong attitudes and values and wrong priorities and expectations. We can pray with David in Psalm 139.23-24 'Search me, O God, and know my heart; test me and know my anxious thoughts. See if there is any offensive way in me, and lead me in the way everlasting.'

So it is our way of seeing or our perspective on the things which happen to us which shapes our reactions. As we will see in the succeeding chapters, the Bible is particularly concerned about our attitudes and values.

'Out of the heart come evil thoughts, murder, adultery
. . . ' (Matthew 15.19). The sermon on the mount takes
our eyes off external actions and turns them to the inner
world of thoughts and purpose.

References

1 George Brown and Tirril Harris, *Social Origins of
   Depression – A study of psychiatric disorder in women*
   (Tavistock Pub.1978) p.103.
2 Ibid p.84
3 S. Arieti and J. Bemporad, The Psychological Organisation of Depression *American Journal of Psychiatry* 1980
   137, p. 1360.
4 Sheldon Vanauken, *A Severe Mercy* (Hodder &
   Stoughton 1977).
5 Dr. Frederick Flach, *The Secret Strength of Depression*.
   (Bantam 1975).

PART II

CHAPTER SEVEN

How . . . 'To put Humpty together again'?

The King's men had been called out on an emergency. Someone had discovered the shattered fragments below the wall. Who (or what) was it? They analysed each part in turn and tried to fit them together. It was rumoured that they were part of a character called Humpty. People had caught glimpses of him near the wall but nobody knew exactly what he had looked like. The King's men speculated for days and drew up many plans of how the pieces might fit together. Some gathered a few of the bigger pieces and decided that the other smaller pieces were irrelevant. A few, perhaps more humble and wise than the rest, went to the king himself and sought his advice. He willingly gave them a diagram of how Humpty looked before the fall with some instructions as to how to piece together the fragments. He also promised to help them in the task of re-building. The others, already busy putting together some of the pieces in the way they thought best, laughed at the king's plans and accused those who had gone to the king of making the plans up themselves. For some time they had been plotting the overthrow of the king, saying that the monarchy was old fashioned and unnecessary. And some sceptics who had never seen the king wondered if he really existed!

Sociological, biological, genetic, existential, demonic, life-events, expectations, values, priorities, . . . it all seems so confusing! How can we ever hope to put all the pieces together or to untangle such a knot of different influences and circumstances? When we honestly examine ourselves in this way we realise that we are all vulnerable in one way or another to depression or other psychological problems. Is there any hope of piecing together the fragments and moving towards health and wholeness? What is health and wholeness anyway? Is psychoanalysis the answer? Or drug treatment? Healing of the memories? Exorcism? If we were made 'in the image of God' it seems pretty shattered and fragmented now. How do we set about the re-building process?

The picture of Humpty Dumpty obviously has its limitations, but it illustrates the importance of our beliefs about the nature of man and his problems in deciding what needs to be done to set things right. Like the king's men who ignored the king's original plan of Humpty Dumpty, most scientists who examine human behaviour have to start with the pieces they find before them and speculate about where man came from and where he is going. Their belief about the purpose of life will affect the way they attempt to help people with problems. So we have many different schools of therapy, some making grandiose claims about putting man together again, others more modest and accepting that they can do little more than relieve symptoms and help people to cope a little better with the struggle of life. Each tends to focus on one or two aspects of man's problems to the exclusion of other aspects.

The limits of science

So, medical studies elaborate on the details of the disease and death of the body. Psychology and sociology studies demonstrate the breakdown we find within ourselves, in our relationships with each other, and with society. Behaviourists focus on the reality of the fact that we are conditioned to some degree by our environment.

Existentialists recognise our sense of isolation in a world without God. They all vividly describe the details of the broken world in which we live. They describe much that is true. But when they begin to describe the cause of the breakdown and alienation, and suggest a cure for it, there are as many views as there are theories of human nature.

Francis Schaeffer has described man as a 'glorious ruin', part glory and part ruin. J. Harold Ellens writes of the 'magnificence and malignancy' of this fallen world.[1] It is interesting to see how different psychiatrists and counsellors have focused on one aspect of man because they lack the framework given by God which explains both the ruin and the glory. For example Freud highlights our broken nature – the ruin! 'Men are not gentle creatures who want to be loved and who at the most can defend themselves when they are attacked. They are on the contrary creatures among whose instinctual endowments is to be reckoned a fair share of aggressiveness. As a result their neighbour is for them not only a potential helper or sexual object, but also someone who tempts them to satisfy their aggressiveness on him, to exploit his capacity to work without compensation, to use him sexually without his consent, to seize his possessions, to humiliate him, to cause him pain, to torture and kill him. Homo homini lupis, man is wolf to man. Who, in the face of all his experience of life and history, will have the courage to dispute his assertion?'[2] Freud sees the unconscious of man seething with aggressive, sexual, and destructive instincts that can only be tamed by repression.

Jung, on the other hand, had a very different view of the unconscious. Paul Stern writes 'whereas Freud imagined the unconscious as a chaos of seething libidinal energies, Jung viewed it as a cosmos with an intrinsic order and creativity of its own. While Freud saw the unconscious as crude storage area of undigested personal traumata, Jung conceived of it as the rich and vast treasure chamber of the archetypes.'[3] And Abraham Maslow, one of the father's of modern humanistic psychology, with his optimistic theory described in his book *The Farther Reaches of Human Nature* stresses something of man's creativity and his aspirations for love and freedom.[4] This is a part of the glory of man made in God's image. Freud is too pessimistic, Jung and Maslow too optimistic. They each take a part of the truth and create a whole system around it. They have no point of integration outside themselves, no absolute reference point, and so they eventually end up as Paul says in Romans 1.25 worshipping (or putting at the centre of their universe) the created being, man, instead of God the creator. They make man in their own image and he becomes God.

False gods

With such a loss of an outside reference point there is an inevitable tendency to make one of the theories into the reference point, so that the particular medical, sociological or psychological theory becomes the most important. It is in a sense making a 'god' out of one particular theory. But there are many 'gods' and E. F. Schumacher quotes Etienne Gilson in his book *Guide for the Perplexed*:

A world which has lost the Christian god cannot but resemble the world which has not yet found him. Just like the world of Thales and Plato our modern world is 'full of gods'. There are blind Evolution, clear-sighted Orthogenesis, benevolent Progress, . . . It is however important for us to realise that mankind is doomed to live more and more under the spell of a new scientific, social, and political mythology, unless we resolutely exorcise these befuddled notions whose

influence on modern life is becoming appalling . . .
for when gods fight among themselves, men have to
die.

Schumacher himself continues:

> When there are so many gods all competing with one
> another and claiming first priority, and there is no
> supreme god, no supreme good or value, in terms of
> which everything else needs to justify itself, society
> cannot but drift into chaos.[5]

So the process for the Christian scientist, psychologist
and psychiatrist is one of moving from the broad
framework of revealed truth about the nature of the
'supreme' God and about man to the details of his
creation. 'The process' writes Dreyfus 'is thus one of
moving from a sense of the whole to its parts, our sense
of the whole determining the significance of the parts.
Thus in recognising a melody, the notes get the values
they have, by being recognised as being parts of the
melody, rather than the melody being built up out of
independently recognised notes.'[6]

The Christian framework

Let me now briefly outline the Christian framework
within which all scientific findings find their full
significance. As we understand our origin and destiny,
we can more clearly see our predicament in the present.
We read in Genesis of a man and woman created for a
relationship of loving dependence and mutual trust with
God. Their whole personality was fulfilled in their
relationship with this personal God, with each other,
and with the creation around them. Their needs for love,
security, significance, purpose, dependence, independence, and for a framework of values of right and wrong,

were fully met in their relationship with God, with each other, and in the tasks that they were given to do. There was no vulnerability to depression because there were no broken relationships, no losses, no frustrations, no genetic abnormalities and no abnormalities of chemicals in the body. There was an integration of body, mind, emotions, and will, all working in perfect harmony together in a relationship with God.

But they were not puppets or robots with no real choice. They could choose not to love and not to obey. It was their disobedience, and Satan's disobedience before them, which led to the tragedy of this fallen, broken world. They had been very carefully warned by God not to eat of the tree of the knowledge of good and evil, and He had made it very clear that the consequences would be too awful for them to imagine. As a result of God's judgement on their sin (the fall) every area of their being was affected. Their bodies became subject to genetic malformations, to disease and death; the soil produced thorns and thistles in abundance thus making work difficult, and there were tragic consequences in rela-tionships. Adam and Eve hid from God; their rela-tionship with him was broken. They were suddenly aware of guilt and of shame and embarrassment in their relationship with each other. Intimacy felt more like vulnerability and companionship more like competitive-ness. Adam blamed the woman for his sin and he began to dominate and oppress her. ('He shall rule over the woman.') Not only did their relationship with each other become more complicated but there was an inner disintegration and disharmony. Emotions, will, mind and body no longer worked so efficiently together. So Paul, like us, an heir to the effects of the fall cries out 'I do not understand what I do. For what I want to do I do not do, but what I hate I do.' (Romans 17.15) Often we feel that we are two or more people!

One of the members of our church who used to be a

gymnast is sadly now paralysed from the neck down. One Sunday he spoke to the children in the service, 'You can see that I am disabled–it's obvious from my wheelchair. But in fact we are all disabled, if not physically, then inside – psychologically.' C. S. Lewis writes in *Voyage to Venus* of 'bent people', an apt description of fallen man. We are in fact born 'bent', with an imperfect nature, prone to disease and sin. From the moment of conception we are surrounded by influences which will either make that 'bentness' worse or will shape it for good and perhaps make its effects less noticeable. As we have seen in our consideration of vulnerability factors, we are affected by parental attitudes, by relationships within the family, by the values and expectations of our peers, and the surrounding culture, by genetic factors and disease of the body. And then Satan too comes and tries to create more havoc in the situation.

Destiny

And what of our destiny? The Bible tells us that as we live in a relationship with God, through Christ, and as we seek to live by the principles he has given us in his word, the Bible, the Holy Spirit is working in us, changing us little by little to be more like him. As we day by day make choices not to be ruled by all the negative influences inside and outside us, we will experience greater freedom to live as he intended us to live. There are some things we cannot change, and we are limited by our genetic and physical structure. One day, when Christ comes back again, and we are given new bodies, those too will be changed. Then we will be restored to the original perfection of creation. 'And we, who with unveiled faces all reflect the Lord's glory, are being transformed into his likeness with ever increasing glory, which comes from the Lord, who is the Spirit.' (2 Corinthians 3. 18) We have an image of what we were supposed to be as we look at Adam and Eve before the Fall, and as we see Jesus, the perfect man and yet also God. Even though we are not perfect we still carry some of the glory of the original creation.

So within this broad framework the biological, psychological, sociological, existential, and demonic factors have a place. Each are to be explored in their own right. Our task is to work against the brokenness in every area of life whether it be by providing anti-depressants, helping a couple to communicate better in their marriage, finding better housing, helping someone to find meaning in life, praying for freedom from demonic influence, or helping someone to change their values and 'way of seeing'.

The myth of neutrality

In most cultures of the world there is, in every community, a priest and a healer who share the role of helping people in distress. With the decline of the church more and more people have turned to the doctor, the psychiatrist, the social worker, the psychologist and the counsellor for answers to their problems in life. These so-called experts on mental and physical health are being expected to help people to be 'happy'. For some, in severe depression, pills will be a great help, but when the problem needs counselling and psychotherapy to sort out relationships, values, and priorities in life, then the therapist's beliefs about the purpose of existence and the nature of right and wrong will deeply affect the direction of therapy. No-one can be neutral even though, for years, social workers have been taught not to let their own beliefs and values affect their counselling. Nowadays most people realise that such a practice is impossible. Anthony Clare in *Let's talk about me* examines various therapies offered to those in distress that have become popular in recent years. The task of

putting alienated, lonely, bored, frightened and fragmented people back together is not so 'scientific' as we
have been led to believe. Commenting on the counselling techniques of humanistic psychology with its
proliferation of different therapies he concludes:

> Many of the people flocking to the growth centres
> . . . the encounter groups . . . seem to us to be
> unhappy, bewildered and disorientated people sear-
> ching for some philosophical principle, some system
> of values by which to live. The questions they ask are
> often the ultimate questions concerning existence,
> purpose, the meaning of life, happiness, pain and
> death. Nor is there any doubt that psychotherapists
> are willing to be cast in the role of 'secular pastoral
> workers' providing values and meaning of their own.
> Yet we do feel that the announced agenda of
> psychotherapy, with its heavy medical, secular and
> pseudo-scientific flavour, insufficiently reflects its
> frankly religious undertones.'[7]

We have looked at a number of factors that make us
vulnerable to depression. In the following chapters we
will try to draw out some Christian principles to help us
with many of the big questions that face people who are
struggling with depression. How much choice do I really
have – it seems as if I can't help myself? How do I deal
with anger and guilt? How much change can I expect?
Will I ever be free from this depressive tendency? What
about death? Although there is much common scientific
ground between Christian and non-Christian it is not
difficult to see that the answers to these questions
involve a commitment to a belief about the nature of our
life and its purpose. There are indeed 'frankly religious
undertones' in all counselling and psychotherapy.

References

1   J. Harold Ellens. Biblical Themes in Psychological Theory and Practice *Christian Assoc. Psych. Studies Bulletin* 1980. Vol. 6 No. 2 p. 5.
2   S. Freud.
3   Paul Stern. *C. G. Jung – The Haunted Prophet* (George Braziller Inc. 1976.) p. 253.
4   Abraham Maslow *The Farther Reaches of Human Nature* (Esalen New York Viking Press 1971).
5   E. F. Schumacher *A Guide for the Perplexed* (Jonathan Cape 1977) p. 69.
6   Dreyfus quoted by John Shotter in *Images on Man in Psychological Research* (Essential Psychology Series F7: Methunen 1975) p. 62.
7   Anthony Clare *Let's talk about me* (BBC 1981) p. 238.

CHAPTER EIGHT

Caught in a web of a broken world

Freedom and determinism

John sat hunched up, depressed and disillusioned with life. 'I feel trapped' he said 'imprisoned by the bars of a cage. My whole life is determined by the past.' The one choice he felt that he had left was suicide. Freedom for him was, as the old song goes, 'just another word for nothing left to lose.' He had never been able to live up to the perfectionist standards of his father. As a child he had been verbally and physically beaten and constantly told that he was a failure. His parents divorced when he was ten and after a few years of experimenting with drugs he managed to get into university to study philosophy. He lived and breathed the world of existentialism, where Sartre and Camus were his heroes and he experienced a deep identification with their struggles. After leaving university he could not decide what to do and began to drift aimlessly. He became depressed, angry, bitter, feeling a total failure and unable to trust anyone, let alone God. He felt a victim of circumstances, a pawn in a sadistic game where real freedom of choice was an illusion. Everywhere he turned he felt hemmed in by deterministic views of life.

An illusion of freedom?

For those who are struggling with psychological problems, whether as counsellor or client, therapist, or patient, one of the central preoccupations is with the question of freedom and determinism. How much can we chose to change? How much are we responsible for our state of mind and emotions? How much are we determined by the past and by our physiology or biochemistry? A casual encounter with most psychiatrists, psychologists and sociologists will give one the strong impression that man has little freedom and that he is merely a product of his inheritance and childhood (and some may have got that impression reading the first few chapters of this book!). Whichever way we turn we encounter similar views. From the geneticists we learn that our physical appearance, and to some degree our intelligence and temperament are fixed from the moment of conception. Listening to some neurophysiologists we may get the impression that life is just a matter of physics and chemistry, of pleasure centres and pain centres, and that it is ultimately the level of chemicals in my brain and the amount of stimulation of the pleasure centre that determines my state of mind and feelings.

Other scientists demonstrate the profound effects of severe malnutrition, producing brain and behavioural deficits which cannot be eradicated. So for at least 200 million pre-school children in the world today life will largely be determined by the amount of food they eat. They look forward to a life of prolonged illness, permanent handicap, generation after generation of inefficiency, unproductivity and impoverishment. B. F. Skinner, a behaviourist, author of 'Beyond Freedom and Dignity', tells us that we are totally controlled, apart perhaps from a few inborn reflexes, by the reinforcing events of the environment and that our freedom is just a myth. Freud believed that our choices are ultimately the result of conflicts of instincts which at root are biological. Through psychoanalysis he elaborated the conviction that it is our childhood experiences which determine who we are today. Freud, at heart, was a

pessimist; he believed that there was some hope in
understanding the things that have conditioned us, but
ultimately one could never break free of the determining
influences of the past. His avowed aim was to destroy
romantic illusions of freedom. 'I regard myself' he says
'as one of the most dangerous enemies of
religion'[1]. . . 'I stand in no awe whatsoever of the
Almighty. If we were to ever meet I should have more
reproaches to make of him than he could make to me.
He couldn't complain that I have failed to make the best
use of my so-called freedom.'[2]

Darwin believed that we are but links in the
evolutionary process and that our highest motive is
governed by nothing more altruistic than the instinct for
survival. Marx, that we are products of our social and
economic circumstances. The primal therapists tell us
that ultimately it is what happened to us in the first few
weeks in the womb, or at the time of birth, that
determines our state of mind and our perspective on life.
Sociologists tell us of the influence of our environment
and of the power of the media in making us do things we
might not have done if we had some freedom of choice.
Peter Berger, a sociologist writes 'most of the time the
game has been fixed long before we arrive on the scene.
All that is left for us to do most of the time is to play it
with more or less enthusiasm. The professor stepping in
front of his class, the judge pronouncing sentence, the
preacher badgering his congregation, the commander
ordering his troops into battle, all these are engaged in
actions that have been pre-defined in very narrow limits
and impressive systems of controls and sanctions stand
guard over these limits.'[3]

Faith in Reason and Science

We are surrounded by these deterministic views of
reality, and it is important to recognise that they

describe only a part of reality. Because some scientists dismiss anything that cannot be described using the scientific method as lacking reality, it appears as if their deterministic systems are all that exist. They dismiss any need for revelation and put their trust in science and reason. This faith in science is sometimes called 'scientism'. Stephen Evans comments that 'brain scientists committed to the scientific method look only for mechanistic causes. Hence they will hardly find any other kind.'[4] Science is not neutral, it is committed to a particular view of reality which affects the questions it asks and the result that it finds. So Professor Gareth Jones, a professor of Neuro-anatomy in Australia, writes in his book 'Our Fragile Brains':

> When the brain or the person is viewed in machine-like terms it is a short step to the conclusion that a human being actually is a machine. If the brain comes to be regarded as a glorified computer any person can be seen as a complex array of interacting gadgetry. If we are nothing but machines and our brains are as determined as clockwork toys, how can we any longer be regarded as free agents? Our freedom to them is an illusion.[5]

It was in this type of mechanistic science that the discipline of psychology was nurtured at the turn of the century. The two dominant schools of psychology that emerged were Freudian psychoanalysis (the so called 'first force') and Watson and Skinner's behaviourism (the 'second force'). Closely related to them was the development of the 'medical model' in psychiatry which explained all abnormal states of mind as the result of physical abnormalities in the brain. In very simple terms, the common themes that emerge from these three schools of thought are that man is determined by his genes, biochemistry, instincts or environment.

Although Freud talked a lot about psychological factors he wrote 'In the physical field the biological factor is really the rock bottom.'[6] Ultimately Freud hoped that man would learn a measure of self-control by understanding himself better. Although Skinner wrote that man 'is indeed controlled by his environment'[7], thus negating the significance of choice, he too hoped that we would be able to learn to control the events that shape our lives. It was difficult for them to be completely consistent in their views, but essentially theirs is a mechanistic, deterministic and pessimistic picture of man. Paul Tournier writes 'Nothing is more calculated to give us this feeling of fate than the deterministic views of man to which science leads. All the elements that go to make up his being seem bound in an inescapable process of cause and effect. Every present is conditioned by the past and every future is conditioned by the present, by a sort of inner fate.'[8]

Freud and Skinner have, of course, discovered some truth about the way we are made. Man *is* partially biological, he *has* a likeness to animals, he *is* partially determined and some faults *are* due to biology and environment, but he is so much more. Inwardly man cries out against such a constricted view of human nature. (see Footnote).

Freedom and Significance

Many people, anxious to preserve man's freedom, significance, and dignity have rebelled against this narrow view of man. They believe we can create our own destiny and are not just cogs in a machine. An example of these two extremes is seen in contemporary psychiatry in the tension between biological psychiatry, with its emphasis on the physical organism, drugs, and other physical treatments, and on the other hand the human potential movement, or humanistic psychology, with its strong emphasis on meaning, growth, individuality and personal responsibility. These two have diverged, one stressing the deterministic physical laws which govern us and other freedom and the possibility of change. Many psychiatrists and counsellors find themselves working somewhere on the spectrum between these two poles.

Many non-Christians share the Christian's concern to rise above the mechanistic view of man inherited from the natural sciences. Abraham Maslow, one of the fathers of the humanistic psychology movement (the 'third force') was concerned to put humanity above the animal world, noting the differences rather than the similarities: 'The use of animals guarantees in advance the neglect of just those capacities which are uniquely human, for example, martyrdom, self-sacrifice, shame, love, honour, beauty, conscience, guilt, patriotism, ideals, the production of poetry, or philosophy or music or science. Animal psychology is necessary for learning about those human characteristics that man shares with all primates. It is *useless* in the study of those characteristics which man does *not* share with other animals, or in which he is vastly superior . . . '[9] And John Shotter writes in a current psychology text book 'It is not nature but we ourselves who are responsible for making and maintaining ourselves as distinct from the beasts and all else that there is . . . man is a self-defining animal . . . In the task ahead, the dignity, self-respect, the confidence to believe that by acting freely we can become more fully human is essential.'[10]

We must save ourselves

Carl Rogers, another of the fathers of humanistic psychology, who even in the face of the horrors of torture and war in the twentieth century remains optimistic about man's ability to perfect himself, writes:

Experience for me is the highest authority. No other person's ideas and none of my own ideas are as authoritative as my experiences. It is to experience I must return again and again to discover a closer proximation to the truth as it is in the process of becoming in me. Neither the Bible nor the prophets, – neither Freud nor research, – neither the revelations of God nor man – can take precedence over my direct experience.[11]

These optimistic views of human nature and with their emphasis on inner awareness and experience and their hope of significance and freedom for man, have deeply influenced contemporary psychotherapy and counselling. An enormous number of different therapies have sprung up under the banner of humanistic psychology (or the human potential movement) as a reaction to the determinism of Freudian psychoanalysis with its interminable treatments (twice a week for at least two or three years and many for much longer). There was dissatisfaction too with traditional psychiatry, which relied so heavily on pills and other physical treatments. There is much that is good in these therapies, such as an emphasis on taking responsibility for one's life and not blaming other people or one's bio-chemistry, and an emphasis on examining problems in the present rather than taking long excursions back into the past. But there is also blind faith in feelings and subjective experience, and a strong belief that man can perfect himself. As the Humanist Manifesto says, 'No deity will save us: we must save ourselves.'[12]

Transpersonal psychology – a spiritual answer?

Many of the people who pioneered humanistic psychology have not been able to live with a denial of a spiritual reality or with the lack of perfection within themselves, and have moved on to develop the 'fourth force' of transpersonal psychology which takes man one step closer to self-worship. This is a combination of western psychotherapeutic insights and eastern philosophy which claims to set us free from the mechanistic, deterministic view of earlier psychology. There are a great variety of beliefs under this umbrella but a consistent theme is that reality is not the way we think it is. We get rid of our problems by redefining reality. We need to remove the glasses of western scientific thinking and replace them with the glasses of eastern mysticism. As one experiences, often through meditation and mystical experiences, the innate unity and perfection of all things, problems should theoretically evaporate. Oscar Ichazo of the Arica Psychotherapy Institute in New York said in an interview for *Psychology Today*:

> When we turn away from our primal perfection, our completeness, our unity with the world and God, we create the illusion that we need something exterior to ourselves for our completion. This dependency on what is exterior is what makes man's ego. Once man is with ego consciousness he is driven by desire and by fear, the things that determine his existence. He can find no real happiness until desire is extinguished and he returns to his essence. That is, until he reaches what Buddhism calls Nirvarna or the Void, there is no peace short of being within the divine consciousness. It should be clear by now that the western secular attempt to live without knowledge of the sacred unity of all things is a failure.[13]

And Zen Master Hakuun Yasutani is quoted in a paper on Meditation and Psychotherapy in *The American Journal of Psychotherapy*:

. . . man, restless and anxious, lives a half-crazed existence because his mind, heavily encrusted with delusion, is turned topsy-turvy. We need, therefore, to return to our original perfection, to see through the false image of ourselves as incomplete and sinful, and to wake up to our inherent purity and wholeness.'

The belief that we are able to perfect ourselves through self-awareness and growth, and the eastern belief that we are already perfect, could both be seen as attempts to escape our limitations and imperfections in a world where we are partly determined by many influences within ourselves and in the world around. The Christian view of man acknowledges that men and women were created perfect and we be perfect again one day, but at the moment, we struggle against our imperfections. It recognises deterministic factors, but also maintains a possibility of freedom and significant choice.

It is fascinating to find that many psychologists and psychiatrists have been moving towards a view which is very close to a Christian view of man. The history of psychology over the last hundred years well illustrates what has been called the 'elastic band phenomenon.' If we assume that man is made in the image of God, then the more he tries to live as if he is something different, either animal or machine or superhuman and perfect, the more he will be stretching the elastic band to its limits and the more tension he will find within himself. The more he lives the way he was intended to live the less the inner tension.

Tension between freedom and determinism

But how does this relate to the practicalities of our lives from day to day? There are profound consequences of stressing either determinism or freedom to the exclusion of the other. When I am caught up in a deterministic way of thinking I have a tendency to deny my responsibility in life. If I cannot control my temper . . . I am drawn into an extra-marital sexual relationship . . . I continuously covet my affluent neighbour's life-style 'I can't help it . . . it's my parents' fault . . . my wife's fault . . . I'm made that way.' Or if I find myself limited by fears and insecurities from wounds and scars in childhood I am full of bitterness and resentment. I have no control over it: 'Its all their fault, not mine.' Paul Tournier sums this up very neatly when he writes in *The Person Reborn*:

> Where others are concerned we are outraged at their behaviour, and consider them responsible. Where we ourselves are concerned we plead that we are not responsible, and point to all the external causes which have determined our conduct . . . If I hold a coin between another person and myself, each of us sees one side of the coin only, either the head or the tail, whichever is facing him, and not the other. In the same way, each of us sees our own responsibility and not that of the other person. And yet, like the coin our infinitely complex human life is one single reality, although with our limited minds we cannot grasp this fact in its entirety. Depending on the side from which we approach it, we see its objective, scientific, technical, determined, non-responsible aspect, or, on the contrary, its personal, subjective, moral, free, and responsible aspect.[15]

Some Christians try in a number of ways to reduce this tension between determinism and freedom.

Firstly there are those who recognise the powerful shaping effect of the early months and years of life but give the impression that an experience of healing of the memories or a reliving of my birth or early womb experiences will set me free from the shackles of the past. While there is much that is helpful in the ministry of inner healing, it is dangerous to stress our freedom in Christ to the exclusion of the other New Testament emphasis of struggle and battle against our sinful nature. Many people have been bitterly disappointed and have had their faith severely shaken because they had been given the impression they would receive a complete cure with freedom from all their troubles.

Secondly there are other Christians who in emphasising the aspect of freedom suggest that we should 'forget those things that are behind', and look forward and up, not backwards and inwards. The victorious Christian life, they say, enables one to reach a plateau where problems are left behind – the old nature is 'crucified' and so is not experienced any more. Christians should no longer be depressed, angry, anxious or upset.

This misinterpretation of Romans 6-8 often leads to a third problem. Because they claim their sinful nature is no longer alive and active, any sin in them can only be explained by blaming the devil. If I have a spirit of lust, envy, anger . . . cast out of me then I will be able to live a truly spiritual life. Again I do not deny the devil's activity, but there is a danger with this interpretation of Romans and the strong emphasis on inner healing and demonic activity that a sense of personal responsibility is greatly diminished.

And then fourthly, others, also anxious to retain freedom, significance and personal responsibility make light of the effects of the past and the shaping influences of our culture. They rightly stress that in contemporary psychiatry the medical, psychoanalytical and behavioural views are so deterministic that they undermine a sense of personal responsibility, and much of their counselling method is based on helping people to take ¬sponsibility for their lives, to renounce personal sin, and not to blame the past. Certainly they recognise the conditioning effects of the past but I fear that they underestimate the pain and brokenness in many people's lives. This, I believe, leads to an impression of a lack of patience and compassion in counselling with unrealistic expectations of the size and speed of change in attitudes, emotions and behaviour.

All of these Christian approaches are attempts to ttranscend or deny the deterministic factors in our fallen world.

I suggest that both extremes – an over-emphasis on determinism or an over-emphasis on responsibility and freedom – lack reality. On their own they are only partial truths. One is sadly pessimistic, or a complete escape from responsibility, the other romantically optimistic. Finding the Biblical position in the tension between these two poles is one of the major challenges in counselling. Some believe in spending much time delving into early life history, while others are reluctant to spend more than a short time recognising the roots of bad habits in the past. How much do we look backwards and how much do we look forwards? I believe that both are important and hope that we will see how to find the balance in this as we explore the issue further. Different emphases may be necessary at different times and in different situations in life.

Footnote

It is important here to distinguish between what is called 'methodological' determinism and 'metaphysical' determinism. All scientific enterprise involves assumptions of laws of cause and effect, so that in examining biological or sociological phenomena one is investigating the causes of an event and attempting to make predictions about future events. This is a valid 'methodological' determinism, because we live in a world of order where God has created laws of cause and effect. But 'metaphysical' determinism makes the much bigger assumption that these laws of cause and effect are all that there is, and that the universe and man within it are mere stimulus-response machines, and man's sense of significance in determining his own future an illusion. B. F. Skinner is the best known example of a metaphysical determinist – he argues repeatedly that all behaviour is determined by natural causes.

All scientists are tempted to extend explanations of phenomena in their particular field of study to all other areas of life. Man is reduced to a biological, mechanical, sociological or economic unit. The reductionist sees only the part and mistakes it for the whole. Donald Mackay and others have described this as 'nothing buttery'. Man is 'nothing but' a machine . . . But it is much more helpful and much closer to Biblical truth to see that as Dooyeweerd and Polanyi have demonstrated in their different ways, man can be analysed at different levels of meaning. A person having a conversion experience or a person deeply depressed can be understood at different levels from the molecular, biochemical and physical structure of his body through the levels of feeling and thinking to the significance of his social relationships and to questions of ultimate purpose and meaning in his presence and actions. He cannot be 'reduced' to one particular aspect of his existence. He is not just a physical organism, nor a thinking animal, nor a social being. There is far more to man than meets the eye.

It is difficult not to keep slipping into a narrow 'scientism' or 'metaphysical determinism'. And such determinism often leads to a sense of pessimism and cynicism about life. If that is all there is, then we have not real freedom and we can only play the game as best we can. For some it leads to a perverted sense of freedom because they no longer have the responsibility of making significant choices.

References

1 Ernest Jones. *The Life and Works of Sigmund Freud* (New York: Basic Books 1955) Vol III p. 124.

2 *Letters of Sigmund Freud* Ernst L. Freud, Editor: (New York Basic Books 1960) p. 307f. Quoted by R. J. Rushdoony in *Freud* Modern Thinkers Series, Christian World Pub.).

3 Peter Berger. *Invitation to Sociology: A Humanistic Perspective* (Garden City: Anchor/Doubleday 1963) p. 87.

4 C. Stephen Evans *Preserving the Person* (IVP 1979) p. 104.

5 D. Gareth Jones *Our Fragile Brains* (IVP 1981) p. 242.

6 S. Freud. Analysis Terminable and Interminable 1937 in *Collected Papers V* (New York: Basic Books 1959) p. 357.

7 B. F. Skinner. *Beyond Freedom and Dignity* (New York: Alfred A. Knopf 1971) p. 215.

8 Paul Tournier. *The Person Reborn* (SCM Press Ltd 1972) p. 123.

9 Abraham Maslow quoted in Frank G. Goble. *The Third Force* (New York: Grossman Publishers, Inc 1970; rpt. New York: Pocket Books 1971) p. 17.

10 John Shotter. *Images of Man in Psychological Research* (Essential Psychology Series F7: Methuen 1975) p. 132.

11 Carl Rogers. *On Becoming a Person* (Houghton Mifflin Co. Boston 1961) p. 23-24.

12 *The Humanist Manifesto II*

13 Oscar Ichazo. A conversation about ego destruction. *Psychology Today*, July 1973.

14 Quoted by J. Tyler Carpenter Meditation, Esoteric Traditions – Contributions to Psychotherapy, *American J. of Psychotherapy* p. 394-404.

15 Tournier. op. cit., p. 118-119.

CHAPTER NINE

Freedom within limits

'Remember the sixties? That was my scene. Counter-culture, free love, be yourself, let it all hang out – if it feels good, do it! And we lived that way. But look where I am now. I feel I've wasted the first thirty years of my life. I've slept with so many girls I don't think I know what love means. I can't stay in a job for more than six months before I'm bored. At times I really hate myself. I'm so lonely – maybe one day I'll have the guts to end it all.'

Freud's theory that much neurosis is caused by sexual repression was very influential in opening the door to the sexual permissiveness of our century. Although he believed in some self-control there were many others who were eager to push open the flood gates. Graham Heath writes in *The Illusory Freedom*:

> For the best part of two thousand years there had been a basic commitment to monogamous marriage. The ideal – if not always the practice – of associating sex with love and faithfulness had been part of the conventional wisdom. But towards the middle of the twentieth century some fundamental changes began to take place, quite different in degree from the minor 'liberalization' of sexual morality which had characterized the previous fifty years or so. Evidence was produced (or popularized) almost simultaneously from zoology, anthropology, history, psychiatry and sociology to show that the sexual morality of the Western world over the previous two thousand years

had been a terrible mistake – unnatural, destructive
of human happiness, repressive; that it had been
sustained by hypocrisy; and that it had in fact been
abandoned in practice by a great part of the
population. The evidence was brought forward by
distinguished academics, whose researches had in
many cases been supported by prestigious founda-
tions. The new doctrine was immensely attractive and
seemed absolutely logical: the age of freedom had
dawned at last; there was no such thing as normality –
everyone had different sexual needs; there were no
guidelines for sexual behaviour, provided that all
parties consented and no conception took place;
there was no need for any social control of the
influences affecting sexual behaviour. And at this
moment, playing the role of fairy godmother, the
pharmaceutical industry produced the first really
effective means of contraception – the 'pill'.
Within less than a generation the new orthodoxy had
replaced the old. Parents and educators who
suggested love, faithfulness and restraint as ideals
found themselves regarded as joyless, under-sexed,
anti-life, anti-youth and anti-progress. The sexual
'revolution' had taken place.[1]

The sexual revolution is a classic example of the belief
that man is basically good and should therefore follow
his own instincts. In the early years of humanistic
psychology there was little talk of self-control and
self-discipline. What was once only in the minds of
existential philosophers is now in the minds of many
ordinary people – real freedom means doing what I want
when I feel like it. It is one thing to believe it but another
to consistently live that way. There are certain
boundaries to God's world. Rollo May writes of the
sexual revolution:

What we did not see in our short-sighted liberalism in
sex was that throwing the individual into an
unbounded and empty sea of free choice does not of
itself give freedom, but is more apt to increase inner
conflict.[2]

Biblical principles

The Bible gives some clear principles defining the
limits of freedom. The first principle is that our freedom
to be who we are is bounded by the limits of how we were
created by God. We are, for instance, unaided by
additional machinery, not able to fly or to dive into the
depths of the ocean. Although there is an amazing
variety of psychological and physical strength in the
human race we do eventually reach limits beyond which
we cannot go. So there is what we might call created
freedom – within certain limits.

Because we are limited by the design of our minds and
bodies, we are made to live within certain external limits
so that if we try to fly we will seriously injure our bodies.
In the same way, if we ignore the maker's instructions
and steal, lie, covet, commit adultery, murder and
worship anything or anyone else but God, then we will
eventually find our freedom limited. The law of God is
not a form of punishment. It is intended to set us free.
Anyone who does follow the maker's instructions,
whether Christian or non-Christian will know a measure
of freedom to be what God intended them to be. So the
second principle is that our freedom is contingent on our
obedience to the Law of God. 'As a bird is free in the air
and a fish free in the sea, each in his own natural
element, so is a man truly free in the will of his God.'[3]

But there is a third principle that our freedom to be
what God intended us to be, is limited in this life. When
Christ returns and redemption is complete we will be

given new bodies which will no longer be subject to disease and decay. Our minds, emotions and wills will be made perfect and we will reach our full potential as men and women made in the image of God. Then, we will be free to live as he intended us, but for the moment we are held back and limited by our sinful nature. Every part of our being was affected by 'the fall'. The most obvious example of this is the physical body.

Limits of the body

After 'the fall' there was not only spiritual death but there were changes in the nature of the body producing disease, decay and eventually physical death. An example of the physical change is given in Genesis 3 where the woman is told that she will have pain in childbirth. We inherit the many consequences of 'the fall' so that a child may be born with only one arm, with spina bifida, with mongolism, mentally handicapped, or with a vulnerability to anxiety or depression as we saw in Chapter 3. In minor ways we are aware of the effects of our bodies for instance in terms of the amount of sleep we need, or for a woman premenstrual tension. Later in my life I may develop diabetes, a stroke, or even severe depression, cancer, or senile dementia – all of these things limiting my freedom and demonstrating my imperfection as a fallen human being. There may be substantial healing of my illnesses but not complete freedom from disease and death.

As a young doctor, one of the most troubling and deeply moving experiences was to walk around the wards of the longstay geriatric hospital and see old people, often neglected by their families, sitting or lying alone for hours on end. Sometimes they were incontinent, unable to speak and unable to relate to anyone except in the very simplest way. They were imprisoned by their bodies. And we have to accept that our bodies do limit our freedom in this life. If we look back into history, before the day of antibiotics for instance, a cut finger would often lead to death. TB and cholera were rife, and life expectancy was short. Thankfully we now have many means of working against the effects of the fall and this is what we are called to do in every area of life. But ultimately, the most inescapable determining factor in our lives is death. Paul writes in 2 Corinthians 4.16-17 'therefore we do not lose heart. Though outwardly we are wasting away, yet inwardly we are being renewed day by day. For our light and momentary troubles are achieving for us an eternal glory that far outweighs them all.' Because of God's amazing grace, even the last enemy, death, the consequence of being a slave to sin, is for the Christian the ultimate liberation to God's freedom. So Paul cries out mockingly, 'Where, oh death, is your victory? Where, oh death, is your sting? . . . Death has been swallowed up in victory.' (1 Corinthians 15.54-55). But for a while, in this life, we have to accept that we are determined. Our freedom is limited by our fallen bodies. When we are given new bodies we will again live out true freedom within the limits of a finite but not fallen frame.

'Flesh' and 'Sinful nature'

The word 'flesh', in the New Testament, is used in a number of different ways. At times it refers to the physical body (1 Corinthians 15.39) but at other times it refers to our sinful human nature. These are so intricately interwoven that one has to examine the context very carefully to see exactly which the writer means. They are so closely related because it is in and through the body that our sinful nature is expressed. Think of Paul's conflict in Romans 7.15-25 where he writes:

I do not understand what I do. For what I want to do I do not do, but what I hate I do. And if I do what I do not want to do, I agree that the law is good. As it is, it is no longer I myself who do it but it is sin living in me. I know that nothing good lives in me, that is in my sinful nature . . . so I find this law at work: when I want to do good, evil is right there with me. For in my inner being I delight in God's law; but I see another law at work in the members of my body, waging war against the law of my mind and making me a prisoner of the law of sin at work within my members. What a wretched man I am! Who will rescue me from this body of death? Thanks be to God – through Jesus Christ our Lord!

This is an amazing picture of Paul's struggle against his sinful nature. He is caught up in an inner battle. In order to see more clearly what he is struggling against I want to separate out three different aspects of our sinful nature, which has been formed by a number of influences in the past and the present.

The fall and inner brokenness

Firstly, looking at the most distant and original root, it is a result of man's disobedience at 'the fall'. We saw in Genesis the amazing account of the disintegration and alienation that came about as a result of Adam and Eve's sin. There was disorder and disharmony at every level of creation – a broken relationship with God, between Adam and Eve, and between man and the creation. Even within himself, man found shame, mistrust, doubt, and confusion, that produced the battle that Paul talks about: 'the good that I want I do not and that which I would not I do'. So our minds, our emotions, and our wills, in some way that it is difficult to define exactly, were twisted and no longer work together as they should. We are fallen, broken creatures, deeply affected by something which happened to us through no fault of our own – the disintegration within us that we inherit from the fall.

The World

Not only are there these struggles with our sinful nature and the effects of disease of the body, but there are also all the influences in the 'world' which try to shape our lives and remove our freedom of choice. Economic, social, and political realities to some extent limit our freedom. One billion people in the world are under-nourished and their lives are governed by one thought – how to survive today. In the Soviet Union, even those who are not in prison have far fewer freedoms than we do.

The sins of the fathers

Our sinful nature is shaped too by the sins of the fathers handed down from generation to generation. To be told, for instance, that you are always a nuisance, to be rejected or neglected as a child, leaves deep scars in the heart and mind. A conviction of being unloveable makes subsequent relationships more difficult and complicated than for someone who has grown up in a secure and loving home where they have been told that they are valuable, loved, significant and respected. The habits of thinking, feeling, and behaving that are ingrained in us in those early and vulnerable years of childhood are part of our 'sinful nature'. So we read in Proverbs 'train a child in the way he should go and he will not depart from it.' (Proverbs 2.2-6) Parents have a great responsibility in shaping their children's minds, emotions, and behaviour, for good or ill. Solomon realised, as he wrote his proverbs, that what parents do to their children is extraordinarily significant, because they are shaping their children's lives for the future. We see an example of this in Genesis 25 in the story of Isaac and Rebekah. When their twin sons Jacob and Esau were born, Esau became his father's favourite and Jacob his mother's boy. The effect of the jealousy between these two was catastrophic, both in their own lives, and also in the life of the next generation where Joseph became Jacob's favourite son and produced jealousy and anger in his brothers. God brought good out of that evil, and thankfully he does that for us too, yet the effect of the parents' sin was seen in the next two generations.

Selfcentredness and pride

Secondly, the 'flesh' refers to life lived without reference to God or the supernatural world (Galatians 6.14, John 8.15). A large part of my sinful nature is that within me which chooses to rebel against God. Sometimes openly with a gesture of defiance, at other times more quietly and subtly even to the point of deceiving ourselves into thinking that we are doing what God wants. This is the source of selfishness and pride – putting myself instead of God at the centre of my life. We cannot blame Isaac and Rebekah completely for Jacob's sin. His deceitfulness was also involved. Often there is an interweaving of others' influences and our responses to that influence. As the dictionary of New Testament Theology puts it 'The outlook of the flesh is the outlook oriented towards the self, that which pursues its own ends in self-sufficient independence of God.'

The devil

And finally but certainly by no means less important, is Satan's direct influence in our lives. He, of course had a hand in the original sin, in the sins of the fathers and in the institutional and social sins by which we are surrounded. But he also, as we see in the study of Job, has a hand in attempting to shape our personal destiny.

As we recognise the influences of the 'world' around us, the 'flesh', that is our bodies and our sinful human nature, and the 'devil', does this mean that we are locked into a deterministic world? Do we have only an illusion of freedom?

There is a striking passage in the Bible which speaks very strongly against this. In Ezekiel Chapter 18 we read 'The Word of the Lord came to Ezekiel saying "what do you people mean by quoting this proverb about the land of Israel?" 'The fathers eat sour grapes and the childrens' teeth are set on edge.'

What this passage seems to imply is that the people were saying that because the fathers had sinned, their sons were caught up in the judgement and that they deserved to be judged for their fathers' sins. Now obviously the children would be affected in some way by their fathers' sins, but the question was whether they were actually responsible for them and did they deserve to be judged for them? God says to Ezekiel 'as surely as I live, declares the Sovereign Lord, you will no longer quote this proverb in Israel because every living soul, the father as well as the son, both alike belong to me. The soul who sins is the one who will die.' Then he goes on into an illustration of this. 'Suppose there is a righteous man who does what is just and right. He does not eat at the mountain shrines, . . . he does not defile his neighbour's wife . . . he gives food to the hungry . . . he follows my decrees and faithfully keeps my laws. That man is righteous, he will surely live, declares the Sovereign Lord. Suppose he has a violent son. . . ?'

Now immediately you can see that it is not inevitable that the good man's children will be good. He has not conditioned them so much that they cannot escape from the values with which they have grown up. They can choose to be different. Suppose this good man 'has a violent son who sheds blood or does any of these other things (though the father has done none of them): he eats at the mountain shrines. He defiles his neighbour's wife . . . Will such a man live? He will not! . . . But suppose this son has a son who sees all the sins his father commits, and though he sees them, he does not do such things: He does not eat at the mountain shrines . . . he witholds his hand from sin . . . he keeps my laws and follows my decrees . . . he will not die for his father's sins, he will surely live.'

Choice and responsibility

Now three things emerge from this example. Firstly we are all responsible before God for our response to the sins of our fathers, but secondly we are not responsible *for* their sins. Each generation must account before God for their own sins. Thirdly, we are not locked into a deterministic world where the sins of the fathers will produce inevitable consequences in the succeeding generations; our choices are significant, they do matter and they do have some effect. Another example is in the history of the Chronicles of the kings of Israel and Judah. It is a fascinating study to see the effects that one king had on the next generation. Think of your own family history. Do you see a progressive deterioration? Do you see the same patterns of rearing children or of relationships in marriage handed down generation after another? Or can you see change where things suddenly became different? One of the surest marks of Christian growth is to see generations of destructiveness in relationships in a family change gradually, and new patterns being set up. Again the biblical emphasis seems to be that we are conditioned to some degree, but that we are not totally determined by what happens to us. Change *is* possible. Stephen Evans in his book 'Preserving the Person' writes, 'Human beings are not just products; they have a hand in shaping themselves'[4] To be human is to make responsible choices. I am the person I am today both because of the experiences which have shaped me and also because of the way I have responded to those experiences. The more choices we make not to be ruled by a difficult past, the more free we will become. The more we live as a victim of circumstances the less freedom we experience.

It is important to note at this point that our belief about how much control we have over our thoughts, emotions and behaviour is as crucial a factor as the actual limits imposed by external circumstances. Malcolm Jeeves quoted a number of examples of 'locus of control' research in the recent London Lectures on this same theme. People obviously differ in how much control they *think* they have over their environment. In a study by Rodin and Langer of elderly people in a nursing home, one group of staff were given instructions about how the home was run, with great stress on the staffs' responsibility for the care, protection and wellbeing of their patients. The other group were given instructions which stressed the importance of the patients looking after themselves and taking some responsibility for their own welfare. The latter group were shown to be considerably happier than the former group and after eighteen months 30% in the first group had died whereas only 15% of the second group had died.[5]

People tend to become what they believe themselves to be. Malcolm Jeeves quotes Prof. Myers: 'The psychology teaching in our colleges in the past two decades has emphasised the strong effects of environmental control and therefore has arguably led to an increased sense of powerlessness amongst many young people. If they believe that forces that control their development are all important then they feel powerless to do anything against them.'[6]

In recent research in child development there has been increasing recognition that although the first few years of life are very important in shaping a child there is still hope that given different circumstances many of the adverse affects of emotional and social deprivation can be reduced.

So we can see that what we believe about the issue of determinism and freedom, where we find the balance between these two is of central importance in counselling and psychotherapy. For each individual who comes to us the balance will be different and it is part of the skill of counselling to tease out the different factors with compassion, gentleness and at times firmness and even confrontation.

Coming to terms with the past

The Spanish philosopher Santayana wrote 'Those who do not remember the past are condemned to repeat it.' Two questions recur again and again in counselling which are interwoven with each other and can only be answered together. Firstly what is our responsibility in coming to terms with things that have happened to us through no choice or fault of our own? And secondly, how much time should we spend delving into the past when there is such a danger of morbid introspection?

I am sure it is unnecessary for everyone to go through deep heart searchings about their past, but for many people at a time of crisis in their lives there is a sense of something holding them back. It is rather like trying to set sail while unaware that two of the ropes holding the boat to the dock have not been cast off. It may be necessary to look back and cast off anything that is preventing the boat from getting underway. The letting go is usually a mental releasing rather than a physical action. It involves changes of attitude towards acceptance, forgiveness, and openness to change. Acceptance means coming to terms, as far as possible, with the reality and truth of who we are and the influences in childhood and more recently that have shaped our lives. It means coming to terms with the reality of the fact that some of us are more vulnerable than others to physical

illness or to psychological tension or depression. We
need to have a realistic idea of our limitations, our
vulnerabilities, and our strengths, and have as Paul says
'a sober judgement' (Romans 12. 3), about ourselves.
Some people try to deny the reality of a painful past and
live with a romantic illusion of a 'happy family'. As they
come to terms with the way they have been affected by
all that happened at home they may need to grieve over a
childhood that might have been beautiful and loving, but
was in fact sad, cruel, and ugly. We have to accept that
we are all, in some way, scarred and limited. There are
some things that we will not be able to change, apart
from a dramatic miracle, in this life. There are other
things that will only change slowly and some that can be
changed much more quickly and easily. St. Augustine
prayed 'God, give me the power to accept what cannot
be changed, the power to change things that I can change
and the discernment to see the difference.'

If we find that there is much 'unfinished business' in
the past – relationships unresolved, anger and bitterness
smouldering, jealousy, guilt . . . then these things need
to be dealt with before God; not, perhaps, in minute
detail, but the major themes which act as weights or
ropes to keep us from moving forward must be seen in
His light for what they are. Often unresolved emotions
will surface in present relationships. A wife's repressed
unresolved anger at her father may emerge in inexplicable anger towards her husband, or a woman's fear of
being assertive in the face of being taken advantage of by
her employers may arise from early fears of parental
anger or disapproval. So facing these issues may be part
of coming to terms with the reality of who we are, and
the influences that have shaped our attitudes and
emotional reactions. It is often helpful to write down the
things that I can change and the things that can only be
changed by my change of attitude towards them.

Open to change

Having faced the issue, we have to decide what needs to be done about it. The most important thing is what happens in our own hearts before God, our willingness to say we are sorry for things we have done to aggravate a situation (even small children can be wilfully destructive) or to forgive others who we feel have hurt us. We need to accept our responsibility, faded in our memories as it may be, and ask forgiveness from God and possibly from the person involved. This is often a very hard thing to do. If the person has died, or is no longer a part of our lives, or would probably not understand at all what we are talking about, there is little point in taking it beyond us and God. However, the ideal is that there should be mutual reconciliation and forgiveness. There is a moving scene in the film *On Golden Pond* when the daughter of an elderly couple, who has always had a bad relationship with her father, finds her own son having a wonderful time with him (his grandfather) at their lakeside house. In a moment of painful insight she realises the poverty of her own relationship with her father – she never had a relationship like that. 'On Golden Pond, I never grew up.' All the childish emotions of wanting to be loved, accepted, and approved of by her father well up in her and she reacts with bitterness and deep resentment. Both of them are aware of the tension and expect bitterness and rejection from the other. Neither is prepared to give in and move towards the other person. Then, after some time, she realises that someone has to make the first move to break the vicious circle. As she moves towards him, accepting him for all he is, with all his limitations, and in some way being able to forgive him for what he has done, so he is able to open up and respond to her. A mutual acceptance and forgiveness is beginning, a healing of some of the pains of the past.

So, we can see that God does not hold us personally responsible for our genetic inheritance, for the wounds and scars, the rejection and hurt of things done *to* us.

But, our responsibility, to some degree, is for how we reacted to those things in the past. Obviously there is increasing responsibility with increasing age and understanding. Is a baby responsible for the experience of frustration and anger when he is the object of his parents' frustration, anger and neglect? We are, as Paul Tournier says, both victims and culprits. Our responsibility is for where we have been culprits. Our responsibility is also for how we react now to the past. The patterns of reaction to the original wound need to be examined and changed. The false beliefs that we accepted about ourselves and our parents when we were small have to be exposed as lies as we begin to see how God views us and them. There is considerable healing in understanding the past, facing pent-up emotions and making sense of the inner confusion and pain. But this is by no means all that needs to be done. Understanding must lead to forgiveness, acceptance and change.

References

1   Graham Heath. *The Illusory Freedom* (William Heinemann Medical Books Ltd. 1978). p. 1-2.
2   Rollo May *Love and Will* quoted in Heath op. cit.
3   Attributed to St. Augustine.
4   C. S. Evans *Preserving the Person* (IVP 1979) p. 74.
5   Quoted by Malcolm Jeeves in *Free to be Different* (Marshalls, 1984) E. J. Langer and J. Rodin. The effects of choice and enhanced personal responsibility for the aged: A field experiment in an institutional setting. *Journal of Personality and Social Psychology* 34, 191-198, 1976. J. Rodin and E. J. Langer,. Long term-effects of a control-relevant intervention with the institutionalised aged. *Journal of Personality and Social Psychology* 34, 897-902, 1977.
6   D. G. Myers. *The Human Puzzle* (Harper and Row, New York, London 1978) p. 235.

CHAPTER TEN

Thorns in the flesh

Elizabeth was a charming woman. Nobody would have guessed from her outward immaculate appearance that inwardly she battled with intense anxiety. She was at her worst when her house and children were not perfectly clean and tidy. When the builders came to fix the roof and the ceiling of the bedroom, it felt as if everything was completely out of control, and she came to see me in a desperate panic. Deep down she knew her perfectionism was unrealistic but without it she felt very insecure. Before the children had been born she had been able to keep everything just as she wanted it, and fortunately her husband was a tidy person and did not object. Now she longed to be free from the paralyzing anxiety and from the instinctive reaction to scream at the children when they touched the wall with sticky fingers on their way up the stairs to bed! She was very like her parents. Their house and garden were immaculate – not a blade of grass out of place. She, from her earliest years had been a very sensitive child with many fears. At a purely biological level, when under stress, her adrenalin would flow and her heart would race at a faster pace than most.

As Colin grew through his teens he increasingly felt attracted to other boys and enjoyed the attention of one of the male teachers. From the latter he got the approval and interest for which he longed from his father. He felt strangely afraid of women and relationships with men seemed much more simple. Gradually he slid into a deep homosexual relationship. When he became a Christian

148

he knew his behaviour was wrong and he tried to relate to women, without much success. He felt awkward, and besides he still could not deny the physical attraction of some of the young men in the fellowship. His occasional failures led to dejection and depression.

Marjorie was only ten when her mother was killed in a terrible accident. Her father was very busy at his job, and when he came home he was withdrawn and depressed for most of the next four years. She took over much of her mother's role at home. She had two younger brothers. There was little time to be sad. Some years later, married and with three children of her own and few friends in the neighbourhood, her father died. She became very depressed. She realised that she had, in fact, been unhappy for years, and when pressures built up she easily sank into sadness and self-pity. It was difficult to talk to Jack, her husband, because he didn't really understand. With help from a psychiatrist she got through the depression but, for many years, she felt very vulnerable. She discovered that her aunt and grand-mother had both suffered from depression. Gradually her relationship with her husband improved, she got involved with a church fellowship and committed her life to Christ. But she still found that under stress she easily slipped back into the old ways of thinking and feeling – into the gray haze of depression.

For Elizabeth, Colin and Marjorie there were a number of influences in their lives which had contri-buted to the formation of habits of thinking, feeling, and behaving – deep grooves into which they easily slipped when under stress. Inherited temperament, parental attitudes and loss of close relationships all contributed to the specific problems and difficulties with which they had to struggle.

Physical and mental 'thorns'

Some people, as a result of genetic abnormalities,

disease, or accidents, are physically crippled throughout their lives. It is possible that Paul's 'thorn in the flesh' was some such limitation. It may well have been a physical disease or weakness that held him back in his work and gave him constant pain. It is perhaps easier to come to terms with an obvious physical disability such as being born with only one arm. You know what you have to accept and you know your limitations. But when it comes to psychological disabilities, what I would call mental thorns, they are not so easy to define and we do not know how much they will change in this life. But if it is something like a vulnerability to depression, that may have to be struggled against for years. The fact that someone has lived in a family where nobody trusted each other, where everyone was bitter and resentful, where they were not accepted, leaves deep scars on their ability to trust other people. That may be a thorn in the flesh, a thorn in their sinful nature that keeps troubling them and they have to learn to work against it. For example, Elizabeth's proneness to anxiety and Marjorie's vulnerability to depression are the things with which they have to struggle.

So, like Paul, we have to learn patience with our disabilities and yet work against them all the time. We have to 'put off the old nature' and 'put on the new' but it will not be completely new until we are with the Lord. Paul pleaded three times that his thorn would be taken away but the Lord said, 'my grace is sufficient for you, for my power is made perfect in weakness'. (2 Corinthians 12.8) We may never know why God does not heal us dramatically and take away some of the things against which we struggle. Sometimes after prayer God does give miraculous healing but more often it is that we have to work against these things and that in our weakness we learn to depend on God more. Through our weakness, through the brokenness of our bodies and minds, God is working out his purpose of changing us into his likeness. When we catch a glimpse of God's perspective we learn to deal with the 'thorns', not with cynical resignation or bitterness, but with grief at the fallen world in which we live and joy that we are being changed, and that there is hope beyond death. (Romans 8.18-24). Then there will be no more tears, no more pain, no more death . . . (Revelation 21.4). Until then, (if we are not miraculously healed – and a few will be) there are some things such as physical paralysis or blindness which we cannot change, but we can work to reduce the sharpness and depth of the emotional and mental 'thorns'.

For example, Elizabeth is working on allowing her children to have rooms of their own where they can do what they want (within reason!); she will help them to tidy their rooms but will not make them spotless three times a day. She is also trying to make time to sit for 15 minutes in the day to relax and to meditate on verses of Scripture and to pray, instead of dusting and vacuuming the living room for the third time that day. She is also learning to deal with her anger towards her dominating and controlling mother and her very critical father. At particularly stressful times she takes a small amount of tranquillizer to help her not to panic and get completely out of control.

Colin is doing all he can to build up a wide circle of friendships within the church and one or two of the married men have taken time to develop friendships with him. He may never get married and may always struggle against homosexual tendencies but as a result of his commitment to the Lord and to the fellowship of the church and their commitment to him, his temptation is greatly reduced. When he is under pressure he knows he can talk to one or two of the members of the church rather than seeking release in some illicit relationship. He may be able to change enough to consider marriage.

Marjorie had to cry a good deal about both her mother's and her father's death. Her relationship with her husband improved, she found support in the life of the church and was able to help others by running a play-group. As she continually reminded herself of her value to God (even though she often felt a failure), her very negative view of herself and her vulnerability to depression decreased.

Throwing off the weights

The writer to the Hebrews uses another image of life – running a race. It is not so much a race against each other but more like a marathon where the aim is to complete the course! But in running 'with perserverance the race that is marked out for us' we have to 'throw off everything that hinders and the sin that so easily entangles' (Hebrews 12. 1). In this race, each of us starts with different handicap, some with physical disabilities, some with psychological problems. Each has his own particular hindrances and sins that entangle. C.S. Lewis, in his wonderful style, contrasts two such people and their own unique struggles:

If you have sound nerves and intelligence and health and popularity and upbringing, you are likely to be quite satisfied with your character as it is. Why drag God into it you may ask? A certain level of good conduct comes fairly easily to you. You are not one of those wretched creatures who are always being tripped up by sex or dipsomania or nervousness or bad temper, everyone says you are a nice chap and between ourselves you agree with them. You are quite likely to believe that all this niceness is your own doing and you may easily not feel the need for any better kind of goodness. Often all these people who have this natural kind of goodness cannot be brought to recognise their need for Christ at all until one day the natural goodness lets them down and their self-satisfaction is shattered. In other words it is hard for those who are rich in this sense to enter the kingdom.

The problem for those who are well endowed, who do not have too many thorns in the flesh, or too many obvious weights to carry is pride and a tendency to look down on others who appear weak. But C. S. Lewis continues:

> If you are a poor creature poisoned by a wretched upbringing in some house full of vulgar jealousies and senseless quarrels, saddled by no choice of your own by some sexual perversion, nagged day in and day out by an inferiority complex that makes you snap at your best friends, do not despair. He knows all about it. You are one of the poor whom He blessed, He knows what a wretched machine you were trying to drive. Keep on doing what you can. One day perhaps in another world, but perhaps far sooner than that, He will fling it on the scrap heap and then you may astonish us all, not least yourself, for you have learned your driving in a hard school. Some of the last shall be first and some of the first will be last.[1]

So there are some who set out with an apparent advantage – 'sound nerves, intelligence, health, popularity and good upbringing' but others appear handicapped by 'a wretched upbringing and some house full of vulgar jealousies and senseless quarrels,' and we must accept the differences. But, before God we all stand equal, there are no super saints. We cannot get rid of the bad things that have happened to us but we can reduce their effects on us–their 'entangling' power–by our attitude towards them. Our responsibility is to take time at points in our lives, to look back and come to terms with our past, our particular handicaps. It is important that we don't make a lifestyle out of morbid introspection and self-pity. Our main orientation is to look forward and fix our eyes on Jesus. Times of hardship and difficulties may make us more aware of our handicaps. Just as when someone is on a run, going up a steep hill, they may become more aware of their vulnerable points, and their resentfulness at not having a stronger body! We may not be able to change our body or our biochemistry or the things that have happened to us in the past, but we can change our attitudes to them, from bitterness and resentment to acceptance and forgiveness.

Against the current

The race I imagine involves crossing a huge river. It means walking across it sometimes up to our necks in water, and with the current pushing us down threatening to overwhelm us at every moment. We find ourselves being shaped by the current of cultural values and opinions, but as Christians we change direction and no longer go with the stream but often against it or across it. Freed from the penalty of sin, we should know ever increasing freedom from the power of sin. We are no longer slaves of sin, Paul says. We serve a new master. He is to be Lord of every part of our lives. This means that we, together with Him, begin to fill in the old grooves of habitual ways of thinking, feeling and behaving and dig new ones. This does not happen automatically. We have to make a very conscious choice. It involves our activity and co-operation. It means admitting our faults – 'Yes I realise that because of the way my father treated me, I have a tendency to bitterness and cynicism but my responsibility is to ask forgiveness from God and to continually resist that tendency'. It is easy to slip back into old, habitual, comfortable grooves especially when under pressure. New patterns of feeling and thinking and behaving do not come easily. It takes hard work. Learning a musical instrument takes regular daily practice for months and years while new reflexes and patterns are forged in the nervous system. So we begin to work against all the ways in which we have been conditioned by the past. Some things will only be undone when Christ comes back again, but there is much that can be changed now. As we begin, by conscious choices, to resist our sinful nature, to serve a new master, we begin to experience new forces within us, new determining forces of a different kind. We are no longer slaves to sin but we are slaves to God.

Obedience and the Grace of God

The cry for freedom from all restraints is a common one today. But freedom can only exist within some sort of form. An attempt to live without boundaries usually ends in being conditioned subconsciously by the surrounding culture and by a growing frustration with the limits of human nature. There are boundaries in God's world from which one cannot escape. True freedom in a world where we cannot escape the determining influences is found in putting ourselves under the right controlling influences – to live true to the way we are made. And those right influences are the Spirit and the Word. The Word of God tells us how we should live and even non-Christians can benefit to some measure by obeying the Law of God. We are called to encourage people, Christians and non-Christians alike, not to steal, lie or commit adultery, because we believe it is better for them and for the rest of society. But living under the Law gives only a measure of freedom and that only in this life. We also long for men and women to know the Spirit who gives life that will go on into eternity, and helps us to know the first-fruits of that future freedom now. Non-Christians may experience in a measure of integration in their lives something of

God's common grace but for the Christian there is also His special grace which gives new strength and vision for change. As we step down from the throne of our lives and ask God to take over, His Spirit is able to flow through us, enabling 'man to go beyond what his own past has made him, giving him new desires, new capacities, new horizons.'[2] God, by His grace, is working in us to remove some of the limits of sin and disorder.

Paul talks about the change of direction from being slaves to sin to being slaves to God. 'Don't you know that when you offer yourselves to someone to obey him as slaves, you are slaves to the one whom you obey – whether you are slaves to sin, which leads to death, or to obedience, which leads to righteousness? But thanks be to God, that though you used to be slaves to sin, you whole-heartedly obeyed the form of teaching with which you were entrusted. You have been set free from sin and have become slaves to righteousness. I put this in human terms because you are weak in your natural selves. Just as you used to offer the parts of your body to slavery to impurity and ever increasing wickedness, so now offer them in slavery to righteousness leading to holiness . . .' (Romans 6. 16-19).

You gotta serve somebody

As we change direction and commit ourselves as slaves to God then other things begin to change. 'If you continue in my words' says Jesus to his disciples 'you will know the truth and the truth will make you free.' John 8.32. If we continue to obey what we know to be true then we will understand more of the truth and will know increasing freedom. We will begin to understand more of the world we live in and what God wants to do in it. If we disobey His words then we will progressively know less of the truth. We will become more caught up by the conditioning effects of the world around us and we will become progressively less free. As Bob Dylan sings 'you gotta serve somebody'. It involves no less than a daily commitment not to serve the influence of the past, our feelings, or the culture around us, but to serve the God who made us for a relationship with himself.

And the balance between freedom and determinism is important there. Sometimes we feel it is all up to us – that it is a battle, a struggle, a fight. At other times we know the Spirit of God at work in us, changing and restoring. Is it all up to us? Or is the Spirit now controlling and dominating us, determining everything we do? Just as we were moulded and determined by the past so now we are moulded and shaped as we are drawn on by the Spirit of God. There is a new determining influence at work. But He requires our co-operation. We still have freedom to choose and act. All through the Bible the twin themes of God's sovereignty and our responsibility run hand in hand. We are told to 'clothe ourselves (put on – an active word) with compassion, kindness, humility, gentleness, and patience.' But we are also told that 'the fruits of the Spirit are love, joy, peace, patience . . .' (Galatians 5.22). We are told that 'His divine power has given us everything we need for life and godliness' . . . but we are also told in the next verse but one 'for this reason add to your faith goodness; to goodness, knowledge . . . ' (2 Peter 1.3-5). God is shaping our lives, yet we have freedom to choose to resist Him, or to work with Him. And we also have the reassuring promise that 'He who began a good work in you will carry it on to completion until the day of Christ Jesus.' (Philippians 1.6).

Being changed

So to summarise: When we feel weighed down by the enormity of the struggle, we need continually to remind ourselves that we are being changed. (2 Corinthians 3.18). The image is being restored, slowly and sometimes painfully now, but one day we will be complete. As the Holy Spirit works within us and as we daily choose to resist the old grooves of thinking, feeling and behaving, we can do something about our particular 'thorns' in the flesh.

Paul cried out in his struggle 'who will deliver me from this body of death?' – from his sinful nature, his besetting temptations and his limited body. 'Thanks be to God' we will one day be delivered completely, but for the moment we taste only the 'first fruits' of that full and final redemption. Occasionally He delivers some from particular thorns instantly, but for most people it is a slow process of change, learning to live with vulnerabilities and weaknesses – 'struggling against sin', 'putting on the whole armour of God', 'running the race', and learning that in our weaknesses we grow to depend on Him more. 'His strength is made perfect in weakness'. As we live in obedience to God and allow the Spirit to work within us, we experience a little of what C. S. Lewis described as 'inklings' of joy – hints of the wonder of the complete changes we will experience when beyond this fallen, broken world, we will be with the Lord forever. (1 Corinthians 15.51-52 and Philippians 3.21).

References

1   C. S. Lewis. *Mere Christianity* (Fount Paperbacks – Collins 1977) p. 178-180.
2   *Dictionary of New Testament Theology* Ed. Colin Brown (Paternoster Press) p. 681.

PART III

CHAPTER ELEVEN

Be angry but do not sin

Dear Mum and Dad,
What I'm asking for, in this my first time to ever show or even know my anger in its depth (so 'disrespectful' it was for us to get angry around our place) – is simply *honesty* on your part. For you know my weaknesses . . . I've not hidden them. However, what *absolutely infuriates* me is that – after suffering a major, seven-year ordeal of depression – at times a clinical one, and, at others, subclinical – you roundly deny any significant mishandling of my upbringing??!! I will not allow such a denial to go unchallenged. I have tried the peace-at-any-cost route for 27 years to no avail, being tolerant and keeping my mouth shut. But I am almost *beside myself* with anger, and it is justified. I will tell you my anger in hopes that you change, also realizing my own problems and imperfections, too. However, if you both continue such a denial of significant mishandling of my upbringing, don't expect me to expose myself to such abuse in the future. I won't be so masochistic as to hang around you much, though I love you very deeply.

Sincerely, Jack.[1]

Anger's disguises

As we come to terms with the past and face frustrations in the present, we often have to deal with such a mixture of anger and love and unexpressed anger is a common cause of depression. If repressed into the unconscious it will tend to simmer within like a grumbling volcano. Spurts of steam or hot lava will escape at intervals and express themselves in a number of different ways. Irritable, critical, and uncooperative behaviour is an obvious sign that the anger is near the surface. Other less obvious disguises are impatience, and boredom. Physical illnesses such as backache, headaches, stomach ulcers and fatigue are also some-times caused by anger: 'A calm and undisturbed mind and heart are the life and health of the body but envy, jealousy and wrath are as rottenness to the bones' (Proverbs 14. 30 – Amplified Version). It is often mild mannered, gentle people with much self control who, when repeatedly provoked, will finally erupt with devasting anger and then feel terrible guilt and depression. Those who often lose control usually feel too little guilt. Sometimes when we cannot accept responsibility for our own anger we blame others for being angry with us first. We often criticise in others what we hate most in ourselves. Self-destructive urges in the form of drug taking, alcohol, or even suicide attempts often arise from anger that has been turned inward against oneself.

Sometimes when a feeling of anger is very frightening and unacceptable it is repressed into the unconscious with rather unexpected consequences. I vividly remem-ber my first day in a psychiatric clinic when a woman was sent to see a psychiatrist because she had a terrible fear (phobia) of kitchen knives so that she could hardly enter her own kitchen. As we talked it became clear that this gentle, mild mannered lady was being seriously abused by her husband. One day, the thought of killing her husband with one of the kitchen knives crossed her mind. She was so horrified at the thought and so afraid that she might lose control of herself that she forgot (in this case, repressed) her anger and was only aware of a great fear of knives.

How should we deal with anger? Is it right just to let it all out? Some, the so called 'ventilation' school or 'exploders' would have us believe so. Shout, scream, hit a pillow, break a few plates, anything to get it out of the system. Others say it is a sin for a Christian to ever get angry.

God's anger

It is helpful, in order to get a right perspective on this subject to step back a little and look at the anger of God. Is his anger just an unfortunate lapse, a moment of self-forgetfulness in an all loving and all accepting God? Is it just a projection of the writer's character, making God in his own image? It is very difficult to believe so when we read verses like Ezra 8.22 'the power of his anger is against those who forsake him', or Romans 1.18 'the wrath of God is being revealed from heaven against all the godlessness and wickedness of men who suppress the truth by their wickedness'. We cannot escape the fact that the Bible is full of God's judgement from Genesis to Revelation. A. W. Pink writes 'A study of the concordance will show that there are *more* references to the anger, fury and wrath of God than there are to his love and tenderness.'[2]

But with His people, the Israelites, we find 'the Lord is *slow to anger,* abounding in love and forgiving sin and rebellion' (Numbers 14.18). 'The Lord is gracious and compassionate, *slow to anger* and rich in love' (Psalm 145.8). He disciplines those he loves but 'his anger lasts only a moment, his favour lasts a lifetime' (Psalm 30. 5).

In Christ, we see the living demonstration of the character of God. His anger is not capricious and out of control. It is appropriate to the situation. We see him speaking amazing words to the hypocritical scribes and pharisees denouncing them publicly as 'whited sepulcures', 'ravening wolves, sons of vipers', and 'children of the devil'. He took a whip to those who desecrated the house of God, and many other incidents are recorded when Jesus 'rebuked', 'charged', 'commanded', and spoke strongly to those with whom he came in contact. A somewhat different expression of anger is seen in his arrival at the tomb of Lazarus. When he saw Mary crying 'he was deeply moved in spirit, and troubled' . . . and as he approached the tomb he was upset again . . . (John 11.33 & 38). The Greek word for 'deeply moved' means 'to snort with anger, as of horses'. This time, not anger at hypocrisy or hardness of heart but presumably at the brokenness of the world, at the results of sin, of sickness, death, and separation.

So we cannot say that being angry is always wrong. As our purpose is to be conformed to the likeness of Jesus we should seek to understand when anger is justified, when it is righteous and when it is unrighteous.

Man's anger

What does the Bible say about the anger of man – not the perfect man, Jesus, but fallen sinful man? The basic principles are summarised neatly in Ephesians 4.26 'in your anger do not sin. Do not let the sun go down while you are still angry' and 'do not give the devil a foothold'. There *is* a possibility of anger without sin – righteous anger – but all other forms must be dealt with before the sun goes down. And it is these other forms that Paul mentions frequently. In Ephesians 4.31 we read 'get rid of all bitterness, rage and anger, brawling and slander, along with every other form of malice.' And in the same vein Colossians 3.8 'but you must rid yourselves of all such things as these; anger, rage, malice, slander, and filthy language from your lips.' In both Colossians and

Ephesians the emphasis is on the fact that we are all sinners and that we must do all we can to help each other fight against our sinful nature. Not only are we commanded to deal with unrighteous anger but in the same passages we are told to be humble, patient, gentle, full of self-control, to speak the truth in love, to recognise each other's gifts, to be kind and compassionate and to forgive one another. It is not just getting rid of anger, it is an active replacement of negative feelings and actions with positive ones.

In Galatians 5.16-26 Paul elaborates on the battle between the Spirit and the sinful nature and you remember how in our discussion about the influence of Satan we noted that Paul does not say 'spirits of rage' but says that it is the acts of the sinful nature which give rise to hatred and fits of rage. It is we who are usually responsible. So in dealing with unrighteous anger we are putting off the old nature, breaking out of old habits and vicious circles, and establishing new patterns of thought, feelings and behaviour. It takes a conscious willing choice.

Bottle or ventilate?

What then does the Bible say to the two extremes of 'bottlers' and 'ventilators'? Proverbs 10.8 speaks of these two alternatives 'he who conceals his hatred has lying lips (bottlers) and whoever speaks slander is a fool (ventilators).' There is much to say to the ventilators or exploders in Scripture. Two of the fruits of the Spirit mentioned in Galatians are 'patience' and 'self control'. The rest of the passage which Paul is quoting in Ephesians 6 is very relevant 'in your anger do not sin; when you are on your bed search your hearts and be silent.' (Psalm 4.4). Because we are so prone to unrighteous anger, the easiest, most downhill route to take, we have to apply the brakes very firmly. We have to stop and think. Proverbs gives some rich images worthy of a few minutes meditation: 'like a city whose walls are broken down, is a man who lacks self control' (Proverbs 25.28). 'A fool gives full vent to his anger, but a wise man keeps himself under control.' (Proverbs 29.11). 'Starting a quarrel is like breaking a dam; so drop the matter before a dispute breaks out.' (Proverbs 17.14).

Until recently most psychotherapists and counsellors belonged to the cathartic or ventilator school of anger. In other words, anger must be let out. Some therapies encourage any form of release of aggression (shouting, kicking, biting, hitting – usually not a person but a cushion or some other inanimate object) to 'get in touch' with feelings. But research has demonstrated that far from defusing anger this technique may inflame it. Children encouraged to get rid of 'pent-up' feelings by kicking furniture and playing with violent toys tend to become more aggressive, not less. Murray Straus, a sociologist in the field of family violence, found that couples who yell at each other do not feel less angry with each other afterwards, but more.[3] Most happy couples learn how to settle disputes and disagreements without leaving scars. Leonard Berkowitz, one of the world experts on aggression says 'telling someone we hate him supposedly will purge pent-up aggressive inclinations and will 'clear the air'. Frequently, however, when we tell someone off we stimulate ourselves to continued or even stronger aggression.'[4] When very angry we may make extreme statements which leave deep scars on the person we are attacking. Carol Tavris writes:

> The psychological rationale for ventilating anger does not stand up under experimental scrutiny. The weight of the evidence indicates precisely the opposite: Expressing anger makes you angrier, solidifies an angry attitude and establishes a hostile habit. If you

keep quiet about momentary irritations and distract yourself with pleasant activity until your fury simmers down, chances are that you will feel better, and feel better faster, than if you let yourself go in a shouting match.[5]

Self-control

So those who tend to let the anger out need to learn self control. This can be achieved to some degree by learning to relax the body tensions which often accompany anger (possibly by learning relaxation techniques or going for a good walk or run) and also by actively changing one's thinking about the person with whom one is angry. So that when I come home in the evening and find the house with toys all over the floor and washing all over the bathroom I don't think 'what a lazy so and so; she has done nothing all day!' Rather I must learn to think 'is she not feeling well? Have there been a thousand phone calls? Is one of the children sick? Did someone visit who wanted to talk for a long time?' We need to learn to re-interpret apparently provocative events and be prepared to believe the best, not the worst of the other person. James writes 'everyone should be quick to listen, slow to speak, slow to become angry – man's anger does not bring about the righteous life that God desires.' (James 1.20). And finally Paul writes 'love is patient, love is kind . . . it is not rude, it is not self-seeking, it is not easily angered, it keeps no record of wrongs.' (1 Corinthians 13.5).

For those who tend to bottle up their anger there is not such detailed advice in the Bible, but many principles. 'In your anger do not sin. Do not let the sun go down while you are still angry.' (Ephesians 4.26). The second word for anger in this verse is a stronger word implying bitterness and resentment. Anger should not be held inside for long, or it so easily turns into bitterness and resentment. It is best to deal with anger on the same day if at all possible. We are encouraged not to hold hatred in our hearts for 'whoever hates his brother is in the darkness . . . ' (1 John 2.11 and 3.15). Honesty and 'speaking the truth in love' are qualities of spiritual maturity.

Why do some people bottle their anger and others explode? It is partly temperament, and partly a process of learning from our parents and friends, so that over the years we develop a particular style, or habit of coping with frustration. Some people typically repress or explode, but most of us are different in different situations. We may explode at home, and repress at work, depending on the consequences!

Either repressing anger or losing one's temper are obviously unrighteous ways of dealing with anger. It is the particular *style* of dealing with the anger that is wrong. But are there some angry thoughts and feelings, that are not wrong in themselves? Is there righteous anger which can be expressed in a righteous manner? There are, I believe, several areas where this may be possible.

Righteous anger

Firstly, we can find examples when God, in the Old Testament and Christ, in the New Testament, express anger at injustice, cruelty, greed, arrogance and hypocrisy. This is not an issue of defending ourselves but rather an issue of human rights based on God's love for justice and the value he places on every human being. Men like Wilberforce and Shaftesbury channelled their anger at injustice into fighting for law reform in the abolition of slavery and the factory act excluding young children from working in factories. If we do not feel angry about child pornography, abortion on demand, racial intolerance, political repression and other gross injustices around the world, then there is something drastically wrong. These issues move the heart of God and so should move our hearts. 'Is not this the kind of fasting I have chosen: To loose the chains of injustice and untie the cords of the yoke, to set the oppressed free and break every yoke? Is it not to share your food with the hungry and to provide the poor wanderer with shelter – when you see the naked, to clothe him and not to turn away from your flesh and blood?' (Isaiah 58. 6-8.) We are not called to be tolerant towards evil and injustice. Anger should motivate us with the appropriate balance of reason and emotion – not losing control nor repressing so much that we become ineffective.

Secondly, anger has its place in the context of disciplining children. 'He who spares the rod hates his son, but he who loves him is careful to discipline him.' (Proverbs 13. 24.) In a relationship of strong affection, friendship and respect, there may be moments of hot displeasure leading to appropriate punishment. But as with God and the Israelites we should be 'slow to anger' and our anger should be 'but for a moment'. If the anger continues for hours or days because it has not been appropriately expressed and leads to a critical and resentful spirit, it will breed an attitude of deep bitterness and rebellion in the child. Spanking properly administered should lead to a child respecting the parent and thus is necessary on only rare occasions.

Thirdly, I suggest that there is a place for occasional expressions of righteous anger in relationships, in marriage, between parents and adolescent children, between friends and in work situations. This is a difficult area because our anger is so easily selfish and unrighteous. A few examples may illustrate the possibilities. Imagine a woman whose husband never listens to her problems and refuses to talk about difficulties and differences in their marriage, and how they discipline the children. Is it her duty to submit, especially when she is crushed as a person and the children are often disciplined harshly and unfairly by her husband? Or in another marriage, the wife starts seeing an unemployed neighbour while her husband is at work, and eventually commits adultery. Should the husband not be angry? Or if a husband is continuously untidy and rarely washes so that there is always an unpleasant smell. If, after repeatedly trying to talk in a calm and gentle way about how much this upsets her and makes her very tense when he expects to make love to her, he still ignores her, is there not the possibility of righteous anger being expressed?

Or if a mother persistently interferes with her daughter's marriage and family life – jealous of her daughter's affection for her husband and children, not listening when they try to reason with her, and telephoning every day? Or consider a fourteen year old adolescent, who is repeatedly told what a failure he is. He doesn't dress right, the music he listens to is terrible, only if he gets an 'A' in all his classes does he sense faint approval from his parents! Would an expression of anger be a wrong response? And finally, if I repeatedly ask for help for a difficult task at work but my requests are ignored, not because of shortage of staff, but because of inefficiency and laziness on the part of my employers, do I have any right to get angry?

Principles of righteous anger

What principles govern all these situations? In all of them I believe it would not be wrong for the aggrieved person to be righteously angry at the injustice in the relationship. The problem is that the anger very quickly becomes unrighteousness because of how it is handled or expressed! We have seen that we should not explode, should not bottle up the anger causing chronic resentment, nor take revenge nor be involved in slander or gossip! So what should we do? The first stage, I believe, is to take time to think and pray and be aware of our own responsibility and faults – the beam in our own eye. We must recognise that no-one is perfect and that everyday we will probably hurt people who are closest to us in a number of ways. Perhaps it is in this context that 'love covers a multitude of sins' (Proverbs 10. 12) so that, for instance, a married couple will not need to talk about every angry thought or feeling. But when the anger remains then we should try to talk calmly and rationally about it, confessing our anger, and trying to see the other person's point of view, and seeking to build relationships peacefully. We need to 'speak the truth in love' asking for forgiveness and being ready to forgive. We must long for reconciliation not revenge.

In many of the situations described this first stage has not worked. They are unresolved long term situations of difficulty. The second stage is then to seek help from an elder or friend that you know and trust, and after thought and prayer, if possible involve all parties in a discussion of the issue. If this fails and still there is gross injustice in the relationship, there are two possibilities. One is that the person perpetrating the injustice is amazingly unaware of what they are doing and needs to be told in very straight terms. This involves expressing anger. God does that with the Israelites. He shows incredible patience and yet ultimately the demands for justice involve an expression of his displeasure. And after repentance there is always mercy and forgiveness. The second possibility is that the person who is being so unjust is doing so maliciously and wilfully and express-ion of anger may not solve anything. In that situation, in a marriage, unless there is continuous violence where a separation may be necessary, the hurt partner can only pray for change and reconciliation and seek support from friends, finding in the situation an opportunity to share Christ's suffering (1 Peter 2. 19-21).

The apostle Paul was not afraid to stand up for his own rights when he was beaten in Jerusalem (Acts 22. 22-29). His anger at the injustice was expressed in a calm and reasoned appeal to the law and his rights as a Roman citizen. On this occasion he was not going to be walked over and glory in being persecuted for Christ's sake, and yet in Philippi, where there was no way he could escape the anger of the people, he did not protest when he was thrown into prison. But Peter commends slaves for suffering for doing good. He does not incite them to rebel against their masters. He encourages them to take the way of the cross. We can learn from these situations that when all legitimate attempts to restore justice in relationships between individuals have failed then the injured person should not resort to revenge or leaving a marriage. They are called to take the difficult path of sharing Christ's suffering on the way of the cross.

Anger for the past

The situations I have described above all involve relationships in the present. What about anger rooted in past injustice and relationships? Is it possible to untie the knots that have been tied deep in our hearts and minds? Because we are made in the image of God, with his concern for justice in the world there is a sense in which anger may be justified when we were hurt and wounded in childhood.

John's father never wanted him. His mother had tried desperately to get an abortion (before it was legal) but had failed. And when he was born he was continuously criticised and eventually at the age of seventeen told to leave home. Others in situations similar to John's have been abandoned to orphanages, neglected, criticised, laughed at and sexually abused. It is known that babies deprived of food and love and affection often pass through a period of rage and frustration at being so deprived before withdrawing and giving up hope. Such children often may not grow as they should and are listless and apathetic.

Sometimes events in the present may trigger deeply

buried emotional memories. For instance a man being criticised by his boss may experience a total devastation of his identity as the experience reverberates with the many times his own father told him he was useless and pathetic. Or a newly married woman whose husband is sexually rough and insensitive may trigger an emotional reaction of terror because of incidents of sexual abuse in childhood.

Knots untangled

It is not wrong to be angry at such injustice but as we face the anger and acknowledge it we have to be prepared to deal with it appropriately. It may take hours of patient talking with a friend or counsellor to tease out the different strands of a knot of anger rooted in the past. Or it may be obvious after only a brief time of discussion and prayer. There are some biblical principles which guide us in dealing with such anger.

Firstly, as we have seen, the Bible implies that Jesus was angry and upset at the tomb of Lazarus. He was probably angry at man's sin and disobedience, the fact that the world is broken and not the way he intended it to be. That anger and sadness He expressed before God, and we can do that too. Secondly, we must recognise that parents who may have hurt us are only partially responsible for what they have done. They too have been hurt by others and are caught up in the sins of the fathers. So we can have compassion for them and see ourselves like them. Sometimes it is helpful to imagine what they would have been thinking and feeling at the same age as you are at the moment. Compassion should lead to forgiveness; being willing to forgive them and being willing to acknowledge our responsibility in provoking them to anger. Thirdly, we must recognise that even as very small children we have some responsibility for how we react to situations. We have to be prepared to make the first move, to say we are sorry for what we have done *without* demanding anything in return. A letter is sometimes helpful to clarify such situations. If parents are able and willing to discuss and recognise wrong, there will be wonderful moments of reconciliation. Sadly they may not understand at all and we may feel hurt and rejected and even more angry. We must leave the rest with God. He can take our anger. He wants us to be honest because it opens us up to Him. David found it was safe to have his outbursts in God's presence. In Psalm 55 he tells God that he is very angry with his friends who have turned against him. In Psalm 13 he is grieved and angry with God, 'How long will you forget me and hide your face from me?' At such times he expressed his passionate hatred of injustice. It is a great comfort for us in the depths of emotional turmoil to find that David shared the same feelings and lifted his eyes and heart to God. He did not run from the pain but faced it squarely and brought it to God. One friend, in working through much deeply repressed anger when coming out of a time of depression, said that it was extremely helpful to write down exactly what she was feeling – swear words and all. 'There was no need to reveal it – I could just tear it up because it was "out" in words – on paper.' It was out in the open – confessed to God.

But I do believe there are some limits to our expression of anger to God. We can question him, but *not* curse him. Job questioned God in no uncertain terms after everything except his wife had been taken from him. She encouraged him to curse God. Satan was determined to make Job turn away from God. Job cried out in his agony 'are you not in control? Why have you allowed this mess?' But he did not curse God.

So there are some relationships in the past and present where we cannot set things right, either because the person involved has died or is unwilling to talk. These we can only leave with God and ask him to bring healing and to help us not to hold onto resentment and bitterness.

Forgiveness

We talk very simply about the necessity for forgiveness but why is it that most of us find within ourselves a deep resistance to actually forgiving those who have wronged us? It is interesting that there is very little mention of forgiveness in the literature on psychoanalysis or contemporary psychotherapy, but it is of course at the heart of Christian relationships. I believe that there are several reasons. Firstly, because within all of us there is a deep sense of justice, of right and wrong, we may feel that if we forgive some injustice then we are somehow going against a natural law of the universe, that we are overlooking or making light of sin. In our desire to see evil punished we feel that forgiveness is incompatible with justice. But in fact justice and mercy often go together and supremely so in the cross of Christ where as C. S. Lewis puts it 'mercy and justice kissed'. The demands of justice were fully met in Christ bearing the punishment of our sin. There are situations where we as created beings can administer justice and forgive. The fact that I punish my son when he is deliberately disobedient does not mean that I do not forgive him. The government is given the responsibility (Romans 13) of ensuring that there is order and justice in the land, but if someone is put in prison for a drunken driving accident which maims my child I can still forgive him. Ultimately justice rests in the hands of God and in some situations we may see no sign of justice this side of heaven. When we have been deeply hurt and rejected or deprived by our parents then we have to leave justice to God. We are called to forgive and to seek for reconciliation. It is always wrong for us to take revenge for some personal insult or injustice. So our instinctive reaction to hit back is a result of a combination of a right concern for justice and a wrong desire for revenge. When Peter writes 'love covers a multitude of sins' (1 Peter 4.8) he means that we must be ready to overlook and forgive others all the petty ways in which they inevitably offend us each day. But where there is repeated injustice then there should be attempts to express our anger in righteous ways so that there may be reconciliation and forgiveness. Ultimate justice we must leave with God. 'Vengeance is mine, I will repay, says the Lord'. (Romans 12.19). Forgiveness is a choice we have to make. Erwin Lutzer in *Managing your Emotions* writes:

> You may be one of those who has been rejected by your parents. In your heart you are saying, and you may well be saying it to your spouse, 'I want to see my parents suffer for what they have done to me. No way am I going to let them off scot-free by forgiving them.' You say that even though in your honest hours you admit they couldn't care less about whether you forgave them or not. They have rejected you – and they will continue to reject you. Your clearest response if you want to live by God's Word, must be 'By God's grace I choose to forgive them.' Don't wait until you feel like it – you never will.[6]

Secondly forgiveness is painful because it involves accepting what the other person has done to us. For example, if a father cruelly beats his child so that she is permanently crippled, the child may well forgive her father but will still feel the pain of the physical consequences throughout her life. The same may happen with psychological damage; the pain of not being loved or accepted by critical parents may continue long after we have been able to forgive. But we are not alone in this because Christ bore the ultimate consequences and penalty for our sin in his own body. Even when we have forgiven once, when we feel the hurt and pain and are reminded of what they have done and we are tempted to be bitter and resentful we have to forgive again. It is important to make a distinction here between the hurt that may go on for years as a consequence of sin and our own response of anger. Many people feel that if they are still hurting then they must still be angry and need to go on forgiving. Often forgiveness is a process which may start with us merely praying for the willingness to forgive.

Rita Nightingale, unjustly imprisoned for drug smuggling in Thailand, was branded a trouble maker by the warden of the prison. In her anger Rita talked to a visiting Christian couple:

> 'I can't help it; I can't forget all the things she's done to me.'
> 'You haven't forgiven her yet, Rita.'
> I gasped. 'But I have, I really have! You have no idea how much I've prayed . . . But God hasn't changed her.'
> 'How have you prayed, Rita?' interjected Jack.
> 'What do you mean?'
> 'You see, there are two ways of praying about a problem like this. You can try to enlist God's sympathy on your side against the other person. Or you can ask God to simply change the whole relationship you have to her. You must choose whether you change or she does.'
> I fell silent. Into my mind flashed an image of the severe-faced, crisply-uniformed woman who ran Lard Yao. I tried to think of her as a friend, as a human being like myself, but shook my head in despair.
> 'I can't do it, Jack. I've such bitterness in me.'
> 'That's right. You can't do it. But Jesus can.'

Suddenly remembering the changes in my attitudes
which I could already recognise, I nodded slowly.
Gladys smiled.

'It won't happen overnight. You have to go on
forgiving. Jesus told his disciples that they should
forgive seventy times seven times. Keep bringing her
to God, Rita. Tell God about your feelings. Don't try
to be something you're not. Ask God to change you
into what you want to be.'

'Satan is trying to make things as difficult for you as
possible,' added Jack. He grinned. 'He's letting all
this anger build up, until your own bitterness hurts
you. You're doing his work for him, Rita.'

As I learned about forgiveness, my understanding of
what was involved expanded, sometimes painfully.
Passages in the Gospels seemed to leap from the page
and bore into my brain. As I read about the attitude
Jesus had towards his enemies, I found it hard enough
to forgive the Warden, because it meant accepting
that I too had been in the wrong. But gradually I had
to face up to the fact that I had to forgive James,
Simon Lo and Alan Soon as well.

It was a slow and painful progression. Each person
had to be prayed over, agonised over, and forgiven.
When I thought I had really forgiven somebody, I
would find myself resenting them two or three days
later, and have to forgive them all over again.

It was only as I looked back, as the days became
weeks and the weeks months, that I saw that my
attitudes were changing. I was learning how to
forgive.[7]

Thirdly, forgiveness is hard, because as Jesus pointed
out in the parable of the beam and the splinter, our
problem is often that we are only too well aware of
others' sins but have little idea of our own. We see
ourselves through the wrong end of the telescope and

others grossly magnified. If we realised how much and how many times God forgives us each day we would be much more ready to forgive others. Jesus highlights this in the parable of the debtor who has a debt of several million pounds cancelled and then goes out and threatens someone who owes him just a few pounds. Paul exhorts us to 'forgive one another as Christ forgave you'. (Ephesians 4.32).

Assertion and aggression

Returning to our theme of the relationship of anger and depression we must notice finally that there are some people who have a particular problem in asserting themselves and coping with anger and they are especially vulnerable to depression. For them any form of self assertion feels like unrighteous anger. They are normally oversensitive to others' opinions, are always anxious to please, and then find it difficult to express their own opinions or to disagree with others. Anthony Storr clearly demonstrates the relationship between this sort of repressed anger and depression:

> It is impossible entirely to separate the violent, destructive, hostile aspect of aggression from the constructive, effective, assertive aspect, without which no decisions would be taken, no leadership proffered, no action to alter events embarked upon. Without a certain assertion of his own personality, a person ceases to exist as definably distinct. In fact, when we loosely affirm that a man or woman has 'a lot of personality', what we usually mean is that he or she is notably assertive. In his relationships with others, the depressive personality generally feels defeated. What he is usually quite unaware of is that there is another side to his masochistic submission of self; a violent, hostile and destructive side of which he is

usually so frightened that he has erected formidable defences to make sure that it does not emerge. No human being can experience repeated defeats at the hands of others without resenting them. What the depressive has done, albeit automatically and without conscious intent, is to throw the baby out with the bath-water. By repressing his destructive hostility, he has at the same time deprived himself of those positive features of aggression which would allow him to assert himself when necessary, stand up to other people, initiate effective action, 'attack' difficult problems, and make his mark upon the world. I said that helplessness and hopelessness march hand in hand: let us add hostility to make a triad of 'h's'.[8]

As we face the dark side of our nature, our 'repressed hostility', and deal with it before God, so I believe we will be more fully human. As we bring these parts of ourselves to God he can work with them and change them to replace the darkness with light, the hate with love. Depression is sometimes referred to as 'frozen passion'. When anger is bottled up for long periods we are often hardly aware that it is present, but when it is 'frozen' within us other emotions are often inhibited as well. The thawing process can be very painful. In order to love others truly we may have to face the reality and depth of our anger, and as we bring that to God we will be set free to assert ourselves, to express anger in a righteous way, and also to love more fully and freely.

References

1   Used with permission
2   A.W. Pink, *The Attributes of God* p. 75 quoted by J.I. Packer in *Knowing God* (Hodder & Stoughton 1974) p. 135.

3   Quoted by Carol Tavris in *Anger – The Misunderstood Emotion* (Touchstone Book. Simon and Schuster. Inc. New York 1982) p. 128.

4   Ibid., p. 128.

5   Carol Tavris, Anger Defused *Psychology Today* Nov 1982, Vol. 16, No. 11 p. 25.

6   Erwin Lutzer, *Managing your Emotions* (Kingsway Pub. 1981) p. 144.

7   Rita Nightingale with David Porter, *Freed for Life* (Marshalls 1982) p. 174-175.

8   Anthony Storr, *The Art of Psychotherapy* (Secker and Warburg/Heinemann 1979) p. 101-102.

CHAPTER TWELVE

Guilt, shame and forgiveness

Macbeth, crazy with guilt and depression after murdering the king in order to take the throne himself, cried out, 'Canst thou not minister to a mind diseased, pluck from the memory a rooted sorrow . . .?' He longed to be able to undo the past. Both he and the doctor know that medicine will not cure straightforward guilt. 'Throw physic to the dogs – I'll have none of it.' Macbeth was left to sort out his inner anguish alone and the doctor says, 'Therein the patient must minister to himself.'[1]

Guilt is a common cause of depression. David describes in Psalm 32 the physical and psychological effects of unconfessed sin and then the enormous relief of confession and forgiveness. 'When I kept silent, my bones wasted away through my groaning all day long. For day and night your hand was heavy upon me; my strength was sapped as in the heat of summer. Then I acknowledged my sin to you and did not cover up my iniquity. I said, "I will confess my transgressions to the Lord" – and you forgave the guilt of my sin.' (Psalm 32.3-5). It is so important to keep short accounts with God and with family and friends. Like bitterness and resentment, guilt can eat into hearts and cause physical and psychological problems.

There are many psychotherapists and counsellors today who regard most guilt as neurotic, a product of a narrow-minded Christian heritage. They talk a lot about getting rid of 'guilt feelings' and rarely about the reality or fact of guilt. Karl Menninger a famous American psychiatrist, has highlighted this trend in his book,

Whatever Became of Sin? There is a great need in our relativistic culture where there are no absolute rights or wrongs, for a renewed emphasis on the holiness of God and the importance of praying daily. 'Search me, O God and know my heart, try me and know my thoughts and see if there is any wicked way in me.' (Psalm 139. 22-24). At the same time the amazing fact is that God *does* forgive even the most terrible sin. David was forgiven for adultery *and* murder and his famous prayer in Psalm 51 has been used by many Christians when they have come to their senses after doing things which they thought might bring them some happiness and satisfaction but later realised were terribly wrong.

But the subject of guilt is not quite as simple as that, for there are some who feel guilt when they have not done anything wrong and a few who even believe they have committed the unforgiveable sin of blasphemy against the Holy Spirit. For example, John was convinced he had cheated on his tax returns. His firm had been in financial difficulties for several years, and he had become progressively more depressed. He had a deep conviction that he had done something terribly wrong, and that this depression was a punishment from God. On examination, his accounts were immaculate and there was absolutely no trace of any dishonesty to be found. He was a sensitive, perfectionist man who tended to feel guilty about even the smallest things that went wrong in his life. For him, it was the state of depression that produced a false belief that he was guilty.

Unfortunately, dealing with guilt may be still more complex than this. Jeanette's parents were always arguing when she was small. Her father was very strict, and her mother a timid soul. Marjorie would try to make peace between them, and somehow always felt the rows were her fault. If she was a good girl, she thought, then maybe her parents would be nice to each other. When she was nine years old her father became ill with cancer and was obviously dying. He was often irrational but she nursed him with devotion. Sometimes he would try to interfere with her sexually and she would secretly wish that he was dead. When she became a Christian, she found it very difficult to believe that God could accept her as she was, and to forgive her evil thoughts. She feels guilty because of her longing that her father would die and finds it hard to believe that God is not like her own father and can really forgive her – even such murderous thoughts. Because of her parents' rows she is very scared of arguments and feels guilty whenever she stands up for herself. Consequently she is always very timid and her desire to please means that others take advantage of her kindness. She blames herself for being afraid to make her father angry by resisting his sexual advances and any thought of sexual intimacy in marriage fills her with shame, guilt, and disgust. Her mind and emotions seem to be a tangle of anxiety, fear, depression and guilt. Her conscience is deeply scarred and seems to be unreliable in that although her guilt at wishing her father dead is real, and perhaps she should have tried to resist her father's advances, the other guilt feelings come when she is not in fact guilty.

What is conscience?

So what is conscience if we cannot trust it? Is it an infallible guide to right and wrong? Is our conscience, as George Byron thought, 'the oracle of God'?[2] It is the part of our being which makes us feel guilty or ashamed when we have done something wrong. It also affirms our sense of acceptability and wholeness when we have done something right – the so-called 'good' or 'clear' conscience (1 Timothy 1.6). The Greeks believed that the conscience was a totally reliable inner faculty: 'There is no witness so terrible – no accuser so powerful – as conscience which dwells within us.'[3] Freud questioned this view, suggesting that the overscrupulous conscience (the 'tyrannical super-ego') might in fact be the product of one's upbringing. He believed that conscience was formed by a child's acceptance of parental standards and values within himself. A very strict father would create a very strict conscience. He recognised the need for some sort of restraints on the sexual and aggressive drives within us, but he certainly did not believe in any absolute moral standards, and therefore guilt was only in relation to parental and societal values. But this emphasis on parental influence on the development of conscience had been largely ignored by many Christians up to that time.

Because our conscience is imperfect, it needs to be shaped by and tested against the word of God. Tyron Edwards wrote, 'Conscience is merely our judgment of the right and wrong of our actions, and so can never be a safe guide unless enlightened by the word of God.'[4]

David in Psalm 51. 5-6 acknowledges that he needs wisdom in 'his secret heart and inmost place'. In Psalm 119. 9-11, he affirms that it is God's word that is the ultimate standard – his conscience is not enough on its own. 'How can a young man keep his way pure? By living according to Your Word . . . I have hidden Your word in my heart that I might not sin against You.' Or Proverbs 14. 12, 'There is a way which seems right to a man but the end thereof are the ways of death.' Inner guidance is not automatically reliable nor responsible. It must be purified to conform to the will of God. Before the fall, Adam and Eve, with the law of God in their hearts, naturally did what was right. After the fall, they and we are confused and broken in every area. Reason, will, emotions and conscience, all tend to swing between extremes and need some inner reference point. A sailor needs to have his compass checked every season against magnetic north, and against his maps and charts, because it is not automatically reliable; it may have been thrown off by pieces of metal on the boat, or by variations in the local magnetic field.

Seared or supersensitive

For someone who has been raised in a family where lying and deceit are the norm and promiscuous sex is accepted uncritically, guilt is a rare experience. Paul talks of those whose 'consciences have been seared as with a hot iron' (1 Timothy 4. 1-2). The image is of nerve endings in the superficial layers of the skin being burnt so that there is no longer any feeling. Then, the conscience is insensitive to those things that really matter. It has become silenced by misuse or abuse. Paul also speaks of 'minds and consciences' being 'corrupted'. (Titus 1. 15).

On the other hand, for someone who has grown up in a family where they have been constantly criticized and as a result have developed very high (perfectionist) standards, a sense of guilt and failure is an almost continuous experience. Paul also speaks of those with an overactive, misguided, 'weak conscience', who did not believe it was right to eat the meat that had been offered to idols. Paul did not see this as an absolute moral law, and therefore while encouraging the other Christians to respect such people, implied that their consciences were a little oversensitive, a little too scrupulous. (1 Cornithians 8).

So, as our conscience is shaped by God, it is also given life by the Holy Spirit within us. 'When he comes he will convict the world of guilt in regard to sin and righteousness and judgment.' (John 16. 8). Satan, as always, tries to get in on the act and confuse things. In Revelation 12. 10, he is called 'the accuser of the brethren'. He loves to beat us with our failures, and to keep prodding us with doubts about whether we have really been forgiven by God.

So, in our consciences there is an interaction between God's law, our parents' law (or values), and cultural law (or values). Rachel grew up in a typical twenteith century family where premarital sex was not frowned upon, as long as she was careful about VD and contraception. All her friends encouraged her in this lifestyle and homosexual relationships were also seen as just another normal expression of sexuality. When she became a Christian and began to read the Bible and to hear teaching on relationships and sexuality, her conscience in this area began to come to life again. Sarah, on the other hand, was raised in a Christian home where sexual relationships were seen as a wonderful gift from God, to be fulfilled only within marriage. All her friends thought she was rather old fashioned and prudish, but her God-given sense of right and wrong had been reinforced (not warped and twisted) from a very early age, by her parents, and she was able to resist the seductive voices of her friends.

Parents have a great responsibility in shaping the consciences of their children, as do teachers in the church. I grew up in a church where any form of dancing, films, or theatre were believed to be sinful. It was a number of years before I could enjoy dancing. (Perhaps also because of my two left feet!) Paul talks about not offending our consciences, but he implies in 1 Corninthians 8 that it might be possible to move from a position of one who believes it is wrong to eat meat offered to idols, to one who is not offended by it. So I believe it is important to distinguish between guilt feelings, and real guilt.

Barbara felt very guilty about leaving home. Her parents were putting enormous pressure on her to stay and keep the peace between them. They even justified their desires by Scripture, arguing that a girl should not leave home before she gets married. Should she go against her conscience? In fact, if she stayed she would feel very guilty for feeling so angry! I believe that if she is convinced that there is no absolute moral law of God forbidding her to leave home, she may have to do something that feels very uncomfortable. She may feel guilty without actually being guilty before God, because of the years of conditioning in that view from her parents.

Getting rid of guilt – the wrong way

A sense of real guilt should stimulate us to take action to deal with it, but it may be handled in a number of unhelpful ways. Very often it is swept under the carpet and repressed. Unfortunately, as Paul Tournier says, 'All unexpressed emotion poisons the mind'. Repressed guilt leads to increasing self-justification and pride, a blindness to one's own faults. Realistically to accept one's own faults is too painful. There is often, at the same time, a deep awareness of something being wrong, which may turn into irritation and anger particularly directed at the person who stimulates the guilty feelings. This often involves shifting the blame, as Adam did to Eve in Genesis 3. 12, 'the woman you put here with me – she gave me some fruit . . .' This was half-blaming the woman, and half-blaming God for giving him such a sinful companion!

Some people attempt to get rid of guilt by subconsciously thinking that if they try to do everything right then they will make amends for what they have done wrong. They feel that they have to pay, by their good works, the penalty for sin. In a few people this may develop into 'perfectionism'. They may not be able to rest until their house is spotless, their bodies scrubbed clean, and their life in immaculate order. This may be a way of coping with all uncomfortable emotions, anger, anxiety, or depression – especially for those who are desperately afraid of losing control of themselves and anxious to please others and especially God. In theological terms it is an extreme form of living under law as opposed to grace.

Another increasingly common way of getting rid of guilt is to deny failure. Guilt and a belief in any absolute standard is, after all, some psychotherapists and counsellors would say, only a neurotic hangup from our old fashioned Christian ways. Freud's followers have tended to throw out the baby with the bath water, the conscience with the overscrupulous conscience. In Transactional Analysis, another form of psychotherapy, parents tend to be blamed for all guilt. One hears such expressions as 'Get rid of the shoulds and oughts in your life', or 'get rid of the witch messages from the pig parents!' (see footnote) This is a semi-humorous caricature of conscience. Because we are supposed to believe we are OK as we are (I'm OK, you're OK) objective guilt is not taken seriously.[5]

So, with the death of God and the loss of any external reference point for reality and values many think that we are at liberty to re-define reality with self at the centre. Then there is theoretically no problem of conscience and guilt. The death of God leads to the death of conscience. Conscience, as a concept of absolute value is a word that will probably remain alive only within the Christian culture. The rest of the world now talks of 'altered states' of consciousness instead of states of conscience. If guilt can be got rid of by throwing out the values which give rise to it, a closely related view takes this process one step further. In some forms of Eastern mysticism, especially the teachings popularised in the West, reality is redefined. We are already perfect. The Maharishi Mahesh Yogi says, 'the answer to all your problems is that there is no problem.' If we can only realize it, there is no suffering, no sin, because all is one. I cannot harm anyone else, because in reality I am that person. Guilt is an illusion.

Conscience may also be simply deadened or drowned with drugs or alcohol. Or at the other extreme guilt may become an obsession, a fixed belief that the person is too bad for anyone to forgive and they may wallow in a mire of self-recrimination.

The existentialist psychotherapists, in contrast to Freud, recognise certain guilt feelings which are not just the products of parental and social conditioning to be removed by psychoanalysis. They see man as genuinely guilty in failing to fulfill all the possibilities of being human. How close this is to the Christian view of guilt but sadly the existentialist has no way to get rid of his guilt and what he calls 'Angst' or dread. He can never be free from it.

Getting rid of guilt – the right way

In contrast to these many unhelpful ways of dealing with guilt, we need to recognise and acknowledge real guilt and appropriate guilt feelings. We need, by talking to ourselves, to friends, and to God to sort out the inappropriate guilt from the real guilt. The lies of a twisted conscience which produces false guilt feelings have to be countered with the truth about God's view of right and wrong. It may take many months of reminding ourselves of the truth about a situation to wipe out the false guilt feelings. However, too often, when false guilt is not recognised for what it is and we do not have a sense of forgiveness or innocence, the outraged conscience continues to demand some form of punishment and may extract it in the form of depression or psychosomatic illness. Our poor minds are often so twisted that we punish ourselves unnecessarily. But we do need to learn to recognise pathological guilt in severe depression or in the person with an obsessional, perfectionist personality. On the other hand I have found that most people are greatly relieved to have their guilt taken seriously when other counsellors or doctors have dismissed it all as neurotic. Ultimately Jesus Christ alone can clear the guilty conscience. Paul Tournier writes in his book, *Guilt and Grace:*

'It is abundantly clear that no man lives free of guilt.
Guilt is universal. But according as it is repressed or
recognised, so it sets in motion one of two
contradictory processes: repressed, it leads to anger,
rebellion, fear and anxiety, a deadening of conscience, an increasing inability to recognise one's faults,
and a growing dominance of aggressive tendencies.
But consciously recognised . . . it leads to repentance,
to the peace and security of divine pardon, and in
that way to a progressive refinement of conscience
and a steady weakening of aggressive impulses.'
And so 'The enemy guilt becomes a friend because it
leads to an experience of grace.'[6]

There is no other way of truly getting rid of guilt. 'If we claim to be without sin, we deceive ourselves and the truth is not in us. If we confess our sins, he is faithful and just and will forgive us our sins and purify us from all unrighteousness.' (1 John 1. 8-9). 'Therefore, brothers, since we have confidence to enter the most holy place by the blood of Jesus, by a new and living way open to us through the curtain, that is his body, and since we have a great priest over the house of God, let us draw near to God with a sincere heart and full assurance of faith having our hearts sprinkled to cleanse us from a guilty conscience and having our bodies washed with pure water.' (Hebrews 10. 19-22).)

Pardon leads to peace and a refinement of conscience and increasing right sensitivity. As we soak ourselves in the word of God we will become increasingly aware of our sin. The Sermon on the Mount powerfully underlines the fact that God is not only concerned about our external actions but far more about the attitude of our hearts.

Shame

We cannot have the subject of guilt without mentioning the experience of shame which is often confused with guilt. The Bible clearly describes two polarities of experience shame and honour, guilt and innocence. We hear much about the latter but little about shame. Dick Keyes has developed this theme at length in his book *Beyond Identity*.[7]

When we do something wrong we usually feel guilty *and* ashamed. But sometimes we may feel a sense of shame when we have not done anything morally wrong but when we have done something which we feel makes us unacceptable to our friends—such as telling a joke at which nobody laughs or dressing inappropriately for a party! Dick Keyes points out that guilt usually relates to 'morals' and shame to 'models'. By 'models' he means those people in our family, friends or society to whom we look for examples of how to live. Most people are subconsciously deeply influenced by the lifestyle and values of our consumer society, especially of Hollywood filmstars and sports heroes. We feel ashamed of our bodies partly because of the sort of self-consciousness that came after the fall ('they were naked and were not ashamed') (Genesis 2. 25) and partly because we do not measure up (or down!) to the bodies of the beautiful people who advertise the latest hair shampoos or body lotion, or who crowd out the set of *Dallas*! Amongst city businessmen I may feel ashamed that I am not dressed in my dark suit and smart tie; amongst artists and musicians I might feel ashamed to be wearing such clothes!

In some schools a boy may feel ashamed if he does not get 'A's in all his exams, in another school where the few intellectuals are seen as snobs he may feel twinges of shame at getting 'Á's. Separating shame from guilt is important because it helps us to understand, for instance, the intense conflict of the situation in which many Christian young people find themselves. They know that sexual promiscuity is wrong but most of their non-Christian friends think that they are odd to be so old-fashioned. It is hard for them not to feel ashamed for doing what is right. If they have the strength to stand out against their non-Christian friends they will feel a sense of innocence (the opposite of guilt) in relation to God and honour (the opposite of shame) in relation to God, their Christian friends and family and themselves. Because we all have a strong desire to be accepted by those around us we may sometimes be ashamed of doing things which are morally right and then ashamed of not doing things which are morally wrong. Many of us feel ashamed when explaining why we are Christians. Paul writes, 'I am not ashamed of the gospel of Christ.' (Romans 1. 16).

Ideally our morals and models should coincide so that our models should be people who live with Christian values. Paul encourages the Christians to imitate him even as he imitated Christ. Dick Keyes encourages us to challenge and expose the false heroes and 'models' of the day, and to recognise when our values are being shaped by them rather than by bibilical values.

More knots untied

So, just as we have to learn to untangle the knots of anger in our lives, so we also have to learn to deal with the knots of guilt and shame. When we are confused about this it is helpful to write down our thoughts or to talk with a friend to separate out the strands of false guilt from real guilt, and appropriate shame from inappropriate shame. Those who do wrong *should* feel shame. 'Those who trust in idols, who say to images "You are our gods", will be turned back in utter shame' (Isaiah 42. 17). If we are innocent we need not be ashamed 'May my heart be blameless toward your decrees, that I may not be put to shame.' (Psalm 19.80). Ideally real guilt and appropriate shame should go together. As we have seen, in reality, guilt and shame are sometimes together, sometimes separate and sometimes in conflict with each other. When we feel ashamed of doing what is right or of being or doing something which is usually morally neutral – such as being the physical shape we inherited or wearing clothes we enjoy – then we have to remind ourselves of how God sees us and glory in His acceptance of us so that other people's disapproval (real or imaginary) come to matter to us less and less.

Accepting forgiveness

As we saw in discussing the difficulty of forgiving others, there is remarkably little discussion in the literature of psychotherapy on the subject of forgiveness. There is little sense of needing to be forgiven for the wrong things we have thought or done. But this is at the heart of the Christian gospel, God forgiving us, so that we too must forgive others.

One would think that forgiving others would be easy. But many people find it very hard and the inability or unwillingness to accept forgiveness and to forgive others who have wronged us is at the root of much insecurity and depression. Why is it so hard? Francis Schaeffer never tired of saying that Christianity is in one way the easiest religion in the world in that we come to God with nothing in our hands to receive His free forgiveness and love. In another way it is the hardest religion in the world because that is all we have to do! There is a deep seated sense in all of us that either we can make ourselves good enough for God by our own efforts, or if some punishment is deserved for justice to be done, then we should take it ourselves. We think that we must make amends for our failures and imperfections. Some forms of perfectionism are driven by guilt, by the sense that only when one is perfect or when one has pushed oneself to the limits of endurance, is acceptance possible. It is especially difficult for those who have been heavily criticised as children and made to feel that there is little, if any, good in them. They may feel that they are unforgiveable and be left with a deep longing for, and yet a distrust in, the possibility of acceptance and forgiveness.

At the other extreme there are those who are raised to have a high opinion of themselves – the self-made man who thinks of himself as a 'good person' – who find the thought of needing to be forgiven insulting and even threatening, as it undermines their whole identity and the basis for their sense of acceptance by others.

Some accept forgiveness too lightly and do not have a serious enough view of sin and the greatness of God's love and mercy. Others do not accept forgiveness easily enough – again because they do not see the greatness of God's love and mercy to cover even what they believe are most terrible sins.

The wonder is that He can and does forgive us as we come before Him as Saviour and Lord. Christ died to take the punishment we deserve. We can stand as Christian did in Bunyan's *Pilgrim's Progress*, at the foot of the cross and watch our burden of sin and guilt roll away down the hill and out of sight. Nothing that we could ever do would be good enough to earn God's forgiveness. He offers it freely as we acknowledge our sin and begin to live for Him rather than for ourselves. He accepts us with all our failings and weaknesses – warts and all – and then begins the process of re-making us so that one day we will be without sin. 'Because by one sacrifice' Christ has made us acceptable to God (Hebrews 10. 14). God will not remember our sins anymore. The guilt of the past is dealt with and can

be put behind us, the future secure because of His
assurance of continuous acceptance and forgiveness.

> Therefore, brothers, since we have confidence to
> enter the Most Holy Place by the blood of Jesus, by a
> new and living way opened for us through the curtain,
> that is, his body, and since we have a great priest over
> the house of God, let us draw near to God with a
> sincere heart in full assurance of faith, having our
> hearts sprinkled to cleanse us from a guilty conscience
> and having our bodies washed with pure water.
> (Hebrews 10. 19-22).
> If we claim to be without sin, we deceive ouselves and
> the truth is not in us. If we confess our sins, he is
> faithful and just and will forgive us our sins and purify
> us from all unrighteousness. (I John 1. 8-9).

Having a clear conscience before God and man is an
amazing freedom. But, there is far more to our
acceptance by God than forgiveness and justification.
There is a greater blessing – the Bible describes it in
terms of 'adoption' into the family of God.

Jim Packer writes in *Knowing God*:

> That justification – by which we mean God's
> forgiveness of the past together with His acceptance
> for the future – is the primary and fundamental
> blessing of the gospel is not in question. Justification
> is the primary blessing because it meets our primary
> spiritual need. We all stand by nature under God's
> judgement; His law condemns us; guilt gnaws at us,
> making us restless, miserable, and in our lucid
> moments afraid; we have no peace in ourselves,
> because we have no peace with our Maker. So we
> need the forgiveness of our sins, and assurance of a
> restored relationship with God, more than we need
> anything else in the world; and this the gospel offers

us before it offers us anything else.

But this is not to say that justification is the highest
blessing of the gospel. Adoption is higher, because of
the richer relationship with God that it involves. The
two ideas are distinct, and adoption is the more
exalted. Justification is a forensic idea, conceived in
terms of law, and viewing God as judge. In
justification, God declares of penitent believers that
they are not, and never will be liable to the death that
their sins deserve, because Jesus Christ, their
substitute and sacrifice, tasted death in their place on
the cross. This free gift of acquittal and peace, won us
at the cost of Calvary, is wonderful enough, in all
conscience – but justification does not of itself imply
any intimate or deep relationship with God the judge.
In idea, at any rate, you could have the reality of
justification without any close fellowship with God
resulting. But contrast this, now with adoption.
Adoption is a family idea, conceived in terms of love,
and viewing God as father. In adoption, God takes us
into His family and fellowship, and establishes us as
His children and heirs. Closeness, affection and
generosity are at the heart of the relationship. To be
right with God the judge is a great thing, but to be
loved and cared for by God the father is a greater.[8]

This is hard to accept for someone who has not known
the love and respect of an earthly father, but it is a
wonderful picture – of being adopted into a new family
where a whole new understanding of the word father will
have to be learned.

Just as Rita in prison had to learn to forgive others so
some people have to learn to accept God's forgiveness.
Often we are tempted to ask 'Does He really forgive me?
Surely I should still feel sorry for that.' We may certainly
regret having done some things and we may have to live
with the physical and emotional consequences and scars

of sin, but continuous remorse is sin in itself. It means that we do not really believe He can or has forgiven us. The Bible says 'He has cast all our sins into the depths of the sea (Micah 7. 19) and Corrie Ten Boom adds 'He has put up a sign saying No Fishing.' He does not keep a record of our wrongs and nor should we! 'I will remember their sins no more' Hebrews 10. 17. And because we have been forgiven so we should forgive others. Paul writes to the Ephesians 'Be kind and compassionate to one another, forgiving each other, just as in Christ God forgave you.' (Ephesians 4. 32).

Carl Rogers discovered that the first step to helping people to change was to accept them with all their hangups and problems. He believed wrongly that they could find all the answers to their problems in themselves, but he was discovering something of the way God has made us. When we are accepted as unique and valuable to anyone it gives a measure of security to take risks and change. When we feel unacceptable to anyone we are often so insecure that we retreat into a corner and build a wall around ourselves to reduce the risk of change. How much greater can be our freedom when we know we are loved, accepted and forgiven by our Creator God who promises to give us His Holy Spirit to help us daily to become more like Him.

Footnote

There is much that is useful in Transactional Analysis in helping people to understand themselves and their relationships, but Christians need discernment to reject false values.

References

1 William Shakespeare. *Macbeth* Act V Scene 3.
2 *The New Dictionary of Thoughts* Ed. Tryon Edwards (Standard Book Company 1960) p. 104.
3 *Sophocles.* Edwards op. cit., p. 105.
4 Ibid., p. 93.
5 Thomas Harris. *I'm Okay, You're OK* (Pan Books 1970) Eric Berne. *Games People Play* 1964 and *What Do You Say After You Say Hello* (Corgi 1975).
6 Paul Tournier. *Guilt and Grace* (Hodder & Stoughton 1974) p. 152.
7 Dick Keyes *Beyond Identity* (Servant Books U.S.A. 1984).
8 J. I. Packer. *Knowing God* (Hodder & Stoughton 1973) p. 186-187.

CHAPTER THIRTEEN

Death, bereavement and suicide

> I look up at the night sky. Is anything more certain
> than that in all those vast times and spaces, if I were
> allowed to search them, I should nowhere find her
> face, her voice, her touch? She died. She is dead. Is
> the word so difficult to learn?[1]

Death is a harsh reality in this world. As I write this I
am daily reminded of its existence by the grim pictures of
starvation in Africa and war in many other countries. Do
we tell dear friends who have lost close relatives through
sudden and unexpected deaths not to be upset, to rejoice
and praise God 'in all circumstances'? Surely not – 'we
weep with those who weep'. Jesus himself, as we have
seen, was 'deeply moved in spirit and troubled' as he
came to the tomb of Lazarus (John 1. 3). The Greek
word implies that he was both grieved and angry at the
fact of death – not at God, but at the abnormality of
death. Death is an ugly intrusion into the world that God
originally made – it came as a result of man's
disobedience and will one day be banished for ever.

Jesus was not only angry, but also sad as he wept for
his friend Lazarus, so much so that those standing
nearby said, 'See how he loved him'. And we too, caught
up in a broken world where separations and death are
inevitable, weep at the breaking of relationships in such
a violent way. Paul writes in 1 Thessalonians 4. 13
'brothers we do not want you to be ignorant about those
who fall asleep (in death) or to grieve like the rest of
men, who have no hope.' Paul is not saying 'do not

grieve' but 'don't grieve as those who do not believe in a more wonderful life beyond the grave.' Martin Luther wrote a lovely letter to a man called Dr. Benedict Paul whose son had recently been killed by a fall from the top of a house 'although it is nowhere forbidden in the Holy Scripture to mourn and grieve the death of a godly child or friend, nay we have many examples of the godly who have bewailed the death of their children or friends, yet there ought to be a measure in sorrow and mourning. Therefore loving doctor, while you do well to mourn and lament the death of your son, let not your grief exceed the measure of a Christian in refusing to be comforted.'[2] We must avoid self-pity or despair.

There is obviously a difference between losing someone through a tragic accident and having a close relative die after a long illness with cancer. For the latter, death is a release from pain and suffering and can in such circumstances be seen in the light of the fact that God prevented Adam and Eve from eating the Tree of Life in the Garden of Eden 'lest they should live forever'. He knew that when suffering became too great in a fallen world, death would be a release. But neither an unexpected accident nor cancer were intended by God in the beginning. There is often a mixture of emotions in grief, thankfulness at the release from pain and also sadness at the loss of a father, mother, brother, sister or child. It is not wrong to feel two emotions at once. In seemingly untimely deaths we recognise the tragedy and weep; yet even there God's grace reaches us and promises to bring good out of evil and that one day there will be no more death.

Many who are grieving think that it is weak, silly, immature or unspiritual to cry. As children they may have been punished for being 'so pathetic'. But there are many references in Scripture to crying – Abraham wept over Sarah, the Israelites for Moses. Mothers wept when their infants were killed in Bethlehem, the women at the cross, Mary at Jesus's tomb, Timothy at Paul's departure, and David, a man after God's heart spent much time weeping 'my tears have been my food day and night'. He wept over the deaths of Saul and Jonathan, over family troubles, and over his son Absalom. In many countries there is an accepted period of mourning when it is almost as if the culture 'gives permission' to the relatives to cry. It would be seen as abnormal and lacking due respect and love if they did not. Our stoic English ways are not necessarily the best. The concept of 'weeping with those who weep' is a very precious one. After her child of fourteen months who had spina bifida died, my sister found that one of the most meaningful things for her was when friends came and were able to talk about her daughter's death and to cry with her. Even six, eight and twelve months later, she had moments when she broke down in tears and felt the intense pain of the loss. Grief makes people feel very alone, and unfortunately what usually happens is that out of embarrassment and not knowing what to say, neighbours and friends tend to avoid them and are especially wary of doing or saying anything that might upset them. But what they often want is someone who *will* talk about the one who had died, and who will listen and share some of the pain.

Stages of Grief

Much research into bereavement describes several stages in accepting and coming to terms with the loss. Freud, in his book *Mourning and Melancholia* pointed out the similarities between bereavement and depression. Others have noted that loss of a job, loss of a part of the body (e.g. amputation of a limb, hysterectomy, mastectomy), a miscarriage or other major losses may precipitate the same stages of bereavement as the loss of a person. A recent study has shown that the grief a woman feels after an early miscarriage or stillbirth is no less than the grief of a woman who loses a newborn child.[3] After an abortion too there may be a complex reaction of grief and guilt. There is usually an initial stage of numbness which may last hours, days or weeks. Things that have to be done, such as arrangements for the funeral are done almost automatically and only vaguely remembered. Susie describes her reaction to her father's death:

> When Daddy's monitor suddenly stopped I seemed to fall into a vacuum. God however is gracious because for a while the shock and horror of it all cannot be absorbed; it infiltrates slowly as the days pass by. Your mind surges into overdrive, which is just as well as there is so much to be done, ringing around, notifying the papers, discussing details with the undertaker.
> When all the formal 'laying to rest' was over I found solace indulging in answering kind letters. I was able to relive happier times and remind others and myself of my father's many strengths and qualities. Pain began to take stabs and I can only describe it as similar to a broken heart, and I imagine like the betrayed's feeling in the sadness of a divorce. I began to feel great anger with my father for leaving me bereft, and having to grow up, and with God for allowing him to die so young (59). God copes so annoyingly well with our resentment and it is comforting to know that He identifies with our tears (John 11. 35).[4]

As the numbness wears off, the painful stage begins, in which many of the symptoms of depression are common. Tearfulness, lack of interest in food, sleeplessness, loss of energy, loss of concentration, anxiety, headaches, and other physical symptoms of tension, even suicidal thoughts. There may be increased use of drugs or alcohol to try to dull the pain. There is a deep sense of loss, of emptiness, of being torn apart inside. C. S. Lewis wrote in *A Grief Observed* 'no-one ever told me that grief felt so like fear. I am not afraid, but the sensation is like being afraid. The same fluttering in the stomach, the same restlessness, the yawning. I keep on swallowing.'[5] The origin of the word bereaved is 'broken up' and that, for many people, is just how it feels. There may be denial that it has really happened – waiting for him to come home from work, expecting her voice on the telephone. There is often a sense of searching for the lost one – thinking you see him in the street or on a bus. Hallucinations are not uncommon – hearing his voice or seeing his figure sitting in a chair or going through a door. 'He is with me all the time. I hear him and see him although I know it is only imagination. I feel he is near me and at times I feel his touch. I cannot help looking for him everywhere.'[6]

Just last night the story *Goodnight Mr Tom* by Michelle Magorian brought tears to our eyes as we read it with the children around the fire after supper. Will, an orphan from a very deprived background has been adopted by a wonderful man called Mr Tom, during the war. Sadly, Will's best friend Zach was killed in a bombing raid on London and Will, a talented artist, could not accept the reality of what had happened.

> Even in drawing and painting classes he would sit and look blankly at the empty page in front of him, devoid of ideas . . . ' 'I en't got anythin' left inside me', he would say repeatedly, for he felt that half of himself had been cut away, that life without Zach was only half a life and even that half was empty.

His art teacher gently encouraged him to talk about what had happened but:

Will didn't want to hear. His eyes were blurred and
his body hurt all over. He stumbled into the darkness .
. . in the direction of the woods and river.
Tripping and falling over the roots of trees, he
scratched his face against unseen branches. A
disturbed owl screeched loudly and flew above his
head but he hardly heard it. At last he finally reached
the river. He stood by it starting at its glassy surface,
his chest and shoulders pounding, his gut aching. He
felt again Zach's presence next to him, felt him staring
up at the starry night and coming out with some
strange fragment of poetry.
'No, no,' he whispered, shaking his head wildly. 'No,
no. You're not here. You'll *never* be here.' With one
angry sob he picked up a dead branch and struck it
against a tree trunk until it shattered. Wildly he
picked up any other branches he could find and
smashed them, hurling the broken bits into the river
not caring if he hurt any animals that might be
hibernating nearby for he felt so racked with pain that
he no longer cared about anything else but the tight
knot that seemed to pierce the very centre of him. He
was angry that Zach had died. Angry with him for
going away and leaving him.

With an almighty force of venom he tore one tiny
rotting tree up by its roots and pushed it to the ground.
Catching his breath for a moment he stood up stiffly and
looked up through the branches of the trees.

'I hate you, God. I hate you. You hear me? I hate
you. I hate you. I hate you.'
He stood, yelling and screaming at the sky until he
sank exhausted and sobbing on to the ground.
He had no idea how long he had lain there asleep. It

felt like a year. Slowly he crawled to his feet rigid and
shivering. He hauled himself up the bank and
tumbled through the woods.

Tom was waiting for him by the gate.[7]

This was the beginning of healing for Will. It is for
many, as the whole mixture of confused feelings –
depression, anger and guilt come out into the open.
Anger towards God for letting it happen, towards the
doctors or nurses, for their apparent incompetence,
towards yourself for what you might have done and
anger at the one who has gone for leaving you so alone.
And then guilt for the things you might have said and did
not, or for the things you said and now regret. Often the
more complicated the relationship, the more complex
will be these mixed emotions. Initially the one who has
gone will often be seen as perfect. It is difficult to
imagine that they ever said or did anything wrong. Then
there may be a swing to the opposite extreme of
remembering all their faults, before a more realistic
acceptance of good and bad and an awareness that none
of us are perfect. It is a time of reassessment of the
relationship. This stage of painful emotions is usually
beginning to fade after six months to a year, but the pain
may continue to come in waves for considerably longer.
Gradually the stage of recovery and adjustment and
reality takes over. Interests and activities are taken up
again and new relationships are made.

During the year or two after the bereavement, it is
vital to have a few people with whom the grief can be
shared. To be able to cry unashamedly, to talk about the
one who has gone, to go over the details of the last
months, weeks, days and hours is very important in the
process in keeping a right perspective and not burying
the pain completely. Birthdays, Christmases, and other
special days will often be sensitive and tearful occasions

as memories and associations come flooding back! It is
not unspiritual to feel upset at those times. Part of our
humanness is to feel the pain of the broken world and the
abnormality of separation and death. We weep just as
Jesus did. But our grief is 'not as those without hope.'
Many Christians are very conscious of a special support
and grace at such times. And some experience amazing
miracles of healed relationships and people becoming
Christians as a result of seemingly very tragic deaths.
God promises to bring good out of very sad situations.

Delayed Grief

Mrs J's husband had died three years before. After his
death she had never really cried and she found it difficult to talk to anyone about him except to say what a
wonderful man he had been – how kind and patient and
gentle. In fact those who knew them well said he had
quite a temper and that she was often afraid of him. In
living room his books on bee keeping were still out
beside his old chair and his slippers lay as if he were
about to step into them. His clothes were still hanging in
the bedroom cupboard and his cap on the hook by the
front door. Poor Mrs J. was obviously having great
difficulty coming to terms with the loss of her husband.

Most people, in the six months to two years after the
loss will manage to make the difficult decision to get rid
of clothes and other possessions or to change things
around in the house. There is a real choice involved in
accepting the new situation. Others will very mechanically deal with such practical things but never really face
the emotional impact of the loss. They may never be able
to talk in detail about the one who has died, and will
remain very busy and active to keep their minds off the
reality of what has happened. Sometimes the grief is so
repressed that it emerges in physical symptoms or

depression months or even years later. A few people will need gentle but firm encouragement to talk, perhaps to share photographs of the one who has died and not to be afraid to express their feelings of sadness, anger, guilt, or anxiety. At first this will be very painful but will become easier as the weeks pass.

Sylvia Plath describes Esther's grief as she visits her father's grave:

> Then I saw my father's gravestone.
> It was crowded right up by another gravestone head to head, the way people are crowded in a charity ward where there isn't enough space. The stone was of a mottled pink marble, like tinned salmon, and all there was on it was my father's name and, under it, two dates, separated by a little dash.
> At the foot of the stone I arranged the rainy armful of azaleas I had picked from a bush at the gateway of the graveyard. Then my legs folded under me, and I sat down on the sopping grass. I couldn't understand why I was crying so hard. Then I remembered that I had never cried for my father's death.
> My mother hadn't cried either. She had just smiled and said what a merciful thing it was for him he had died, because if he had lived he would have been crippled and an invalid for life, and he couldn't have stood that, he would rather have died than have that happen.
> I laid my face to the smooth face of the marble and howled my loss into the cold salt rain.[8]

For some people such an experience may come many years later, and although painful at the time, may prove to be a tremendous release.

Death – the cultural taboo

Our ancestors were probably better prepared for death than we are today. For them it was a reality of their everyday experience. By the age of ten most children would probably have attended several funerals of brothers, sisters or other relatives. They would have seen people dying in their own home. Today we are separated from this reality by some of the achievements of modern medicine. Although our children will have seen many thousands of violent deaths on television by the time they are ten years old they are not prepared for the reality of suffering and separation when it happens in their own family. Death has become the cultural taboo and many live trying to deny its existence.

So we must be realistic in facing the possibility and not be afraid to talk about it in straight forward terms with practical realism about the pain and yet also wonderful hope. This hope was illustrated by my niece, who at the funeral of her little sister Georgina, turned to her mother and said, 'Mummy, will we see Georgina at the great party in heaven?'

For those who have loved ones who were not obviously Christians, there is a deeper sting to death. We have to come to terms with the reality of the possibility of eternal separation, and to trust God's justice and mercy. This sounds very harsh, and is far easier said than done, but God has made us so that our choices are significant for this life, and for eternity. We will never know what happened in the heart of the one who died, and we can only hope and pray that there was a change in their last hours and leave the rest with God.

Grace – in time of need

As we face our own death, with the possibility of the prolonged suffering and dependency of terminal illness, and the pain of separation particularly for those left behind, do we rejoice? In one sense, yes, and in another no! Paul rejoiced *in* sufferings but not *for* them. I'm sure he felt the pain of the rocks crushing on his body when he was stoned and left for dead; I'm sure he felt the pain of the lashes when he was beaten and put into prison. Being human, he experienced pain; and yet I'm sure he was given 'grace to help in time of need'. Stephen saw 'Jesus standing at the right hand of God' and was able to pray for forgiveness for his murderers (Acts 7.55). Death from cancer, senile dementia or other diseases is often ugly and humiliating. Nowadays, with good medical care, it should be possible to control the pain without making the person completely unconscious. But many feel guilty, thinking that good Christians should not be afraid of the weakness, dependency and sense of being out of control that may come when dying. But we are not promised complete freedom from suffering; so this is a realistic fear and we deal with it by praying for grace and strength to be patient in suffering. The temporary suffering leads on to greater things. Death is like a door, a dramatic change from a world torn apart by sin and suffering to a world of peace and beauty where, in the presence of the Lord, 'He will wipe away every tear from their eyes. There will no more death or mourning or crying or pain, for the old order of things has passed away' (Revelation 21.4).

Suicide

In thinking about death, bereavement and depression we cannot avoid the uncomfortable subject of suicide. In the first chapter we saw how thoughts of suicide are not uncommon in serious depression. There are some Christians who are appalled to think that anyone should ever take their own life and regard it as an almost unforgiveable sin. They have never been seriously depressed themselves and find it hard to imagine such a state of mind. Others, living under the weight of considerable handicaps, may live for many years with the thought of suicide not far from their minds. John Berryman was an American poet. From the age of ten he lived with the possibility of his parents' marriage breaking up and with his father's constant threats of suicide. When John was twelve years old his father shot himself outside John's window. His life was a constant struggle against alcoholism and depression but in his poems *Eleven addresses to the Lord* there is clear evidence of a time of real Christian commitment.

> Under new management, Your Majesty:
> Thine. I have solo'd mine since childhood, since
> my father's blow-it-all when I was twelve
> blew out my most bright candle faith, and look at me
> . . .
>
> You pierced the roof
> twice and again. Finally You opened my eyes.

and

> . . . You have come to my rescue again and again
> in my impassable, sometimes despairing years.
> You have allowed my brilliant friends to destroy
> themselves
> and I am still here, severely damaged, but functioning
>
> . . .

Even with these and many other beautiful expressions of faith he still struggled against depression.

> Panicky weekdays, I pray hard,
> not worthy.
> Sucking, clinging, following, crying, smiling,
> I come Your child to You.

Struggling to keep going, his last but one poem demonstrates his torment of mind, his faith and perhaps a sense of relief that his suffering will soon be over. He

THE ROOTS OF SORROW

has decided to take the quick way home. 'In January 1972, he jumped to his death from a bridge. In his pocket was the notification of yet another literary award.'[9]

Although it is understandable to take one's life in the face of such suffering I do not believe that it is ever right. Even as I write these words I am aware that for some people in the depths of severe depression there is an appalling strength to the inner urge of self-destruction. There are some who are so 'sick' that they are no longer responsible for their actions. Their view of reality is so distorted that there seems no other way out of their prison of pain. Only God knows what is going on in their minds in the minutes and hours before they died. For some the determining factors of biochemistry, perhaps the repressed pains of early childhood and even Satan's destructive influence may, at the end, overwhelm the last island of resistance in the mind and will which had been struggling to resist the impulse of suicide. Someone, like John Berryman, who was a true Christian will I'm sure be forgiven, but the solemn fact is that they will have to stand before God, the judge of all the earth, the One who gave them life and give account of their actions. God knows and understands the pain and suffering we experience and He sent His own Son to die so that we might be given the strength to cope with the struggles of this broken world. God has not given us the right to take our own lives and we must do all we can to help those who feel so desperate that they wish to destroy themselves.

Why did he do it?

Why do people destroy themselves? It has been shown that the risk of suicide is increased in those who are 'mentally ill', especially with severe depression and alcoholism, in those with unstable personalities, in the lonely and socially isolated particularly after bereavement, breakdown of marriage, loss of a job or retirement and in those who have had previous suicide attempts.

The suicide rate has been rising at around three and a half per cent a year since 1975 especially amongst the 15–35 age group although the elderly are still the highest risk. As people get older they begin to lose their family and friends, they experience more illness, they may go deaf or blind, and often may realise that they have not lived up to their youthful dreams of success in career or relationships. All of these factors contribute to the possibility of severe depression. Very often depression in the elderly is misdiagnosed as 'senility' or 'they're getting old' when effective treatment might well be very helpful.

The number of attempted 'unsuccessful' suicides has risen dramatically in recent years to what the psychiatrists call epidemic proportions – approximately 200,000 each year. For every one successful suicide in the 15–20 year old age group there are approximately 20 suicide *attempts* in males and 400 in females! In stark contrast, for every 65 year old who commits suicide only two men and six women attempt suicide. Most unsuccessful attempts are made by teenage girls or women in their late teens or early twenties. Many do it as a 'cry for help', some as a gesture of defiance after a row with parents or a quarrel with a boyfriend. It is interesting that two striking incidents in the Bible, of Jonah and Elijah wanting to die, occur after difficult crises in their lives and when both of them were exhausted physically and very angry with God. Many suicidal attempts are angry responses to difficult relationships or situations. But there are always some who seriously intend to end their lives. So it is important that all suicide attempts should be taken seriously so that the various motives can be assessed. All may need help but some more urgently than others. In the vast majority of cases suicide is a very permanent solution to what is usually a temporary problem.

Suicide may appear to be a final solution but if the person is not a Christian it is especially sad as they will go into eternity without God. Even if the person is a Christian there is a sense in which it is a selfish act because it leaves many problems for relatives and friends. I have met a number of people who have been haunted by their father or mother's suicide, unable to get it out of their mind, unable to forgive them for abandoning their children and spouse and always fearful lest they too may become so depressed as to do the same thing. A suicide often hangs over the family like a dark shadow. Hence the importance of being able to talk about it openly in the family. It may also leave behind unresolved guilt in those who were trying to help or in relatives who may have ignored that one desperate telephone call out of the hundreds they had had in the previous year. A row with his wife may be the last straw to break the camel's back in someone who is already depressed and he may kill himself partly as a gesture of anger ('see how she feels when she finds out what she's done!) and partly out of guilt and self-recrimination at having been so horrible.

How can I help?

What then can one do to help someone who appears depressed and hints at thoughts of ending it all? It is important to take all talk of suicide seriously and not to be afraid to discuss it openly. Even jokes about it may be half serious and should not be dismissed lightly. If someone makes references to feeling trapped or wanting to get out of the situation, don't be afraid to ask them what they mean and if they have planned to do anything. It is often a help to be able to share such thoughts with someone else. Don't offer simplistic solutions like 'come on, pull yourself together, you'll feel better in the morning' or 'believe in Jesus, He'll take all your problems away.' If they have already made plans (for instance purchased tablets or razor blades or a hosepipe to put through a car window) then the situation is potentially more serious. They may allow you to look after the tablets for them. They may need someone to stay with them until the crisis is past. Encourage them to get some sort of professional help from a doctor or counsellor. If there is a serious death wish then they may need to be admitted to hospital for their own protection.

Some people who have considerable difficulties in relationships may use threats of suicide as a form of blackmail. It is an ace card which it is difficult to ignore or respond to without giving in to all the demands. In such situations it is very important to know a lot about the person and to have discussed the problem with a professional counsellor before ignoring such a threat. There is always a risk that the attempt will be successful even if only because of accidentally taking too many tablets or not realising how strong they were.

So those who are severely depressed may need both medication and counselling or psychotherapy to help them to overcome their hopelessness and self-destructiveness. Others, not severely depressed, but who have longstanding difficulties in coping with life may go from one crisis to another, at times willing to receive help and other times unwilling to receive help or to help themselves. There may be little that one can do in such a situation except to reassure that you are willing to help when they are in a more constructive frame of mind. Ultimately, of course, many problems are solved by focusing not on ourselves but on Christ. It is hard for most people in the depths of suicidal despair to grasp this amazing truth and even when they do there will still be problems in their lives as they learn to apply the truths of Scripture to each situation. Although it is true in an ultimate sense to say that 'the gospel will solve all your problems', we must also recognise that we still live in a fallen world, where even for Christians there is much pain and suffering.

References

1   C. S. Lewis. *A Grief Observed* (Faber and Faber Ltd 1964) p. 16.
2   Martin Luther. Table Talk Ed. Will Hazlett (G. Bell & Sons 1909) p. 277.
3   L. G. Peppers and R. Knapp. Maternal Reaction to Involuntary Foetal/Infant Death. *Psychiatry* 1980. 43: p. 155–159.
4   Used with permission.
5   C. S. Lewis. op. cit. p. 7.
6   Colin Murray Parkes. *Bereavement – Studies of Grief in Adult Life* (Pelican 1975) p. 79.
7   Michelle Magorian. *Goodnight Mister Tom* (Puffin Book 1983). p. 287–288. Some parts of this book are not suitable for very young children.
8   Sylvia Plath. *The Bell Jar* (Faber 1966) p. 177.
9   John Berryman Taking the Quick Way Home by David Porter. May 1983. Published in *Straight* Magazine.

CHAPTER FOURTEEN

Love yourself?

Only now, as I am coming out of depression, am I beginning to realise what effect my father's absence and my mother's bitching nagging had on my sense of self-esteem. Oh, yes they gave me everything I needed materially but . . . What my absent father communicated to me is that I was not really that special. Then, as inexorably as any law of nature or mathematics, compulsive psychodynamics began to kick in within my personality. The need and drive for love and self-esteem were so great that I did anything to get them (and the drive will rationalize away the *real* reason for doing them, i.e., I thought I was doing them for pure or altruistic reasons) . . . I even got straight A's from age 7 onward wanting to be a doctor just like Dad. What was communicated subliminally was that I was not worth very much as I was 'or, else, why wouldn't Dad spend time with me?'; so, the subconscious drive is triggered to have to perform in order to elicit any positive response from Dad . . . perhaps then he will want to spend more time with me, the subconscious thought goes. From such defense mechanisms sprung the compulsions to be in the football team for two years running like I did, for Dad loves football ('and, after all, Dad's the one to emulate in our family, right? Surely not Mom who is so obviously the bad guy,' . . . I thought . . . valedictoria, student president, for Dad likes good grades and is into school and stuff . . . magna cum laude ('For med school is the only way to go, right?') . . physician, for Dad is one, too. Sound like me?[1]

Yours, Jack

217

Self-esteem

Several times in this book I have used the term self-esteem and have noted how many studies show that low self-esteem makes us more vulnerable to depression and high self-esteem acts as a protective factor against depression. There is much confusion amongst Christians about the rights and wrongs of self-love and self-denial and it is important to grasp the biblical balance between these two concepts if we are to see the true source of self-esteem. There are some who say that we cannot love anyone else until we obey what they see as the third commandment in Jesus' summary of the law – to love God, love our neighbours and to love ourselves. (Matthew 22:39, Mark 12:31). But others say that self-love is always wrong and quote such verses as 'There will be terrible times in the last days. People will be lovers of themselves, proud, abusive . . . lovers of pleasure rather than lovers of God'. (2 Timothy 3:1–2). Both are partial truths and depend on how we understand the expression love of self! As Walter Trobisch wrote 'One difficulty lies in the fact that the word self-love has a double meaning. It can mean self-acceptance as well as self-centredness'.[2] Perhaps the words self-acceptance or self-affirmation are less easily misunderstood for we are encouraged in the Bible to affirm and accept that which is God-given and good i·, ourselves and to deny and work against that within ʌs that Paul describes as our 'sinful nature'.

A religion of self-worship

A confusing factor is that so much contemporary psychology is focused on a wrong sense of self-affirmation. As we have seen, humanistic psychology, seeing no need for God, has to help people to find their sense of purpose, their values and their identity within themselves, and has thus become as Paul Vitz puts it 'The religion of self-worship'.[3] There is much talk about one's rights and needs, about self-fulfilment, self-actualization, self-awareness and the pursuit of happiness. We are encouraged to get in touch with our feelings, to be our real selves without inhibitions or guilt, to discover for ourselves the best values by which to live. For the optimists, like Carl Rogers and many other psychologists, there is a faith that within us we will find all the resources we need to perfect ourselves. This inevitably leads to a preoccupation with ourselves and our need for identity. The most extreme example of such self-love is called 'narcissism' where there is an overwhelming concern for self, a deep insecurity and a marked lack of sensitivity to the needs of others. The term narcissism comes from the myth of the handsome youth Narcissus who after cruelly spurning the love of Echo fell passionately in love with his own image reflected in a quiet pool of water. So preoccupied was he with himself that he lost all desire for food and sleep and pined away and died leaving a little flower behind him. Many psychiatrists have commented on the apparent increase, in recent years, of the number of young people with 'narcissistic personality disorder'. All of us are egocentric to some degree but the twentieth century culture of sensation-seekers and 'selfist psychology' only serves to enhance our self-centred tendencies.

In previous chapters we have seen how, after getting rid of God, (or so they say) the humanist psychologist is left only with himself as the centre of all things. The only way to happiness is to believe strongly enough in his own uniqueness and goodness. So my self-esteem comes, he tells me, from telling myself that I am 'the most beautiful, exciting, worthy person ever'. And some, as we have seen, tell us that *everything* is in reality perfect already if we could only see it. It is an awesome thing to be alone in the universe, believing there is no God, and man does his best to persuade himself that everything is really all right. 'I'm OK,' he says and 'you're OK'. This psychological 'wisdom' is translated to the man in the street in the flood of popular self-help books and 'power of positive thinking' courses that are available. The influence of humanistic psychology is much more obvious in the United States partly I believe because it resonates with the American mentality of optimism and 'rugged individualism' which motivated the early pioneers. There is great pride in being a self-made man. The English are perhaps less optimistic and more cynical about life but most English psychologists preach the same gospel of self-sufficiency, and its influence is perhaps more subtle but still very powerful in changing peoples' values and beliefs. If you think well enough about yourself, they say, everything will begin to go right in your life. But William Kilpatrick asks in his book *Psychological Seduction* if we should really like ourselves under *all* circumstances – when we lie, cheat, spread vicious rumours or callously manipulate others to improve our social standing?

> Now the psychological answer to this question is to say that if we truly like ourselves these other things won't happen – or they won't happen as much. According to this view, people who realize their self-worth don't have any need to do ugly or unkind things. And this is the point, please note, where Christianity and psychology part company. People will continue to behave badly, says the Christian, because human nature is twisted, and liking yourself doesn't remove the twist. But psychological theory doesn't take account of the Fall; it takes the position that there are no bad natural inclinations. As a consequence there is no reason we shouldn't accept ourselves as we are.[4]

Sadly, many Christians have been seduced into abandoning a doctrine of sin and the fall and now explain all our problems in terms of negative self-image. The gospel then becomes a message of salvation through self-awareness, self-actualisation and positive thinking. Many of those who have been affected by this mentality have become so preoccupied with their own problems and self-image that they have lost the biblical emphasis on self-denial and service.

Total Depravity

On the other hand there are some Christians who understand the Scriptures about denial of self, and 'being crucified with Christ', to mean that there is absolutely nothing of value within us and that there is never a place for affirming or loving ourselves. They take Paul's words 'I know that within me, that is in my flesh, there is no good thing' (Romans 7. 18 A. V.) to confirm this view without recognising Paul's division of himself into his flesh or sinful nature and the rest of him which seeks to love and serve God. They emphasise John's words 'Do not love the world' (1 John 2. 15) but play down Paul's teaching in 1 Timothy 4. 4 'Everything created by God is good, and nothing is to be rejected if it is received with thanksgiving.' They misunderstand the doctrine of 'total depravity' to mean that no part of man is of value to God. Certainly this doctrine means that man, by his own efforts, can do nothing that will earn his salvation but there are, as we have seen, remnants of the glory of the image of God in the 'glorious ruin'. It means also that every part of man is affected by the malignant disease of sin but not so that everything he does is totally evil. What is important to God is our use of the things He has given. He wants us to enjoy our minds, emotions, bodies and the trees, flowers, music and other beautiful things He has given but to reject all that is sinful in ourselves and the world around us. So we both affirm and deny ourselves.

How do we know what right self-love or self-esteem is? We know that those who have been loved and accepted by their parents have a better sense of self-esteem and are usually more able to love others than those who have been neglected and criticized. In loving their children parents are demonstrating what it means to be made in the image of God whether they are Christians or not. They minister something of God's common grace to their children. But such love, good as it is can only go some way towards helping us to understand what true love really is. Behind all human love is the One who is the Source of Love. 'We love because He first loved us' (1 John 4. 19). Loving 'our neighbours as ourselves' is the result of loving God 'with all your heart and with all your soul and with all your mind.' (Matthew 22. 37–39). Our self-esteem and our ability to love ourselves and others in the right way rests in the fact that God loves us. Each person is unique and infinitely valuable to Him. It is difficult to love *truly* until we know we have been loved by Him.

Love is more than acceptance

The biblical concept of love is not the same as much shallow, sentimental twentieth century love but is a far deeper and richer concept of sacrificial love. Love is more than acceptance. Love longs for the best for the other person. God knows what is best for us and longs for us to change to be like Him. Acceptance says 'I accept you the way you are, with all your problems, faults, imperfections and sin.' And the wonder is that God accepts and loves us in this way. He says 'I accept you and want you to be even better than you are now even if I have to die to make that possible.' God loves us so much that He sent His Son to die for us and Paul uses this example when he says 'Husbands, love your wives as Christ loved the Church and gave Himself up for her' (Ephesians 5. 32) and 'Be imitators of God therefore, as dearly loved children and live a life worthy of love, just as Christ loved us and gave Himself up for us as a fragrant offering and sacrifice to God.' (Ephesians 5. 1). So, in the context of this sort of love we can begin to be set free from fear and insecurity and can begin to change. We know that even if we fail He still loves us and we have clear direction of the ways in which we need to change.

Self affirmation and Self-denial

Some say that we have to love ourselves in order to love others but it seems that both go together and mutually reinforce each other. The more we truly love ourselves without being self-centred, the more we will love and serve others, and conversely the more we love others, the more we are affirmed in ourselves. But the more self-centred we are, the harder it is to love others, and the more selfish we become. True self-affirmation goes hand-in-hand with self-denial. This seems to be what Jesus means when He says 'If anyone would come after me he must deny himself and take up his cross and follow me. For whoever wants to save his life will lose it, but whoever loses his life for me will find it.' (Matthew 16. 24-25). When our lives are totally self-centred then we lose them, when they are God-centred then we find them. We must 'deny' our selfishness but love all the wonderful ways He has made us and the things he has given us to enjoy.

When Jesus talked about 'the man who hates his life in this world' keeping it for eternal life (John 12. 25) He was using a well-known form of speech, a hyperbole, which is an exaggerated statement not meant to be taken literally. Jesus also said 'If anyone comes to me and does not hate his father and mother, his wife and children, his brother and sisters – yes, and even his own life – he cannot be my disciple'. (Luke 14. 26). But we know that Jesus did not actually hate His own mother but a time came when His first priority in life had to be recognised, 'I must be about my father's business'. Also other passages of Scripture command us to honour our parents and to love our wives and children. And Jesus did not hate His own life. He took time to rest, to pray, to be alone, to eat, to be with his friends, to enjoy a wedding feast, but He was not self-indulgent. He was often tired and sometimes He pushed himself to the point of exhaustion, but He did not heal everybody. He was seeking in all He did to be obedient to His father.

Practically this means that I need time to be alone, and times when I lock the door and take the telephone off the hook so that I can be alone with my family. Some people need to be helped to look after themselves better, others need help to be less self-indulgent. Self-denial does not mean that we become doormats or martyrs so that people take advantage of us. There is a close relationship between right self-assertiveness and anger. As we saw in Chapter 11 Paul appealed for justice as a Roman citizen; he did not allow people to walk all over him. Just as with righteous anger we saw that there is always a tension in this fallen world between the way of justice and the way of the cross, so there will always be a tension between self-centredness and self-denial throughout our lives on this earth.

The more we search for self-awareness, identity and happiness *within* ourselves, the less we will find it. A sense of identity and an experience of happiness come as a by-product of losing our self-centeredness and seeking to know, love and obey God.

Love yourself

Some say that Jesus explicitly gives *two* commands in Matthew 22 (27–39) about loving God and our neighbour and there is no third command to love ourselves. Man, they say, naturally loves himself and does not need to be told to do so.

Our motivation in loving ourselves is always slightly and often very twisted. We need to examine the roots of the wrong sort of self-love in order to understand its true place. There are some who come from indulgent homes who have experienced little discipline restraint who are arrogant, proud and selfish. The motto of the psychopathic personality is 'I want what I want when I want it'. They are past masters at subtly manipulating situations to get what they want, even if it means doing something apparently loving. The narcissistic person is very similar. Such a family background which does not teach humility and self-acceptance only exaggerates to egocentric tendency and pride that is within all of us.

Others who seem to have a very low self-esteem, who think they are useless and a waste of everyone's time, have often been heavily criticized in childhood and told that they are hopeless failures. Even if the displeasure is never voiced, they may be nurtured in an atmosphere of 'you are not intelligent or beautiful enough for me to be proud of you and accept you.' Without the basic needs for significance and security being met, they grow up with an aching void within and a deep longing for approval, acceptance and love. Their whole life may then be motivated by the desire to get rid of the inner pain and fill the void. Again this only serves to reinforce their natural self-centredness and pride, only for a completely different reason. And if they do not believe in a God who can meet those needs, then there is a desperate craving for love from other people. Some struggle to be perfect, believing that they will be acceptable. Others move from one intense relationship to another, finding temporary release of the tension in physical intimacy but because their needs are so great they cannot give freely to the other person and the relationship dies. C. S. Lewis writes of the balance of 'need love' and 'gift love' in any mature relationship. Others become 'super helpers', a large part of their motivation in apparently loving others is their own need to be needed. Some are able to deny their needs, even to themselves, and develop a tough, self-reliant image. When this fails they may resort to drugs or alcohol to drown the pain, or become depressed. William Kilpatrick writes:

> The depressed person would like nothing better than to get outside himself, but he can't. The world seems as hopeless as the self. The depressed person knows that he needs to be rescued, but he doesn't believe in the possibility of rescue. He can't abandon himself because he fears there is nothing or no one to rely on. Unlike the one who is paranoid, the depressed person has no illusions about autonomy. Yet the basic similarity, the thing you notice in both cases, is the centrality of self. The paranoid person believes the self is all there is and tries desperately to control it. The depressed person fears the self is all there is and is in despair.
>
> If I were depressed, the last thing I would want to hear is 'At least you've got yourself.' The depressed person has already tried self-reliance, and when the real test came, it failed. If the self is all he has to live for, he'd rather die. Of all people, he is in the best position to appreciate George MacDonald's observation: 'The one principle of hell is – I am my own.'[5]

While I agree that Jesus speaks of only two commandments I believe that there are some people who need to learn to love themselves *properly*, either because of deep self-hatred stemming from rejection and lack of love in childhood or because of deep self-centredness and pride. Sometimes these are two sides of the same coin! There are other passages in the New Testament which clarify this theme. Paul says that a man who truly loves his wife with self-sacrificing love and service shows that he knows what true self-love is (Ephesians 5. 28). He uses the example of our bodies, a part of ourselves he says which 'no-one ever hates' (Ephesians 5. 20). But most people do in fact seem to dislike their own bodies. So what does he mean? I believe that we can paraphrase the verse as 'no-one, in his right mind, ever hated his own body, but he feeds and cares for it,' so 'husbands ought to love their wives as their own bodies.' (Ephesians 5. 28). Perhaps it is precisely *because* we love our own bodies too much that we are so proud and vain that because they are not perfect (by the cultural norms!) we dislike and even hate them. True love, as we have seen, means accepting ourselves, including our body with all its faults and imperfections, not with resignation but with a recognition that improvement may be necessary. God did not intend us all to be like Charles Atlas but He does want us to care for our bodies as 'temples of the Holy Spirit'. We should be concerned about fitness and not being overweight, recognising our own individual limitations and our abilities. We can glory in the *right* use of our physical abilities and sexuality. But our bodies are not to be worshipped and physical fitness or dieting are not to become the focus of our lives. The Psalmist with a touch of humour says the Lord's 'delight is not in the legs of a man; the Lord delights in those who fear him, who put their hope in his unfailing love.' (Psalm 147. 10–11).

Self-acceptance not self-centredness

So true self-love or self-affirmation is a realistic acceptance of ourselves as Paul says 'Do not think of yourself more highly than you ought, but rather think of yourself with sober judgement.' (Romans 12. 3) and 'Do nothing out of selfish ambition or vain conceit, but in humility consider others better than yourselves. Each of you should look not only to your own interests but also to the interests of others.' (Philippians 2. 3–4). And Paul goes on to say that our example should be Christ Himself:

> Who being in very nature God, did not consider equality with God something to be grasped, but made himself nothing, taking the very nature of a servant, being made in human likeness. He humbled himself and became obedient to death–even death on a cross! Therefore God exalted him to the highest place and gave Him the name that is above every name, that at the name of Jesus every knee should bow, in heaven and on earth and under the earth, and every tongue confess that Jesus Christ is Lord, to the glory of God the Father. (Philippians 2. 5–8).

> And he died for all, that those who live should no longer live for themselves but for Him who died for them and was raised again. (2 Corinthians 5. 15).

Just before Jesus's self-denying act of washing His disciples feet there is an amazing declaration of self-affirmation. 'Jesus knew that the Father had put all things under his power, and that he had come from God and was returning to God.' (John 13. 3).

So a right sense of self-esteem and self-love is rooted firstly in God's love for us. Knowing that we are loved and accepted just as we are means that we do not have to earn love from others. This is the only real escape from the vicious circle of self-criticism and self-destruction for those who have never known love and acceptance from their parents. They need to remind themselves every day of the truth, in order to counteract the negative old tapes in their heads and the satanic suggestion that they are useless failures. In C. S. Lewis's 'Prince Caspian', Alsan says 'You come of the Lord Adam and the Lady Eve. And that is both honour enough to erect the head of the poorest beggar and shame enough to bow the shoulders of the greatest emperor on earth. Be content'[8] And the knowledge that God loves us is not based on wishful thinking or myths, but it is rooted in history, in the life, death and resurrection of Christ. For Paul knew that without that solid historical fact, his sense of significance and hope would evaporate. 'If Christ has not been raised . . . then we are of all men most miserable.' (1 Corinthians 15. 17-19 A. V.)

Secondly, we need other Christians in the family of God, to help us to have a realistic view of our gifts and weaknesses. And they can show us something of God's love in the tangible form of human affection. There is a right dependence on God and on other people so that we may become more truly independent. Christ's depend-ence on the Father did not mean that He was less of a person. Also, we are encouraged to think of ourselves as members of the body of Christ, an image of extraordin-ary mutual dependence on one another.

Thirdly, the Bible tells us that as we 'deny' our self-centredness and learn to serve others, following Christ's example, so we have a deeper understanding of who we are. As we learn to truly accept and love ourselves and struggle against our sinful nature and the brokenness we find within us, in the same way love of others involves a realistic recognition of both the 'glory' and the 'ruin' that is within them. We then do not expect too much of others but we learn to love them as we love ourselves.

References

1 Used with permission
2 Walter Trobisch. *Love Yourself* (Editions Trobisch 1976) p. 14.
3 Paul Vitz. *Psychology as Religion: The Cult of Self-Worship* (Eedermans 1977).
4 William Kilpatrick. *Psychological Seduction* (Thomas Nelson 1983) p. 37.
5 Ibid., p. 68.
6 C. S. Lewis. *Prince Caspian* (Penguin Books 1962) p. 185.

PART IV

CHAPTER FIFTEEN

A little self-indulgence

If you have travelled with me thus far, a little self-indulgence may be in order! Another aspect of our responsibility before God is that of looking after ourselves. Sleep, exercise and food are all very important for our sense of well being. You remember how Elijah had his dramatic encounter with the 450 prophets of Baal on Mount Carmel, proving that his God was the true God. He then ran ahead of Ahab's chariot 'all the way to Jezreel'. When Ahab told the wicked queen Jezebel what had happened, she threatened to kill Elijah and he ran for his life. Utterly exhausted, he collapsed on the ground. 'I've had enough Lord,' he said, 'take my life. I'm no better than my ancestors'. Suicidal thoughts . . . desperately low self-esteem! 'He lay down under a tree and fell asleep.' Then there is a beautiful simple detail—'and all at once an angel touched him and said "get up and eat". He looked around and there by his head was a cake of bread baked over hot coals and a jar of water. He ate and drank and then lay down again. The angel of the Lord came back a second time and touched him and said, "get up and eat, for the journey is too much for you". So he got up and ate and drank. Strengthened by that food he travelled 40 days and 40 nights until he reached Horeb, the mountain of God. There he went into a cave and spent the night.' (1 Kings 19. 4-9)

Good food, sleep and exercise

Within many of us there is a self-destructive streak

and when we are depressed this sort of self-destructiveness is often greatly exaggerated – as it was for Elijah. 'I just want to die, Lord. Leave me alone everyone, don't touch me. I don't want to bother to get up and get food for myself.' But God knew that he had not slept for nights, was physically exhausted after running so far and emotionally exhausted after the victory on Mount Carmel and the fear of Jezebel. He also had not eaten for many hours. God knew he needed rest, food and sleep to restore his perspective on the situation. We can expect to feel depressed after sleepless nights, exhausting work schedules and dramatic speaking engagements. At times we have to force ourselves, almost against our will, to be responsible for our own bodies. Regular exercise, a balanced diet and adequate sleep are important. Without becoming a health 'freak' one can take a healthy interest in one's physical needs. Reading a few good books on nutrition and exercise and then taking their advice will contribute to reducing vulnerability to depression. Just to read them may make you feel even more depressed! Eating the wrong food reduces one's resistance to all forms of stress. The effect of all the chemicals, preservatives in our food remains to be seen but they may have a long term effect similar to pollution in the atmosphere. But the simple fact of feeling reasonably physically fit is enough to raise anyone's self esteem a few points. It is also good use of the body God has given you: 'Physical training is of some value' (1 Timothy 4. 8). In other words our physical needs are not to be ignored. If our bodies are physically unfit our minds will probably be sluggish too. As we saw in Chapter 3 there is some evidence that exercise releases natural pain killing substances from the brain and that this may help to relieve depression.

Lack of sleep – burning the candle at both ends – may contribute to depression through exhaustion. But depression itself usually brings difficulty in sleeping and this can be very distressing.

> It is at times of half light that I find forsaken monsters shouldering through my mind.[1]

Waking in the early hours of the morning, with consequent exhaustion in the day, becomes a painful vicious circle. Again, adequate exercise and activity in the day time, relaxation exercises and simple remedies like herbal tea may help. Too often people who are depressed and not sleeping well drink far too much coffee or tea which only makes the situation worse. But if there are severe problems then sleeping-tablets or anti-depressants may be necessary for a while to help break the vicious circle. Some people have a terrible fear of taking such 'mind bending' drugs thinking that they will change their whole personality and make then into a 'zombie'. Certainly if too much medication is taken there may be some side effects and this is why they should be taken under careful medical supervision. But they do not alter personality, or slow you down, and no-one else will know that you are taking them just by looking at you or talking to you. Nor are they a 'magic wand' – anti-depressants take time to work, often five to ten days before they have any effect.

Practical work

We also have to be responsible in the area of work. This is the last thing one feels like doing when depressed, but it is a very important factor in contributing to our sense of self-esteem. We feel like giving up and doing nothing, but it is important to do something that gives a sense of our own value. One of the most helpful things for people who are in the middle of depression is to help someone with their family, house or garden. Talking is of some value, but being able to contribute something, however small, to the lives of others is also very helpful. This may mean such things as helping with cooking, cleaning, helping with the children, digging manure, planting beans, and the many other activities of the life of a family. Ideally, work should give a sense of serving others and of contributing to the community of people amongst whom we live. We are made by God so that some of our sense of significance and self-esteem should come from those around us and from the knowledge of having used our creative gifts responsibly and well. The apostle Paul knew that idleness was very unhealthy – physically and mentally and he wrote in stark terms 'if any man will not work, let him not eat'. (2 Thessalonians 3. 10). It is considerable challenge in the present economic situation to help each other to find creative ways of coping with unemployment. A constructive use of the time, perhaps in doing some voluntary work, when one does not have regular paid employment, will reduce vulnerability to depression.

There are of course some people traditionally known as 'workaholics' who have no problem working because it often prevents them from coming to terms with unpleasant aspects of themselves. For them sitting still and doing nothing is probably the most painful thing you could ask them to do. Morton Kelsey tells a story about Carl Jung:

> . . . A clergyman came to see Dr Jung on the ragged edge of breaking down. He had been working a fourteen hour schedule and his nerves were played out; his hands even trembled. Jung began by asking him if he wanted to get well and the minister said indignantly that of course he did. Jung gave him a simple and inexpensive prescription. He was to work just eight hours a day and sleep eight. The remaining hours he was to spend all alone in his study, in quiet.

This seemed easy enough and he agreed to try it and seemed quite hopeful that the tension would be relieved.

That day the clergyman worked only eight hours. At supper he explained to his wife what he was going to do and went into his study and closed the door. And there he stayed for several hours. He played a few Chopin etudes and finished a Herman Hesse novel. The next day he followed the same routine, except that in the evening he read Thomas Mann's *Magic Mountain* and played a Mozart Sonata. The following morning he went back to see Dr Jung, complaining that he was just as badly off; and obviously he was.

Jung carefully enquired about how he had followed the instructions and heard what he had done. 'But you don't understand!' Dr Jung told him. 'I don't want you with Herman Hesse or Thomas Mann, or even Mozart or Chopin. I wanted you to be all alone with yourself.' At this the minister looked terrified and gasped, Oh, but I can't think of any worse company!' To this Dr Jung made the reply that has been repeated so often: 'And yet this is the self you inflict on other people for fourteen hours a day.'[2]

Such a person needs considerable help in the area of self-acceptance and self-worth.

Recognise warning signals

So we need to recognise the signs of distress in our own bodies and in our minds and emotions and do practical things to help ourselves. Many depressed people tend to take on too much. 'If only I can finish building this extension on my house – finish writing that book, – then I will feel better!' Instead of taking on something small that they can complete, like knitting a small scarf, they start knitting a huge complex sweater! Such successes feel vital at a time of threat of total failure. We must build on small successes with slightly bigger ones, not failures with bigger failures! We have to be realistic about our limitations.

This applies too in prayer. When depressed we often feel that God is far away and we feel guilty that we are not praying or reading the Bible as we should. I am sure the Lord understands our single word cries for help. We do not have to pray and fast for hours on end. He understands our simple prayers. It is important to pray not only for ourselves but to try to continue to pray for others as this helps to take us out of our own self-absorption.

Study and meditation on Scripture is important too. Many have found the psalms comforting in times of deep troubles. Unhelpful teaching about reading the Bible can contribute to depression. Some people are taught to depend on a sort of emotional fix in their daily quiet time. Many Christians read the Bible as if it were a magic book, waiting for a thought for the day to strike them. Although God does sometimes speak to us like this, it is a very superficial approach to the word of God. When David says 'I have hidden your word in my heart, that I might not sin against you' (Psalm 119. 11) he is not using the word like a charm or amulet, but he means that he has soaked himself in God's word and absorbed the values and attitudes of Scripture. This may not be something that one can do when concentration is so bad in the midst of depression but it is something that will help to build up our strength and decrease our vulnerability to depression. This involves *serious* study of the Bible – 'I reach out my hands for your commandments, which I love and I meditate on your decrees.' (Psalm 119. 48) It means reading and studying the whole Bible, seeing how one book connects to another, getting a sense of the flow of history from Genesis to

Revelation, and then reading specific verses in this whole context and applying them to our own situation. Sometimes it is helpful to allow one's imagination to play over a biblical story and to imagine oneself one of the characters – thinking and feeling as he or she does in reaction to what is happening.

Then, reading positive books is important. In severe depression, concentraton is so poor that getting beyond the headlines in the newspaper is a major achievement, but in milder depression, in resisting the downward slide, it is important not to read pessimistic books, or to go to too many plays or films which are full of tragedy and nihilism. Such themes will pour water on the fires of the spirit which is fighting not to sink into the depths of depression. Christian biographies, not the super-saint variety, but realistic pictures of those who have wrestled with suffering and failure are often a great encouragement. Biographies of men and women like Martin Luther, John Bunyan, George Burton, Joni Erickson and others who have suffered much and wrestled against some thorn in the flesh. A number of friends have commented on how much they have appreciated children's books when physically ill or depressed. C. S. Lewis, *Narnia* stories, *My Side of the Mountain* by Jean George and others.[3]

Martin Luther found music and singing helpful in his times of depression. For Saul it was the sound of David's harp that sometimes calmed his troubled spirit. Listening to music can be helpful or harmful. In a period of mild depression some years ago I used to enjoy the songs of Leonard Cohen. It was not until I listened to his songs again sometime later, when 'in my right mind', that I realised how depressing they are! We usually identify with the music or lyrics which resonate with our state of mind at the time. There is comfort and security in this, but also a snare, for it may not help us to get out of the pit. Listening to the aggression or depression of some rock music, the anxiety of some modern jazz, or the chaos of some contemporary classical music, will probably make things worse. When we are struggling to find boundaries to our lives firm ground for our feet that threaten to slip, the sense of order, of beginning and end, of harmony and beauty will be helpful.

So it is vital that we make some effort to keep in touch with reality in all sorts of practical ways and not to retreat into our own inner world of unhappiness and self-pity. Martin Luther writes:

> When I am assailed with heavy tribulations, I rush out among my pigs rather than remain alone by myself. So the human heart, unless it be occupied with some employment, leaves space for the devil who wriggles himself in and brings with him a whole host of evil thoughts, temptations and tribulations, which grind out the heart.[4]

Satan, as Luther says, is only too anxious to undermine our self-confidence. As the 'accuser and deceiver' he will be quick to remind us that we are failures. Luther, besides throwing an ink pot at the devil, said that whenever he is tempted to think in this way 'I say to Satan: "Like as thou camest to confusion by Christ and Saint Paul even so Mr Devil shall it go with thee if thou meddlest with me." '[5]

So these things are not 'self indulgent' in a bad sense, although they could become so, but rather a right valuing of oneself as a person made in the image of God with gifts of body, emotions, mind, creativity . . . which are to be cared for and used responsibly before our Creator and Lord.

References

1   Mervyn Peake, *Selected Poems* (Faber and Faber 1972) p 42.
2   Morton Kelsey, *The Other Side of Silence* (Paulist Press. New York 1976) p. 84.
3   C. S. Lewis, *The Lion, The Witch and The Wardrobe* and others. Jean George, *My Side of the Mountain* (Puffin 1959)
4   Martin Luther, *Table Talk* Ed. Will Hazlett (G. Sell & Sons 1909) p. 275.
5   Ibid., p. 270.

CHAPTER SIXTEEN

Getting help

Counselling, psychotherapy and medicine

'Nancy?' When my name was called my heart felt like
it was beating from somewhere within my stomach.
'I'm Dr Michaels. Would you like to follow me to my
office?'

'Have a seat.' There were two chairs. I sat in the chair
nearest the door. 'Can you tell me a little about why
you came?' 'Well, er, I've been a little bit down.' I
smiled. 'Down?' 'Depressed.' Silence. 'A friend
suggested that maybe a counsellor might be able to
help me.'

After asking me about my job and my family Dr
Michaels said 'You mentioned that you were
depressed. What's that feel like?' I was amazed at
how I was at a loss to describe a feeling that had been
with me for so long. 'It's, well . . . it's really bad.' I was
now staring very intensely at the carpet. 'I get lonely.
It's just empty. I don't know what to do with myself.'
'Nancy, do you ever think of suicide?' She stabbed
close to home with those words, but I was relieved
that she asked the question. 'Yes.' I looked at my
hands. 'I've thought about it. But I'd never do
anything.'

She nodded her head as though she understood the
intensity of my struggle. I wanted her to know
everything now. I wanted this stranger to stop the
hurt. I wanted her to reach down and pull the ache
out. But how could I let her know? I could never

make anyone know or understand. The past had erupted, the present was drowning me. The future was lurking with waves of emptiness, empty days, empty nights, empty flat, empty soul. What was there to lose in telling this stranger about what had happened with my stepfather? I knew it would happen. She'd give me the solution to the problem and everything would be fine. At least that's what was supposed to happen.[1]

Walking on a small path along a steep grassy hillside I realised that if my foot slipped I would fall. I might be able to check my fall by grabbing hold of tufts of grass and hauling myself back onto the path. But if not I would soon be sliding so fast that even if I could hold onto the grass it would almost certainly come away in my hand. All I could do would be to shout for help and pray that someone or something would stop my fall. In the early stages of depression it is possible to help oneself, but if it lasts a while and there is a continuous slide downhill, with gathering speed, then help will be needed from others. For some who repeatedly slip off the path or are too weak to pull themselves back up they may need help to make them walk more carefully and also to build up their strength.

Who and where?

In England, most people's instinctive reaction is to advise someone who is depressed to visit a doctor. This is certainly important in order to rule out any physical causes for the depression. But perhaps we are expecting too much of the medical profession. With the decline of the church as a strong influence in society many people look to the doctor to be priest, counsellor and healer of all personal and societal ills. Do people with serious personal problems in fact get the help they need? A study in Manchester has shown that in an average population of one thousand people, in any one year, two hundred and fifty will have fairly serious psychological problems (anxiety, depression etc). Only about half of these will be recognised as psychological problems by the G.P. and a mere handful will be referred to a psychiatrist.[2] The rest he will try to help with perhaps some assistance from health visitors and social workers, but with an average of six minutes for each patient what can the poor doctor do but give a prescription and arrange another appointment – for another prescription and a brief chat? Some G.P.s make a special point of seeing a few patients at the end of their clinic for a longer time and this is certainly a move in the right direction. Of 458 women surveyed in a London study, 30% had been significantly depressed in the previous year or were depressed at the time of the survey. Half of this depressed group were not being treated by their G. P. and only four received psychiatric care.[4]

Thankfully most people do eventually recover from an episode of depression on their own, or with the help of family and friends. But many would get better much more quickly with counselling and might also learn things about themselves which would help to prevent them from becoming depressed again. So the need for alternative resources for counselling and help is enormous. Within the health and social services there is an attempt to meet some of the need by training more social workers, psychologists and nurses in counselling and psychotherapy. But when money is in short supply 'talking treatments' are not given priority in health care. We can certainly be thankful for the benefits of our Health Service but there is a danger that we rely too much on the services provided by the government. Particularly in a time of recession we may have to re-pioneer areas of health care that the church started hundreds of years ago with the founding of hospitals. We will have to give our own time, money and emotions to care for the handicapped, elderly and emotionally troubled. Gerald Clerman commenting in 'Psychology Today' on historical traditions of caring writes 'The three most common support systems have been the family, the church and the immediate neighbourhood. A characteristic of the present time is that all these societal support systems are in various degrees of disarray.'[5] It is because of this disarray that we expect the state to become the major support system and at the same time we become frustrated and angry when it cannot cope with the enormous needs. Thankfully many churches are taking up the challenge to counteract these fragmentary tendencies in society and are emphasising the importance of the family and a caring community.

Ideally, for the Christian, it should be to family, friends and church that he turns first. With many minor problems we can help each other as fellow members of the body of Christ. But for more serious problems there should be a few people in the church with pastoral gifts and training to whom one can turn. Those who have particular counselling gifts should work in close cooperation with local doctors, social workers and psychiatrists. However, because many churches are too small, or too ill equipped and underexperienced to handle the many problems that emerge as people begin to really care for each other, Christian counselling centres have been set up in several major cities. In the USA there is a danger that the proliferation of Christian counselling centres is undermining the responsibility of the local churches to care for their own people. My own concern is that Christian counselling centres should primarily be a resource centre, training others to go back to their churches and also perhaps helping with difficult cases.

Before we glibly accept such developments perhaps it is important to examine the nature of counselling and psychotherapy and to ask if they really do work!

Does talking help?

We have seen how, in severe depression, it may be necessary to use antidepressants to break a biological vicious circle but in nearly all cases of depression it is also necessary to talk about the problems that precipitated the depression. Counselling and psychotherapy of whatever school offer:

1   A caring and friendly relationship.
2   Acceptance and encouragement and hope.
3   A regular, hopefully predictable, period of time to talk.
4   Reasonable objectivity. A family member may be too close and too involved emotionally to be objective.
5   A sharing and acceptance of emotional pain.
6   Some explanatory system to make sense of the suffering and confusion.
7   An opportunity to talk about, and thus become more aware of, conscious and unconscious conflicts, thoughts and feelings and then to evaluate values, priorities, expectations, goals, and behaviour in the light of these.
8   A opportunity to learn new ways of thinking, feeling and behaving and to test them out without fear of rejection.

Insight and Understanding

It is clear that there is considerable common ground between Christians and non-Christians in this area. Much psychotherapy and counselling undoubtedly owes a great debt to Freud and his followers. As with most theories and schools of therapy his was a mixture of truth and error. Most psychotherapy based on Freudian psychoanalysis, and there are many variants of it, emphasises the importance of the child's first few years of life in shaping enduring attitudes, values and emotions. Freud particularly emphasised infantile sexuality. Many of his followers have put less emphasis on sexuality and more on the developing sense of identity that may be hindered by difficulties in relationships with parents and siblings, and this we have already seen is a important cause of vulnerability to depression. Freud secondly emphasised the ways in which we unconsciously cope with conflicts which are too painful to face consciously. A central and very helpful part of psychotherapy and counselling is to bring to consciousness what has been kept unconscious so that conflicts can be dealt with more realistically. For example, repressed anger, guilt or fear are powerful causes of depression. Only as painful thoughts and emotions are brought to the surface and allowed to enter conscious awareness can they be dealt with appropriately.

A third important focus of psychoanalysis is the emphasis on the relationship of the patient to the therapist. Freud noticed that very often his patients would develop similar emotional conflicts in relation to him as they had had in childhood with their parents – especially their fathers. This he described as the 'transference relationship' – a 'transference' of feelings for one person onto another. An example of this is seen in the way June was desperately frightened that I would reject her when I knew all the bad things she had done (in fact they were not such terrible things, but in her mind she was far worse than everyone else). Her father was harsh and critical and she had had a number of disastrous relationships with boyfriends. Over the months of counselling she began to see that not all men were like her father and that her characteristic negative thoughts about herself only produced the very rejection that she feared. Many of her usual reactions to her father and other men were 'transferred' to me and it was by openly talking and praying about this that change and healing was able to take place. As she was able to face the negative things within herself and deal with them before God, the positive sides of her personality began to appear.

We see in these three areas how important understanding and insight were to Freud and they are certainly very important parts of all counselling and psychotherapy. In fact Freud, later in his life, was pessimistic about the possibility of much change, but he believed that with understanding one would have the ability to face the inner and outer world more courageously. He believed that stoic acceptance of our confused world and all the influences which act upon us was the best way to cope with life.

The process of psychoanalysis where a therapist sees his patient two or three times a week for many years is perhaps the secular counterfeit of the Creator's original intention of man living in a close relationship with God – the 'Wonderful Counsellor' (Isaiah 9. 6). Freud was in a sense trying to be God to his patients, helping them to understand their past and to find a way of living in the present. The growth and change hoped for by the humanist psychotherapist is the secular equivalent of sanctification. Such therapy is limited in what it can achieve. The Holy Spirit, the divine counsellor, who comes alongside us to comfort, encourage and challenge promises to lead us into the truth.

Humanistic therapies

As mentioned earlier in Chapter 8, in reaction to Freud's pessimism and resignation, Carl Rogers and others in America developed a more optimistic vision of man with greater hope of change and wholeness. Rogers believed that by listening to a 'client's' problems, whether present or past, with 'genuineness, empathy and warmth' and real 'acceptance' then they would normally find their own answers to their questions. This is surely a description of part of what it means to love one's neighbour. His emphasis on really listening to people and attempting to step inside their shoes and to see the world as they see it is a basic lesson in counselling. Too often we prescribe cures and pronounce judgement before we have really understood a person's problems. However, because of his implicit faith in man's innate goodness and ability to move naturally in positive directions he was also responsible for the belief that counsellors should remain completely neutral and 'non-directive'. It is now being increasingly accepted that it is impossible for any therapist or counsellor to be neutral. Even Rogers has a belief about human nature and a theory about the cause of psychological problems. All therapists will attempt to help their client or patient to make sense of their distress in terms of that theory. This will involve suggestions for ways of changing their situation so that stress is reduced. It is certainly best for someone to discover for themselves what is wrong but there are ways of being gently 'non-directively directive!' And for some people very firm 'directiveness' is necessary.

A combination of psychoanalytical ideas with Rogers' techniques and optimism and other ideas from eastern and western philosophy has given birth to an enormous number of 'therapies' . . . transactional analysis, gestalt therapy, psychodrama, bio-energetics . . . the list is endless. All of these provide a theory and a particular technique which help people to 'get in touch with' present conflicts and usually relate them back into the past. This means becoming more aware of the source of conflicts and expressing some of the emotions generated, with the aim of gaining understanding, and experiencing cathartic release of pent-up feelings. Again, there is a mixture of helpful and unhelpful, good and bad beliefs, insights and techniques.

Partial truths and false beliefs

Some Christians would say that there is no value in any of the insights of secular counselling and psychotherapy at all. But as we saw in Chapter 7, just as man in all other areas of science discovers truths about the way we are made, so in this area too we have to separate false beliefs about the nature of men from the helpful insights of secular therapy. For example, most of the newer therapies, gestalt therapy, bio-energetics etc. were developed by humanists with a very optimistic view of human nature. They believe man is essentially good and that through self-understanding he can develop towards perfection. No-one can tell anyone else what is more important than change of attitudes. Forgiveness is rarely mentioned. There is no need for a belief in God, except some would say that we are all God if we could only recognise it.

However, if separated from these assumptions and if used within a clear Christian framework then some of the techniques and ideas are useful in helping people to become aware of repressed conflicts and to make sense of confused emotions.

Does psychotherapy work?

Until recent years there have been few studies that have shown that psychotherapy and counselling have any demonstrable helpful effect. In fact, a number of studies in the fifties claimed that psychotherapy had no more beneficial effect than being on a waiting list for psychotherapy! But more recent studies are more optimistic. In the 1978 edition of the *Handbook of Psychotherapy and Behaviour Change* the authors write:

> In contrast to the chapter on this topic in the previous edition of the Handbook, wherein it was concluded that psychotherapy had an average effect that was

modestly positive, recent outcome data look more favourable. A growing number of controlled outcome studies are analysing a wide variety of therapies. These findings generally yield clearly positive results when compared with no treatment, wait-list, and placebo or pseudotherapies . . . Our review of the empirical assessment of a broad range of verbal psychotherapies leads us to conclude that these methods are worthwhile when practised by wise and stable therapists.[6]

To test whether psychotherapy works is a very difficult task because of the number of different factors involved. Different problems and people need different approaches, and often at different stages in recovering from a breakdown, different approaches will be relevant. As we have seen psychoanalysis focuses on the past, gestalt therapy focuses on the present and behaviour therapy focuses on helping someone to change unhelpful habits of thinking, feeling and behaving. All three can be linked together and used at appropriate stages of therapy. Understanding the root of the problem in the past may be enough to help someone to change. But often people will say 'I have been over the past again and again and although it is valuable to understand why I am like this I don't seem to be able to change.' Recent therapies have recognised this problem and have directed their attention to helping people to go beyond mere understanding and to change their patterns of thinking and feeling. For example 'cognitive therapy', the 'nouthetic' counselling of Jay Adams[7] and 'behaviour therapy' all tend to focus on this half of the problem.

Working for change

This new emphasis on actively helping people to change may explain why research studies are beginning to demonstrate the positive results of some forms of psychotherapy. In particular 'cognitive therapy' has recently been found to be more successful in helping with depression than treatment with antidepressants alone or no treatment at all.[8] This particular form of counselling fits well within the Christian framework that I have outlined in earlier chapters because it focuses on the need for change in attitudes and beliefs in order for significant change in emotions and behaviour to occur. It emphasizes talking to oneself as David did in Psalm 42– 'Why are you cast down, O my soul?' Cognitive therapy encourages patients to test out negative beliefs and assumptions about themselves and the world by talking openly about them and by trying out alternative ways of thinking and acting. We saw in Chapter 2 that things that happened to us have their affect not only because of the events themselves but because of the meaning that the events have for us. People who get depressed easily have been shown to have a tendency to see situations in negative terms, often with recurrent themes of rejection, failure, loss and punishment. These 'automatic thoughts' are like tape recordings which switch on as a reflex response to certain situations.

Automatic thoughts

It is usually such negative thoughts which pre-dispose to depression, but it is important to note that in some forms of depression, and especially as the depression gets worse, negative thoughts arise from the depressive process itself, perhaps as a result of changes in brain chemistry. Often these are gross exaggerations of pre-existing mild negative tendencies. In order to help someone become aware of other options and alternatives to the 'automatic thoughts' it is necessary to analyse a number of common situations in their life in considerable detail. Often people under stress find it difficult to see more than one option open to them.

When a bull is chasing me across a field I will probably see only one escape route whereas an observer on the other side of the fence may see several options open to me! So it is important to be able to step back and consider possible strategies of response to situations that occur frequently in life from a distance and without the emotional involvement of the actual event.

Take, for example, a wife whose husband arrives home from work, tense and irritable and immediately begins to clean up the living room. What is her reaction? Anger? – 'Nothing I ever do is right. Why does he always find fault with everything I do? I'll show him.' Door slams and vicious circle of tension is well under way. Depression? – 'I'm a useless wife what's the point of everything? I'll never live up to his standards.' She retreats to bedroom to cry. Notice first that both of these statements may have a grain of truth in them but they are extremely exaggerated and contain a number of words like useless, never, always, and everything! To prevent the vicious circles of anger and depression beginning, the wife might consider alternatives to her original thoughts. 'He realised I had a bad day, and is only trying to help!' or 'He's just finished seeing a difficult client and is very tense. He will calm down soon if I ignore him and just get the supper as usual.' Or 'I can understand he is finding it a bit difficult. I've been wanting to get around to cleaning it up myself, but with phone calls, and visitors, I never got around to it. I'll apologise and help him.' Or finally 'He is trying to tell me something indirectly – that the house is a mess. Even if I'm not too good at that I know he respects me for other things I do.'

Another example is seen in my reactions to a fellow lecturer who asks me to stand in for him at the last minute. My gut response would probably be a combination of anger and panic. Anger because my 'automatic thought' would be 'he has asked me because he thinks I am too weak to say no.' Or panic because my 'automatic thought' would be 'I will do it badly and make a fool of myself.' On reflection a number of alternative reactions emerge. Instead of suspecting me of being too weak to say no, perhaps he has confidence in my ability to do well, or perhaps there is nobody else available and then of course I did ask him to fill in for me at short notice last year. Or, instead of thinking I will make a fool of myself, I realise that in fact it is quite an easy topic to teach, and anyway the students will realise I'm standing in and will not expect a first class presentation. If it goes reasonably well I may gain considerable respect from my colleagues. After identifying various possible reactions it is important to practice the new responses of repeated situations as often as possible so that they become more automatic.[9]

Phil set very high standards for herself. Her life was lived with an image in her mind of an 'ideal self'–the person she would like to be or perhaps felt she ought to be. Her mother and grandmother were both extremely efficient, capable and anxious women. Subconsciously they had become her major 'role models' for her life. Whenever she was busy 'doing something', achieving some goal, she was reasonably content although it was very demanding and exhausting for those around her. She could never sit down and relax for more than a few minutes before she would notice something else that needed doing. Every few days or weeks she would become painfully aware that she was not living up to her own image of who she would like to be and would then collapse in a heap of self recrimination and self-pity, feeling useless and hopeless. Her problem was an extreme example of what we all do to some degree – she lived in the extremes of on the one hand idealism and on the other hand cynicism and despair. Somehow she had to learn that her automatic extreme thoughts were a complete loss of perspective and hence the cause for her enormous fluctuations of mood. The reality and truth about herself was somewhere between the two poles. Her ideal self needed to be brought down to a place where at least some of it was within reach. She needed to recognise that we cannot be perfect in this life and God does not expect us to be. We can certainly move towards perfection but cannot achieve it. And when we fail we are still of great value and significance to God and hopefully to family and friends who love us, so that to wallow in self recrimination is also wrong. One of the major problems for those who live between these extremes is that they have learned to rely for their sense of identity and 'aliveness' on extremes of mood and activity. It is hard but necessary to learn a whole new way of seeing and being!

Social skills

Another area where understanding is not enough is in those who have become depressed because they are very shy in social situations and consequently feel an enormous sense of failure when comparing themselves with their peers. They are often lonely, isolated individuals who avoid rejection and failure by not taking risks to reach out to others, and they need a lot of help to break out of this vicious circle. They need a few 'success experiences' to gain confidence. One form of therapy, called 'social skills training' involves helping such people to practice taking risks by rehearsing the situations that they fear as one might rehearse a scene in a play. Practicing going for a job interview, joining in a conversation with a group of people or learning simple conversational skills like what one says after 'hello, how are you?' Ideally, in a fellowship group within a church those who are shy should be encouraged in their relationships so that they don't become increasingly isolated. But for a few who have never had the benefit of a good family or an accepting group special help may be needed.

In one study of depression, this 'social skills training' was demonstrated to be better than antidepressant tablets alone, and like cognitive therapy took only twelve weekly visits to the therapist to show significant change. So many people who see themselves as 'failures' slide into apathy and depression. A supportive group can be a real help in giving them encouragement and some experience of success. The authors of one study commenting on the success of the social skills therapy note that the women who were depressed may have been looking for support, encouragement, and warmth from other people rather than pills![10] One of the major ingredients of the healing process is an accepting, caring and sometimes challenging relationship. In these and other studies severe depression was found to respond best to a combination of antidepressants and psychotherapy of different types. Not only are we made to live in relationships, we are also biological organisms!

In these examples we can see that Biblical principles are very important in evaluating our reactions to situations. This is I believe Jay Adams' great contribution in demonstrating that the Scriptures give very practical advice on all the situations that we encounter.[11] We have already looked at some Biblical principles in relation to guilt, anger and self-esteem. We have to recognise that 'unrighteous anger' is not only 'unhelpful', it is sinful, as are bitterness, jealousy, pride and covetousness and must be dealt with as such before God and in relation to anyone against whom we have sinned.

Digging up roots or forcing shoots?

There are two extremes in counselling. At one end there are those who would sit down with someone who is depressed and after brief discussion enumerate the ways in which they need to change. At the other end there are those who will sit and listen for hours to talk of misery and woe and delve endlessly into the past to uncover the roots of the problem. Both extremes are unhelpful. The person who is depressed needs time to be heard, accepted and loved so that they will trust us enough to want to work with us to change things in their lives. For some this will take many months and years to change deep rooted personality characteristics and to heal past hurts. In others only a few hours or days are needed to sort out a particular problem in their lives. All Christians should be able to learn how to help each other with basic problems of living, but more complex situations often need longer training and some form of supervision by an experienced counsellor. There is a spectrum, from one end where much time is taken to explore the past, especially infancy and childhood, to the other end where the focus is on changing thoughts, feelings and behaviour in the present. As we have seen throughout this book I believe both have a place. Amongst Christians, Jay Adams seems to lie on the latter half of the spectrum,[12] and the primal therapy, inner healing movements are towards the other end, dealing with causes in the early months and years of life. Some therapies focus more on the mind and will, others on emotions and feelings. All are important.

Primal therapy – Inner Healing

In the last 25 years there has been an increasng interest in the possibility that children and babies may be able to remember events much earlier than traditionally thought. Arthur Janov (a humanist) in the USA and Frank Lake (a Christian) in the UK have developed counselling techniques to help people re-live the events of the early months of childhood, the birth experience, and more recently taking them back to the first three months inside the womb. Frank Lake writes:

> All the common diagnostic entities of psychiatric practice, hysterical, depressive, phobic, obsessional, achizoid and paranoid, have their clearly discernible roots in this first trimester (the first three months of pregnancy) . . . The evidence now available shows how severely the foetus can suffer at this early stage of its development. Most adults who have taken this retrospective journey recognise how closely the afflictions of later life, which had driven them to despair or near suicide are faithful reproductions of crises first encountered in the earliest weeks of their foetal life. Before birth the foetus may be seriously damaged if the mother is dependent on alcohol or nicotine or other drugs. It is also damaged by the less readily identifiable changes that transmit to the baby a mother's rejection of a particular pregnancy and of the life growing within her. Any severe maternal distress, whatever its cause, imprints itself on the foetus. These damaging experiences are now accessible to consciousness without undue difficulty.[13]

Although there is much that is helpful in Frank Lake's writings I seriously question his assumption that all psychological problems are rooted in the first three months of life in the womb, and also that in order to overcome these problems it is necessary for everyone to relive the 'primal experience'. For some this may be helpful and healing, but for many I do not believe it is necessary.

The ministry of the healing of the memories which is so popular in many churches today also uses various energetics to help people to remember and re-experience emotional pains. Ruth Carter-Stapleton believes that negative memories can be replaced with a positive godly reconstruction of those memories. She calls this 'faith imagination'.

> A woman came for counselling who had just attempted suicide. She said that total despair arose from her husband's unfaithfulness. What she didn't realise was that her extreme reaction to the infidelity was founded in the death of her father when she was two years old. His death had left her with deep, largely, repressed, feelings of male rejection. Her husband's conduct had confirmed her fear of being deserted by men.
> During counselling the woman was able to see and deal with this fear. Through the timeless miracle of Jesus she went back to her father's death. By faith imagination she was a little girl of two and she sat beside me looking at her daddy in the casket. But Jesus who stood beside her touched her father as He did the widow's son whom He resurrected in the city of Nain centuries before. The father arose from the casket and took his little daughter in his arms – she had her daddy again . . . In the new confidence that all men are not deserters, a new relationship could now begin with her husband.[14]

Although there is an impression from her books of dramatic healings and rather superficial use of what sounds more like the power of positive thinking, she accepts that cures may take many months or years because psychological insights are usually not enough on their own, there must be changes in behaviour patterns as well. Other healers, notably Francis McNutt, a Catholic priest, who is widely read and accepted by most Protestant evangelicals, focus on prayer as they delve into·the psychological origins of illness. He writes 'An hour is a good amount of time: 45 minutes to talk and 15 to pray . . . I find that most deep emotional problems go back into our distant childhood.' He has over his 20 years of experience increasingly recognised that healing takes a long time and recommends 'soaking in prayer'. I find myself in complete agreement with him when, for people with severe problems he recommends three aspects of healing–prayer counselling, being part of a Christian community and help with breaking destructive habits.[15]

The central focus of all these forms of therapy and healing is the attempt to make sense of present confusion and distress in the light of its connection with past experiences. The past can be brought to God in prayer, and anger, grief, guilt and other uncomfortable emotions can be faced for what they are. Then changes may have to be made in attitudes and behaviour which involve breaking old habits and resisting or putting off our sinful nature. For some this will take many weeks of gently helping them to face up to things they have never dared to admit even to themselves, let alone to another person. For others they will be able to deal with the past much more easily and quickly. Rita Bennett describes in her book *Emotionally Free* how, by asking people to imagine themselves in unresolved painful situations (past or present) and then to imagine Christ coming into the situation and seeing how he responds to the cruelty, pain and injustice they can see more clearly how they should respond.[16] 'I know he would forgive my mother,' said Susan, 'so I guess I should too.' Our deepest concern should be to know the truth about ourselves and the past and to see ourselves and others as far as possible from God's point of view.

Not 'does it work?' but 'is it true?'

There are some forms of healing and psychotherapy which elevate a theory about the cause of psychological problems to the status of a fact and thus impose on early events a particular framework of meaning which may not be true. Some would say that this does not matter much as long as the therapy works and is helpful. But there are many things that appear to be helpful in the short term which may be very harmful in the long term. For instance, I may gain great benefit by joining the Divine Light Mission and having an experience of 'enlightenment' with the Guru Maharaji but in the long term this will lead me away from the truth about reality and the truth about myself. The central question should be not 'does it work?' but 'is it true?' I believe that many Christians are dangerously naive in accepting as fact explanations of healing which at best are still only tentative theories.

Another example of the many views on inner healing, all of which have some truth in them is seen in Dr. Kenneth McAll's recent book *Healing the Family Tree*.[17] He believes that some mental illness can be caused by 'bondage of the living to the dead, whether to ancestors, to those not related, to stillborn, aborted or miscarried babies, or to those who once inhabited a particular place now occupied by the living' and claims dramatic healings after prayer for deliverance. His emphasis on the central themes of Christian healing – prayer, forgiveness, love for those by whom we have been hurt, deliverance from the power of Satan and bringing all our relationships past and present to Jesus Christ is very helpful. But there are some disquieting themes running through the accounts of healing. In the final chapter he elaborates his belief that the healing takes place because the spirit of the dead relative or ancestor is brought into a relationship with God by the prayers of the living, especially a Eucharist said on their behalf. My concern is that he is building a theology to match his experiences rather than interpreting the experience through the framework of Scripture. The idea that the living are helping the unbelieving dead into a relationship with God, and thus being released from their influence, is straying dangerously far beyond the bounds of biblical truth.

Should I see a Christian counsellor or psychiatrist?

This brings me to the question of whether it is necessary for a Christian always to see a Christian counsellor or psychiatrist. I have worked alongside a number of sensitive and caring non-Christians, social workers, psychologists, counsellors and psychiatrists, to whom I would have only a few problems referring a member of my family for help. They are people who would respect Christian beliefs and who would be very slow to suggest changes of beliefs or value. They are people who, although not Christians, have a strong sense of the appropriateness of Christian values and live within a Christian memory and heritage. Sometimes a 'good' non-Christian psychiatrist may be better than a 'bad' Christian psychiatrist! On the other hand as the Christian memory fades and humanism becomes the dominant philosophy in people's hearts and minds, I think it is going to become increasingly necessary for Christians to see Christian therapists. We have talked much about attitudes, values, and goals of life and these, as we have seen, may be different for the non-Christian psychiatrist or counsellor and he may encourage thinking in directions which are not at all helpful for the Christian.

It is important too to know the particular point of view of a Christian counsellor or therapist. With one there will be an emphasis on pre-birth experiences, with another inner healing, another sinful habits of thought or feelings, and with another an emphasis on the victorious Christian life and the sinfulness of depression. So whether they are Christian or non-Christian, if you have a choice find out a little about them first. Personal recommendation from someone you trust is probably the best guide in the end.

A slide into 'sickness'

As we saw in Chapter 1 there is a whole spectrum of depression ranging from brief down periods after disappointments or frustrations to the profound enduring depression where one's perspective on life is completely out of touch with reality. As someone moves towards the latter end of the spectrum their depression becomes more and more like a 'sickness' that needs to be treated by someone outside themselves rather than a problem which involves a change of attitude or circumstances. John White's book 'The Masks of Melancholy' is an excellent description of the illness end of the spectrum.[18] How do we recognise when someone needs more than counselling help? Loss of appetite, early waking at 2 or 3 a.m., constant fatigue, loss of interest, difficulties in concentration, general slowing up or excessive overactivity and agitation, and thoughts of suicide are all warning signs that professional help should be sought. Often it is possible to see that there is a change of personality, either an exaggeration of normal negative traits such as pessimism or selfishness or a complete change to the opposite personality. This disruption in normal patterns of functioning is a strong indicator that the depression has become so extreme that it needs to be treated more as an illness than a problem needing only counselling or psychotherapy.

References

1　Condensed from *Winter Past* by Nancy Anne Smith. Used with permission. (IVP. USA).
2　D. Goldberg and P. Huxley. *Mental Illness in the Community. The Pathway to Psychiatric Care* (London. Tavistock Pub. Ltd 1980).
3　Richard Winter and Michael Whitfield, General Practitioners, Counselling and Psychotherapy *Update* 15 March 1980 p. 637-647.
4　George Brown and Tirril Harris. *The Social Origins of Depression* (Tavistock Pub. 1979).
5　Gerald Klerman The Age of Melancholy *Psychology Today* April 1979 p. 42.
6　S. L. Garfield and A. E. Bergin, *Handbook of Psychotherapy and Behaviour Changes* (New York: John Wiley 1978) p. 179-80.
7　Jay Adams. *Competent to Counsel* and many other books. (Baker Book House 1970).
8　I. M. Blackburn et al. *Brit. J. Psychiatry* 1981 139, p. 181-189.
9　Example from Dougal Mackay *Cognitive Therapy in Depression* S. K. & F. Publications Vol 1. No. 8.
10　A. S. Bellack et al. *Am. J. Psychiatry* 1981 Vol 138. No. 12 p. 1562.
11　J. Adams op. cit.
12　Ibid.
13　Frank Lake. *Tight Corners in Pastoral Counselling.* (Darton, Longman & Todd Ltd. 1981) p. 24 & p. 16.
14　Ruth Carter Stapleton *The Experience of Inner Healing* (Waco. Tex. Word Books 1979) p. 27.
15　Francis MacNutt *Healing* and *The Power to Heal* (Ave Maria Press. Notre Dame, Indiana 1977).
16　Rita Bennett *Emotionally Free* (Kingsway Pub. 1982).
17　Kenneth McAll *Healing the Family Tree* (Sheldon Press: London 1982).
18　John White. *The Masks of Melancholy* (IVP 1982).

CHAPTER SEVENTEEN

Marriage and family

Escaping From You

> Many times life has offered me
> the chance to escape you;
> not to run away with someone else;
> but just to withdraw imperceptibly
> – to become involved with my job,
> with my children
> with books or trips,
> with digressions of many kinds
> – all at the expense of my involvement with you.
>
> Perhaps I found it too strenuous
> to communicate with you,
> or feared for my own sanity
> if I became too deeply involved
> with your ideas,
> or I found that I didn't get through to you.
>
> Then came the temptation to escape from you
> – to take the easier way out,
> to be less involved with you,
> to spend less time,
> to tune out when you talked,
> to say, I am tired,
>> I have a hard time listening,
>> I don't understand (often meaning that
>> I don't want to understand)
> – to slowly divorce my inner person from you.

And because it begins so subtly
We would not notice the beginning cold
between us;
but our marriage would start its slow decline,
its gradual dissolution.
And the eventual destruction
would be complete
if neither of us noticed
that anything was wrong.[1]

This poem expresses clearly what I have heard from so many people who have slowly, often over years, sunk into a state of depression. For Christians, marriage difficulties can be frightening, because working through them may be very painful. Many, believing that divorce is wrong, withdraw from conflict and settle for co-existence rather than companionship, and forfeit the possibility of a deep sharing of souls and personalities. For the brave ones, marriage can be the place where the greatest growth occurs – each person seeking to provide an environment where the other can grow and be enriched as a person, each seeking to put the other's needs first. There will be inevitable times of tension, disagreement, forgiveness, and reconciliation as two very different personalities learn, over a lifetime, to get to know each other better.

Signs of strain

Often when breakdown of a marriage occurs, the first thing that anyone knows about it is when one partner becomes depressed, or when the children start to get into trouble at school or develop physical or psychological symptoms of their own.

Philip was referred to the child and family guidance clinic by his doctor. At the age of eleven he had recently started to wet his bed at night, and the doctor could find no physical abnormality. To the social worker who interviewed Philip he appeared as slightly nervous but an intelligent and well integrated child. Reports from his school showed that he had done well until the last year when his confidence and concentration seemed to be dropping. He admitted that things were not too easy at home and that his parents seemed to have been rowing a lot recently. His mother had been in hospital for four months previously after taking too many of her tablets. Father had refused to come to the clinic as he was busy at work and anyway he could not see how his presence would help. Philip's elder brother was apparently 'brilliant at everything'. When his mother came into the room it was obvious that Philip was not the major problem. Mother looked drawn and tense. She had not been sleeping well for months and was irritable, tearful and depressed. Her mother had died in the past year and her husband had been out of work for a while. Philip, the youngest of the family and perhaps less gifted of the two boys, tended to get criticised by everybody and he often used to lie awake at night listening to his parents rowing or his mother crying. His problem was just a symptom of his parents' problems. When Philip's mother was able to grieve properly for her own mother, and was able to begin to talk more rationally with her husband, her depression lifted and Philip's insecurity, that had led to the bed-wetting, disappeared.

Communication the key

When I was training in psychiatry, one of us would have to visit the general hospital in the city centre every morning to see the three or four patients a day who had been admitted after taking overdoses. A few were seriously depressed and tried to kill themselves. Most were in their teens or early twenties and were angry or depressed after a row with family or boyfriend. Many were wives whose marriages were in trouble. The overdose was a symptom of a problem in relationships, a problem between husband and wife, parents and children, boyfriend and girlfriend. There was a breakdown in communication and this became the only means left to tell the other person that they were desperate. They felt misunderstood and rejected. It often took several sessions of forty minutes to an hour patiently refereeing while husband and wife or parents and teenage daughter began to communicate again. It needed a third party, someone to come alongside, to help them to be reconciled to each other.

It was the realisation that change in one member of the family often leads to changes in all the others that led to the development of family and marital therapy. There are some therapists or counsellors who would refuse to see a patient without the friends or relatives who are most significant in his life being with him. They feel that there is little point in trying to change the individual because so often it is not his or her problem alone but a problem of relationships. Many times it is problems in relationships which have caused the depression, and then a vicious circle is set up when the instability and fatigue of the depression exaggerates the original relationship problem. Sometimes the partner who gets depressed has less problems in life than their spouse who seems sublimely unaware of the pain they are causing. Their insensitivity and unwillingness to admit there is a problem is a major influence in their spouse's distress. We noted earlier that many more women than men get seriously depressed. This may be partly due to the fact that most women tend to internalise their anger and frustration whereas many men find external outlets for their emotions. It is interesting that while there are more women than men admitted to psychiatric hospital, there are many more men than women in prison!

Because many marriage problems are solved when communication is restored and there is a renewed ability to understand and support each other, it is important not to treat just one half of the partnership as 'the patient' and ignore the other half. Both partners need to know what is happening in the sessions with the counsellor. After all they have to live with each other the remaining 167 hours of the week. Unless they are both prepared to change it is very difficult for one partner to make significant progress. If medication is being used or hospitalization contemplated then the spouse needs to know the reasons for this.

A wife's pain

At times a husband or wife may have become so depressed that it is impossible to work together with the counsellor or therapist. Then, the spouse, children, or close friends will need almost as much help as the one who is severely depressed and identified by the medical profession as 'the patient'. One woman whose husband had been through a deep valley of severe depression has given me permission to reproduce her long and heart-felt letter:

My mind was filled with questions, why this depression, what causes it? How much is my fault? Where have I failed in our marriage? Why doesn't he turn to me for comfort now? Why doesn't he even share his battles and doubts with me? Will he ever be happy with me again? How can I help him? Will this go on for ever? How can I stop myself cracking too? How can I protect the children from all this gloom! It was a time of uncertainty about the past, the present, and the future. A time of great sadness to see my husband in such distress. It was so hard to live close to so much pessimism. He was convinced he was living in a tunnel from which he would never emerge. I felt myself beginning to believe him. I began to think depression was normal for him, and the times of relative happiness were abnormal. When he was deeply depressed there were times when I felt desperately alone with my own fears and sadness. I seemed to become 'hard' and feelingless but I think that was just a defence against the pain. I could not suffer every agony with him. I had to maintain my sanity for the children's sake. When he recovered I found that I was still detached and emotionless and it took some months of reasonable stability before I could respond to his new found needs or love with normal emotion. I still tended to see him as 'a person with problems' needing my care and protection. I felt I was always lagging behind and out of phase in my responses to his moods.

Most of the time, during the depression, I felt cut off from him. He withdrew into his own inner world and became less anxious or willing to share. This was very painful as we had been used to a deep level of communication. Perhaps I demanded too much because it was denied. I longed to know what he was thinking. I longed for some demonstration of affection, appreciation, and sexual love. I felt guilty for putting such pressures on him when he seemed least able to cope. I probably made the whole situation worse. Or did I? Should I have left him to sit or lie in silence? Should I have asked all the questions on my mind and encouraged him to talk? My patience would sometimes run out and every few days I would probe for information. The response was delivered with anger, but I felt better for some contact again. How much should I have expressed my own needs when he was so pre-occupied with himself? Should I

have let him know that I was suffering too or would
that only have increased his overload of guilt? When I
did give voice to my anxieties I think he became even
more reluctant to share his worst thoughts, for fear of
upsetting me further. Nevertheless, I am convinced it
was better to know what he was going through –
better than remaining 'totally cut-off'.

All this time I had many bad dreams, food seemed
unappetising, and I suffered from a continuous
'butterfly stomach'. I would often disappear into the
loo and weep.

How much should I have protected him from the
pressures and responsibilities of life? Should I have
removed sources of tension and thus enabled him to
collapse more easily? Should I have encouraged him
to go away for a complete rest or would this have left
him with too much time for negative thought? Where
was the balance between expressing sympathy
towards his despair and expressing quite natural
annoyance and anger as he appeared to become more
and more self-centred? There were no definite
answers to these questions, and I had to try out
possible alternatives. It did not help to fuss over him
as if he were a child, but I tried to express
understanding and concern and sometimes I had to be
pretty firm with him. I guess some couples benefit
from expressing their anger. Both can ventilate their
resentments and frustrations and they are jolted into
making positive changes. I was afraid it might drive
him deeper into despair. His threats of suicide made
me very cautious and fearful. I had to be sensitive to
what I thought I knew of him. I learnt to take every
remark he threw out seriously. Earlier in our
marriage I had naively brushed aside his discouraging
words as 'exaggerated' or as the outcome of feeling
depressed. But I learned to listen and to question.
There were clues to the cause of the depression. I

learned to take any mention of fears, doubts, guilt, or remorse seriously. I would question him carefully if he talked of leaving home, of losing himself, of giving up, or of suicide. It was certainly worrying but there were often concrete reasons for such statements that we could do something about.

I learned too that I must not preach at him in reply to his sharing of feelings of emptiness, fear, loss of faith and hope. If he did want to hear my opinions, I had to tell him very carefully and sensitively.

And then the children. Their noise and activities irritated him, and his strange moods were very disturbing for them. His limits of tolerance were extremely unpredictable. The whole household seemed to be enveloped in a cloud of gloom whenever he was present. I think that when he was most depressed it was best that he stayed with a friend, others might have to be in hospital. As he improved I had to help him and the children to adjust to being together again. The children of course needed more of my time. I had to simplify meals, shopping, and housework to sit with them and answer their questions. The youngest asked 'why is daddy cross with me?' as if it was their fault. He seemed to do the very things for which they had been rebuked themselves. They were worried about me too, they could see I had been crying. How does one explain 'breakdown' or 'depression' to a child? How do you explain why he cannot 'just pull himself together' or 'snap out of it'? I wasn't even sure myself – could he choose to get better or was he a prisoner of his 'illness'? I had to be as honest as I could with the elder ones, even sharing some of my confusion. The youngest were satisfied with 'Daddy is not well'.

I don't think I would have survived without being able to share it all with a couple in the church. I knew they were praying for us and they were able to be more objective about what was happening. I could express my conflicting emotions and gain some confidence when I was doubting my own perceptions and feelings rejected by the one to whom I should have been closest. It was good to have friends in such desperate loneliness. I felt guilty telling them so much. I felt I was betraying my husband, but I believe it was necessary for my own sanity. And when it was all over I had to be careful to loosen those links and relate more closely with my husband again.

On reflection I can see that I may have built my existence too much around my husband and children before and when I later began to develop some of my previous interests and activites I found that I had more confidence in myself and this helped me to remain more stable in the situation at home. I also found that it was important to take every spare moment to turn to the Lord in prayer and to read and imbibe his promises in the Bible. The Lord's loving reassurances meant so much more than other human comforts. It was essential to do this, even at the expense of household tasks, which certainly piled up. And now we are out of that long dark tunnel. It is difficult to believe everything was so bad, and also difficult for either of us to remember all the details of what happened.

This letter vividly describes the frustrations and conflicts of living with someone who is depressed. Many men, whose wives are depressed, cannot understand their wives withdrawal into themselves and loss of sexual desire. They easily misinterpret it as rejection and may become angry or depressed themselves. It is difficult for someone who has never been depressed to understand the pain of the experience. They also usually think that it should last only a few days or at the most weeks, not realising that severe depression may sometimes last many months and that much patience is needed. Those who believe in willpower only and 'mind over matter' are the most impatient and experience intense frustration, especially with the slowness, indecision and dependency of the depressed person. There is often a strong feeling of guilt and responsibility for the other's mood and this leads to irritation in the presence of the one who stirs up these feelings.

Dr. Frederick Flach writes in *The Secret Strength of Depression*,

> The more intense kinds of depressive reactions can be frightening. 'My husband slept only two or three hours a night,' said a thirty-four-year-old woman. 'In spite of this he went to work and put in a full day. By the time he came home, he was wiped out. He often went into the bedroom, closed the door, and cried. I could hear him. If I went in to talk to him, he would accept my comfort for a while, but sooner or later he would get up from the bed and pace around restlessly. He wouldn't watch television or read. He never talked about suicide, but he seemed so upset I was terrified that he might do something to himself. He said he wouldn't. He said such ideas had never entered his mind. But I just couldn't understand why he was so upset.'
> 'I've been down, but I usually know why, and it rarely lasts more than a day or so. With him, it kept going on for weeks. I couldn't stop being afraid until, with therapy, he started to show some improvement. And even now, six months later, if he gets up during the night or seems a little preoccupied, I become frightened. I have to learn to trust all over again.'[2]

There is always confusion over how much a depressed person can help themselves and how much they need help from others and this can be sorted out to some degree with the doctor or counsellor.

The good wife!

We saw in Chapter 2 how a caring, confiding relationship is so important in reducing a woman's vulnerability to depression. Both men and women need to know that those whom they love, respect and value them, and believe there is real value in what they do, whether it be in cooking meals, looking after the children, cleaning, fixing things around the house or working outside the home . . . Much confusion and stress is caused by unhelpful ideas in the culture around us and sadly often by misguided teaching in the church on the woman's position and role in the family. It is interesting that depression is much less common in single than in married women.

Many Christian women are taught that their place is in the home and that they should find adequate fulfillment in being wives and mothers while their husbands are protectors and providers. However, there is considerable pressure from others, especially the feminists, to liberate the poor housewife (the very word implying marriage to her home!) from the kitchen sink so that she can find true self-fulfillment in a job outside the home. Economic pressures to maintain a comfortable lifestyle have only added to this.

There is some truth in both these emphases. Women should find fulfillment and take pride in being wives and mothers, but the feminists have rightly recognised the need for women to have a broader base for their sense of self-esteem. A woman has many other areas of her personality which are not fulfilled in rearing children, just as a man has other areas of his personality which are not fulfilled in his job. Men too have been limited to the role of 'breadwinner' rather than being allowed the full expression of personality as father and husband! Women have been limited to their roles as 'mother and wife'. Many women (and men) are caught in this tension and experience a major identity crisis. Commenting on the isolation and confusion of many Christian women, and I would add, men, Elaine Storkey writes:

> The Bible does not have all that much to say about 'women's roles'. It does not in fact teach that child-rearing and the care of the home are to be ascribed only to women; both parents are given the responsibility of bringing up children. Nor does it anywhere teach that women are subject to men. The only area where the 'headship' of the male is spoken of is in marriage, and then it is clearly as a headship of love and service – not of rule and dominance. There are passages about appropriate behaviour in worship where the male-female relationship is referred to, but we cannot deduce from these, as some would like to, anything about the kinds of job a woman might hold. It would involve considerable distortion of Scripture in fact to justify unequal job opportunities, unequal pay or unequal educational possibilities. The biblical point is rather that, regardless of sex, both men and women are called to exercise their talents to be more responsible servants in the Kingdom of God. Nor does it mention special qualities of 'manliness' or 'femininity' for the different sexes. Only one set of attributes is regarded as significant: the fruits of the Spirit.[3]

The Bible teaches that the *ultimate* authority and responsibility in the family and the church is given to the man but this does not imply that he is in any way superior. Men and women are equal but different.

Brown and Harris found in their study that a job outside the home was a significant factor preventing depression in women who have three or more children at home under the age of fourteen and who lived in London. Their study took them to the Outer Hebridies to compare women in a rural crofter community with the women that they had studied in London. In this island village, the wives were involved to some degree in helping their husbands with the fishing and also in the general running of the home. There was a significantly religious atmosphere in that many still attended church and there was a real sense of an integrated community life. They discovered that there was much less depression, but more anxiety about external factors such as the weather, which directly affected their corporate livelihood and safety.

The blurred margins between the roles of husband and wife and the sense of community of the rural crofter village seem to me to be much closer to the biblical view of the roles of men and women within marriage and their responsibility for others in the community. If we look, for example, at the 'good wife' described in Proverbs 31 we find that besides caring for her husband and family, she finds fulfillment in many other areas. She 'selects wool and flax and works with eager hands . . . she considers a field and buys it; out of her earning she plants a vineyard . . . she opens her arms to the poor and extends her hand to the needy . . . she makes linen garments and sells them and supplies the merchants with sashes.' She does not necessarily need to have a job *outside* the home to be fulfilled as a mother, wife and member of the local community.

Martin Luther was very aware of the need for his wife to have other interests outside the four walls of his home. She kept pigs! He addressed a lovely letter 'to the rich lady of Zulesdorf, my Katerina, Mrs Luther, mistress of the pig market!'

So, both men and women will be more vulnerable to depression when their sense of self-worth is exclusively dependent on just one aspect of their personality – either the woman in the home or the man in his role as 'breadwinner'. We must respect the differences and the similarities there are between men and women so that we can help each other to be more fully human. Too often, in the past, the church has resorted to 'sterotyped roles' of men and women with little emphasis on the similarities of being human beings made in the image of God. On the other hand, there is pressure in our present culture to blur the difference completely and thus lose the sense of wonder and joy at the original creation intention of men and women being made for each other – equal but different.

References

1   Ulrich Schaffer, *A Growing Love* (Lion 1977) Used with permission.
2   Frederick Flach, *The Secret Strength of Depression* (Bantham 1975).
3   Elaine Storkey, Feminist Signposts *Third Way*. Nov 1983. Vol 6 No. 10 p. 22.
4   George Brown and Tirril Harris, *The Social Origins of Depression* (Tavistock Pub 1979).

CHAPTER EIGHTEEN

Another family – the Body of Christ

A few years ago I visited a church in America. It was beautiful – and so were the thousands of people in the congregation. Not a hair out of place, not a blemish in sight. I felt that any kind of weakness or vulnerability would be embarrassing. The only black person in church was the cleaner who appeared at the back when only a few people were left after the service. The smallest fellowship group in the church had over a hundred members. If people were struggling with depression or marital problems they would go to the local Christian counselling centre rather than first trying to help each other. It was almost as if there was a denial of the fact that we *all* have problems and that we are commanded to bear one another's burdens.

There is a tendency in some of the bigger churches in America to professionalise counselling so that individuals in the church do not take up their responsibility for each other. In England we have swung to the other extreme and have, I believe, too few Christian counsellors. Perhaps the balance is between these two extremes. First, we must learn to help each other as much as we can, as brothers and sisters in Christ, as members of a body. Then the pastors and the elders of the church may be involved, and if the problems still remain, professional help should be sought. The real pastoral needs of the congregation can only be met if there are small groups (e.g. home fellowship groups) of approximately twelve people meeting regularly. This demands a lot of organisation in congregations where there are thousands of members. Perhaps churches should think of dividing into two or three different congregations once they reach a size of more than two or three hundred.

How then can the church help someone who is slipping into depression and also help the rest of us to be less vulnerable to depression! One of the greatest needs of those who are depressed is acceptance. They often feel that they are a burden to everyone and that others will be impatient with their weakness. God's gracious acceptance of us, not for what we achieve, but just who we are, should ideally be mirrored in our acceptance of each other. We should be ready to listen, to recognise that no-one's perfect, to share problems and pains and thus 'bear one another's burdens' (Galatians 6. 12). We all have great needs for approval and love. Carl Rogers was right to stress acceptance and listening as being a crucial prerequisite for healing and growth. He was highlighting one aspect of real Christian love. With the community of the church we can encourage each other and help each other to grow. We can also gently but firmly challenge each other in our Christian lives. As we have seen love is more than acceptance and seeks to help people towards maturity in Christ.

Teaching

In order to have our values and attitudes shaped so that we are less vulnerable to depression we need clear teaching from the Bible. This may be from the pulpit or in smaller study groups but we need constant reminding of who God is and what he has done and is doing in our lives. We also need teaching on the principles of God's law – the Maker's instructions – which give us guidelines for how we should live in God's world. And the pastoral ministry of the church is in helping people to apply these principles to their everyday lives and relationships. At times, a pastor, teacher and friend will 'weep with those who weep,' encourage and comfort, but at other times may have to lovingly confront, exhort and rebuke.

Worship

There should be a balance between teaching, worship, prayer, and fellowship. Worship helps to lift us out of our self-centredness to focus on the One who is the true source of our life and self-esteem. As we praise Him for who He is, we gain a clearer perspective of who we are. Worship is not just singing caressing songs for hours on end to obtain an emotional 'high'. Both mind and emotions must be involved so that we worship from the heart – with the whole of our being. Singing should lift up our emotions, but the content is as important as the music and our hymns and songs should remind us of the great truth of who God is and what He has done for us. The psalms are a wonderful example of the relationship of prayer, love of God's word, praise, thanksgiving and worship. 'Why are you downcast, O my soul? Why so disturbed with me? Put your hope in God, for I will yet praise Him, my Saviour and my god.' (Psalm 42. 11). We see in Psalm 8. 2 that praise silences the enemy.

Another family

The church should also, ideally, be a sort of alternative family. Unfortunately the car, and the demands of city life, and the increased mobility of many families, tends to make this very difficult. Some churches have been encouraging their members to move nearer to the church and to each other so that they can know more of this 'body life'. They have also encouraged people to commit themselves to working and living in the area for more than just a year or two because it takes several years for most people to build more than superficial relationships.

We have seen how one factor causing vulnerability to depression is the quality of early family life. Relationships within the church and within church families can act as an example for those who have rarely experienced and have become cynical about good relationships, such as those who have been starved of real love, have lost their parents at an early age or who have had experiences of deep rejection. Some of the people who come to L'Abri and work and live alongside our families say that the most helpful thing was not the study time or the lectures, important as those are, but just seeing the different relationships within the families. One girl wrote to one of the families:

> Amazing, isn't it, that it used to make me hurt inside to watch you with your children (particularly the father daughter relationship you demonstrate with them is oceans apart from my own experience), but now, watching you together gives me great joy and especially HOPE – ah yes, that families can be good and relationships can work and husband and wives can love each other and enjoy, really enjoy, their children. Yes, there is still a twinge of sadness, but overwhelmingly and increasingly, I just feel that it is a privilege to know you and share in your lives, play and talk with your children, sit around the meal table . . .[1]

Although none of us have perfect marriages or families or friendships, we can at least hold out hope that change is possible, that crises in relationships are not a sign of total incompatibility and therefore a recipe for disaster, but that they can be worked through and lead on to growth and real love and mutual caring. They may also experience something of what it means to be loved and accepted by 'parent' figures and friends within the church. Obviously they will not be able to have the same relationship as they might have had in childhood but it will make up for some of the loss. There will be a measure of healing of some of the scars.

An interesting study on homosexuality appeared in the *American Journal of Psychiatry* a few years ago. E. Mansel Patterson described the situation of a number of homosexual men, who within the context of a church had been able to experience friendship with other men within the fellowship who had given them approval, caring, and love in a totally non-erotic way. This in some measure made up for some of the difficulties they had experienced in childhood. Most of them had had very bad relationships with their fathers and in seeking for approval and affection from other men, in their teens, had resorted to relationships which quickly became erotic and homosexual. Nearly all of these men were released from the bondage to their homosexuality as a result. It seemed to be the caring, prayerful atmosphere of that alternative family, with a deep concern to help each other live up the biblical standards, that produced the change.[2]

Simple friendships can be an enormous help to many lonely people. I know how much my own wife valued the friendship of a wonderful motherly lady in the church that we belonged to soon after we were married. The Atlantic lay between my wife and her parents, and I was living a busy doctor's life! Some people have a wonderful gift of a combination of real love, care, wisdom, prayerfulness, and sometimes appropriate firmness when self-pity tends to take over. Churches which have a very youthful congregation have a hard time fulfilling this particular part of the healing role of the Christian family.

Some people have sadly been so starved of basic security, significance, and love they seem to have an inexhaustible need for attention and caring from others.

This is often a result of a mixture of deep pain at feeling so unlovable and insecure and also their own selfishness and unwillingness to take responsibility for their own lives. In trying to help such people it often feels as if one is walking a knife edge. Sometimes one feels desperately sorry for them and is able to sit down and listen while they pour out their problems. At other times one feels like shaking them and shouting 'why can't you pull yourself together'. There is no easy answer, we usually all need a bit of both in life and to know the times and seasons for each is a matter of discernment, prayer, and seeking help from a trained counsellor or psychiatrist.

Team work

We need to know our own limits and that too is something one learns from experience. Unless the person with the problem is really 'sick' and truly has little responsibility for his actions he needs to learn to respect the counsellor or helper's time and privacy. Sometimes we may need to lock the door, take the phone off the hook, and effectively tell the world 'today my need is greater than yours, unless I have time to recover and see my family . . . I will be of no use to you whatsoever . . . in fact you will have to help me!' This is where working as a part of a team is so important. When one has a day off, another can be available. This is why it is also helpful to structure regular meetings according to the particular needs – an hour or two once a week, once every two weeks . . . This is a means of the counsellor saying 'I will try to help you, in this hour I will concentrate totally on the problem with which you are struggling and we will work on it together. Unless you are absolutely desperate, that is the limit of what I can do for you until next week. Others in the church may be able to help by having you for a meal or giving you a job which will help to fill the time and be useful to them.' We have to learn to set limits and share responsibility for the good of the sanity of all!

Prayer

Praying for each other is also part of our responsibility to care. This should be a continuous activity of the church but there may be special times to pray for particularly difficult problems and people. We cannot ignore the instruction in James 5. 14-16–'Is any of you sick? He should call the elders of the church to pray over him and anoint him with oil in the name of the Lord. And the prayer offered in faith will make the sick person well; the Lord will raise him up if he has sinned. He will be forgiven. Therefore confess your sins to each other and pray for each other so that you may be healed. The prayer of a righteous man is powerful and effective.' Confession of sin is important for healing because as we have seen bitterness or wrong attitudes can cause physical and psychological problems. As we pray for healing, can we ever expect God to deliver us instantly and miraculously from suffering, depression or physical illness? Certainly we are encouraged to pray for it. But there are some mysteries in God's ways with us that we cannot fully understand. We are not told why he heals or delivers one person and not another. He works in us and with us in different ways. There is an amazing section in Hebrews 11 where the writer has been making a huge list of men and women of faith and he ends up:

> And what more shall I say? I do not have time to tell about Gideon, Barach, Samson . . . who through faith conquered kingdoms, administered justice, and gained what was promised; who shut the mouths of lions, quenched the fury of the flames, and escaped the edge of the sword; whose weakness was turned to strength; and who became powerful in battle and

routed foreign armies. Women received back their
dead, raised to life again.

Notice here a sudden and dramatic change:

> Others were tortured and refused to be released, so
> that they might gain a better resurrection. Some faced
> jeers and flogging, while still others were chained and
> put in prison. They were stoned, they were sawn in
> two; they were put to death by the sword. They went
> about in sheepskins and goatskins, destitute, perse-
> cuted and mistreated – the world was not worthy of
> them. They wandered in deserts and mountain, and in
> caves and holes in the ground. (Hebrews 11. 32–38).

Sometimes people are delivered dramatically from
depression and other psychological problems. Most of
us live with the scars and wounds of a fallen world and
know a measure of healing and change. Some are bound
in extreme forces of mental and physical handicap and
have to wait patiently, in hope, until the Lord comes to
change them. Often healing comes in the form of a
change of attitude to our suffering. With others a
combination of medical help, counselling or psychotherapy which may involve healing of memories, support
and prayer brings about slow but sure healing.

Service

There are also many opportunities in the church for
serving others. Jesus is our example in 'coming not to be
served but to serve.' In helping others, especially the
elderly, handicapped, or unhappy, our own lives are
brought back into perspective. We become aware that
there are others with worse problems than we have.
There are people for whom we can do something. There
are people who need our care and love and attention. As
we have seen there is some truth in the fact that we need

to love ourselves to some extent in order to be able to love others. As we saw in Chapter 14, by loving ourselves I mean realistic self-acceptance not self-indulgence. But the converse is also true, as we love others we also learn to love and respect ourselves more.

As I mentioned earlier, all these aspects of the life of the church are most effective if there is a small group structure within the larger congregation. Many churches have home fellowship groups which relate back to the pastoral elders or leaders of the whole congregation. Tom Oden, in a critique of humanist group therapies and encounter groups, pointed out the similarities with John Wesley's class meetings in the 18th century:

> Puritanism is doubtless the worst of words in the encounter vocabulary. The irony, of course, is that it is precisely the pietist wing of the puritan protestant tradition (so strongly influenced by English Calvinist descent) which is being re-appropriated in current encounter groups. We hypothesize that the deepest roots of the encounter groups are in the least likely of all places; more generally in Calvinism than in any other religious tradition . . .[3]

He refers back to the time of George Whitefield and John Wesley. Their preaching, together with the formation of the small groups of men and women, especially working class, to encourage each other in the Christian life, bear one another's burdens, and confess their sins to each other, was one of the major factors in bringing about the evangelical awakening in 18th century England. John Wesley wrote:

> I desired a small number to spend an hour with me every Monday morning. My design was not only to incite them to love one another more, but also to have

a select company to whom I might unbosom myself on all occasions without reserve . . . We spoke each of us in order, freely and plainly, the true state of our souls, with the faults we have committed and the temptations we had felt since our last meeting . . . As we had a more intimate acquaintance with so we had a more endearing affection for, each other.[4]

Getting to know a few people well is a risky business. It may mean that you will be challenged by their life and example to change your own values and attitudes. So those who are scared of change, should keep their distance from other people! It is in relationships that we have awkward corners knocked off and the blind spots brought to light. It is in relationships that we learn the nature of love, of forgiveness and of self-sacrificing service.

So just as a good marriage is a protection against depression, so a caring church with good biblical teaching and pastoral care is another. But this is idealistic, few of us have the perfect church or the perfect marriage. Some of us find times in our lives when we are close to despair, our defences crumbling, and we fear that we will not cope much longer. Friends may be helpful, the pastor or minister sympathetic, but it may need the skill, sensitivity, and wisdom of a trained counsellor or psychiatrist to help to sort out the different strands of depression that I have outlined.

Realism about change

We must remember too that most episodes of *serious* depression last for a considerable time. Without any form of special help or treatment it has been estimated that they may last anywhere from six months to two years. In my own experience I have found, and other friends have confirmed this, that it takes a year or two to adjust to any major change or crisis in life. Being creatures of deeply ingrained habits of thinking and feeling, it takes a while to come to terms with change. And depression is often a product of attempting to do just that. Ideally we should take corrective actions to prevent ourselves getting into a vicious circle of negativity. We should be able to seek support and counsel from friends before we are sliding too fast down the slope. But for those who have slipped too far it may take much time and patience to help them climb up again. This involves willingness on the part of those who care, to commit themselves and their time, perhaps over many weeks and months.

A letter from a girl who stayed at L'Abri for a while illustrates the many factors which contributed to her recovery from depression:

> Even though everything is still up in the air about my future and there is a lot I must think about in regard to that, I 'feel' better than I have for years. It is I'm sure, partially due to these 'wonder drugs' I'm taking (I never thought I would be able to say that!). But I give credit to my time at L'Abri as well—even though it was a very difficult time (or should I say because it was difficult?). Dare I say I feel stronger in myself? I don't mean it vainly. I have still a long way to go but I feel more patient with myself and with God to get there. Before I left L'Abril, I didn't dare talk to this God we all talked about and around. I was afraid of not knowing, or feeling like He was really there, but now I feel more relaxed about that and more curious about what the Bible says about Him and about us, His image-bearers. (Yes, I'm even reading my Bible now and then!) Reading the Narnia books helped me have more understanding in combination with the tape I transcribed about the law in the Old and New Testaments, understanding truth a little more and

being continually assured that being human is what we're made to be and we will be who we are in eternity as well, only perfect. It's all rather overwhelming. I trust everything will be more and more clear as I think and study more. But you know what I realised when I left was most helpful? That when I was lowest and most depressed, struggling with hardly any energy left – you all didn't forsake me and give me up for lost (as I often did). You hung in there with me and tried your best to help. I realised as I was saying goodbye that I was loved and that made leaving worth it and it helps to comfort me when I miss you. I suppose this all sounds sentimental but that's the way it is. If you all could love me with the ugliest hanging out of me, there must something okay in there! And God, who loves perfectly, well, if that's really true then suddenly there's bushels full of hope.[5]

There has been much talk in recent years of 'caring and sharing' in the church, and this is an important part of the life of the church family. But as people have begun to share, many have been taken by surprise at the depth of pain and sadness and fear that they have uncovered. This concern has brought us back from a total pre-occupation with evangelism to a right concern for the healing ministry of the church. Both are important. This is an important change but it has given rise to a number of healing techniques which need to be infected with a consumer orientated, quick results mentality. There is danger of asking only 'what can I get from God?' rather than 'how can I know Him better and serve Him more faithfully?' Techniques of exorcism or instant healing, although sometimes effective are often a means of avoiding the costly, sacrificial caring for one another over months and years which will produce a much deeper and more lasting work of healing.

So we see that there are many aspects of the life of the

church which will help those slipping into depression and hopefuly build others up so that they are less vulnerable to depression and able to cope with life more effectively.

References

1   Used with permission.
2   E. Mansel Pattison & Myrna Loy Pattison, Ex Gays: Religously Mediated Change in Homosexuals *American J. of Psychiatry* 1980 137:12 p. 1553–1562.
3   Thomas C. Oden *The Intensive Group Experience: The New Pietism* (Westminister Press 1972).
4   John Wesley. Quoted by T. C. Oden in *The Intensive Group Experience: The New Pietism* (Westminister Press, 1977) from John Wesley A. Outler (Ed) (New York: Oxford, 1967) 180ff and J. Emory (Ed) *The Works of John Wesley* (New York: Lane and Scott, 1850, V) 184ff.
5   Used with permission.

EPILOGUE

A door of hope

A matter of perspective

'In the world's biggest airline disaster 482 people were killed last night as . . . martial law continues . . . 80,000 refugees, many dying of starvation were gathering in camps . . . the body of a girl who was brutally raped and murdered was found . . . a new study of the effects of nuclear fallout shows . . . suicide rates amongst young people have reached a record level . . . the number of divorces . . . abortions . . . children in care . . .'

The world has not changed much since Biblical times. Paul lived under a Roman dictatorship with persecution, imprisonment and death as do many Christians in the world today. And our hearts are still full of the same things that the Bible talks about – criticism, hate, pride, self-destructiveness, selfishness . . . it is tempting to crawl into bed and take a few tablets and be out of it all. Sometimes we wonder if God has given up too or even whether he is really there. Life seems as Woody Allen says 'to be divided into the horrible and the miserable'. Most people cope by shutting out the 'bad news' and hoping that everything will turn out all right in the end.

Our perspective on what is happening is vital to our sense of hope. So much depression arises because of a loss of perspective. Without realistic hope all is lost. This was the key, for David and Jeremiah, to the door out of the blackness of depression and despair.

I remember my affliction and my wandering, the bitterness and the gall. I well remember them, and my soul is downcast within me. Yet this I call to mind and therefore I have hope: Because of the Lord's great love we are not consumed, for His compassions never fail. They are new every morning; great is your faithfulness . . . it is good to wait quietly for the salvation of the Lord . . . For He does not willingly bring affliction or grief to the children of men' (Lamentations 3. 19–26, 33).

and

Why are you downcast, O my soul? Why are you so disturbed within me? Put your hope in God, for I will yet praise Him, my Saviour and my God' (Psalm 42. 11).

When they were down in the depths they talked to themselves, reminding themselves of the true perspective on life. When everything seemed to be going against them, they could not see things very clearly, but they clung on to the one whom they had seen in easier times to be the real source of hope – the only one who had a true perspective on the situation – God. It was in their knowledge of Him and in their trust that He was ultimately in control of things that they found hope.

False hope

In Chapter 4 we saw how Victor Frankl demonstrated that a sense of purpose and hope was a vital part of the psychological survival kit of prisoners in concentration camps.[1] We saw how people find some temporary sense of hope and meaning in career, possessions, family or in the search for self-understanding. Some put their hope in evolution and science, in self-understanding and taking control of our own evolution. Trotsky's original

utopian hope was in man's capacity to improve himself.
In 1924, Trotsky wrote:

'Man will become immeasurably stronger, wiser, and
subtler; his body will become more harmonized, his
movement more rhythmic, his voice more musical.
The forms of life will become dynamically dramatic.
The average human type will rise to the heights of an
Aristotle, a Goethe, or a Marx. And above this ridge
new peaks will rise.'
In 1965, two Soviet ideologists effused 'We have in
our hands a truly miraculous method of transforma-
tion, our "philosopher's stone" – the philosopy of
Marxism-Leninism.' 'With this,' they went on,
'Soviet society is rearing a man whose spiritual and
moral qualities are worth more than any treasures in
the world.' This alone, supposedly, can eradicate all
negative traits such as individualism, bourgeois
nationalism, chauvinism, indolence and religious
prejudices.[2]

Marx accused the Christian hope of being the opium
of the people – something that prevented them from
dealing with their real situation. Eastern philosophy
offers hope in a new view of reality where the ultimate
aim is to escape the cycle of birth and death and rebirth
and to realise our essential unity and identity with God.
Some even reduce hope to biology. 'Thinking rosy
futures is as biological as sexual fantasy; optimistically
calculating the odds as basic as seeking food when
hungry . . . Perhaps the promises of Marx, Mohammed,
Jefferson, and Jesus are engraved not on stone but in
chemistry.'[3] Many secular thinkers of the ancient world
regarded hope as a temporary illusion – something we
invent to keep our spirits up.

A basis for real hope

The word 'hope' is defined by the Oxford Dictionary as 'desire joined with expectation of getting what is desired.' We use the word with varying degrees of expectation of getting what we desire. I sense that in our culture it has become a very feeling-orientated word. 'I hope that everything will work out alright' without much certainty that it will. Perhaps our use of the word not only reflects a culture which lives more on feelings than facts, but also reflects the uncertainty of the world in which we live. The prophets of doom and gloom in the economic, social and ecological disciplines, together with the daily news of wars and murders, have shattered our illusions of a happy future. Biblical writers, in contrast, used the word hope with the meaning of a strong desire joined with a deep conviction and expectation that what they desired would actually happen. Their hope was not based on speculation but on belief in God and what He had revealed about Himself. There were good reasons to believe.

What is this hope of which the Biblical writers spoke so frequently? In the Old Testament we find Jeremiah reminding himself of God's character – that God is loving, faithful and just (Lamentations 3). Then we find David with hope in God's word–'I have put my hope in your word' (Psalm 119. 74, 81). In God's word he found an explanation of the purpose of his life–where he had come from and where he was going to. He also knew that as he obeyed God's word he would be living the way God intended him to live and so would be most fulfilled. God's word also told him of salvation–of the promised Messiah (Isaiah 8 and 9) and of life after death (Job 19. 25-27, Psalm 16. 8-11).

In the New Testament the same themes recur but in much more detail. Again and again the theme of hope is sounded in the context of encouragement in trial and difficulty. We are encouraged repeatedly to get our perspective right, to look up and beyond the immediate situation, to see the wood from the trees. So easily we lose perspective and fall into cynicism and despair or we become unrealistically idealistic and swing back into pessimism when we fail to reach our goals. So, like David, we must talk to ourselves and remind ourselves of the biblical perspective on suffering.

Paul, in the middle of all his hardships and troubles says that he is 'sorrowful yet always rejoicing.' (2 Corinthians 6. 10). In this broken world we will often experience two emotions at once, sadness at sin but at the same time rejoicing at what God is doing in us and in the world and at what He is going to do in the future. 'Rejoicing' does not always mean happiness, it is an attitude of mind which may bring a feeling of happiness. As Martin Lloyd-Jones says 'Seek happiness and you will never find it. Seek righteousness and you will find you are happy.'[4] So Paul encourages the Philippians to hang onto their new perspective of life and to 'Rejoice in the Lord always' (Philippians 4. 4). Both David and Paul knew that it was not enough to talk to themselves when they were down, but they should 'by prayer and petition, with thanksgiving present their requests to God.' We should bring all our anxieties and fears to Him in prayer and as we day by day remind ourselves of who He is and what He is doing in us we will know something of 'the peace of God, which transcends all understanding', which 'will guard our hearts and minds in Christ Jesus' (Philippians 4. 4–6). So the more we see things from God's point of view, the more we will know His peace which will set a wall around our mind and emotions and protect them from the extremes of depression, fear and anxiety.

The roots of sorrow

In earlier chapters we have seen that we are in a struggle against the world, the flesh and the devil and when depressed we have to do what we can to work through the different strands of our particular situation. We are caught up in a fallen world and deeply affected by it. Parents' neglect or abuse, an accident caused by a drunken driver, the horrors of torture, imprisonment and war may leave scars and wounds on us. These are the effects of others' sin and rebellion against God.

Our own sinful nature with its strong bias towards independence and rebellion against God may bring suffering through our own choices. Selfishness in marriage may lead to divorce and depression – not only problems for us but for our own children and perhaps their children too. We may bring suffering on ourselves by our neglect of the principles God has given us in His word.

But we are also told 'we wrestle not against flesh and blood but against principalities and powers'. We do not fully understand this aspect of the battle but we have glimpses of it all through Scripture. Job, himself, did not know what was going on in the heavenly places but we have the curtain drawn back in retrospect for a moment to give an additional dimension to his and to our struggles. Satan threw out a challenge to God. He would make His faithful servant Job curse Him (Job 1. 9-10). So God allowed Satan to do whatever he wanted except to take Job's life. Everything was taken from him, but Job remained faithful. We cannot see this dimension of suffering very clearly but we can pray for protection, and trust the One who said 'He will not let you be tempted beyond what you are able to bear' (1 Corinthians 10. 13).

There are two other aspects of suffering which I have not yet mentioned. Firstly, God's judgement. There will one day be a final judgement. But the Bible tells us that God judges individuals and nations, both Christian and non-Christian, to some degree, in the present. In the Old Testament we see God pleading again and again with His people to return to Him; He gives them many chances to repent but eventually judgement comes. We see Him also destroying nations who have turned their backs on Him. It may well be that we will be caught up in the judgement and destruction of a godless nation. In the Bible we see illness, famine, and death sometimes as a long term result of God's judgement at 'the fall'. Sometimes it is a result of our sin, so that I may experience the consequences of a sin such as stealing, cheating or sexual promiscuity in my own life. And finally it is sometimes a direct act of God–such as the death of Ananias and Sapphira described in Acts.

Closely related to this is a second aspect of suffering – God's discipline. When we sin and experience the consequences of that sin so that it causes us to turn back to God in repentance, God is using these circumstances to discipline us and teach us something new.

In your struggle against sin, you have not yet resisted to the point of shedding your blood and you have forgotten that word of encouragement that addresses you as sons: 'My son, do not make light of the Lord's discipline, and do not lose heart when He rebukes you, because the Lord disciplines those He loves and He punishes everyone He accepts as a son.' Endure hardship as discipline; God is treating you as sons. For what son is not disciplined by His father? If you are not disciplined (and everyone undergoes discipline), then you are illegitimate children and not true sons. Moreover, we have all had human fathers who disciplined us and we respected them for it. How much more should we submit to the Father of our spirits and live! Our fathers disciplined us for a little while as they thought best; but God disciplines us for our good, that we may share in His holiness. No discipline seems pleasant at the time, but painful. Later on, however, it produces a harvest of righteousness and peace for those who have been trained by it (Hebrews 12. 4-13).

When illness, death of a loved one, or persecution come, it may be a nasty shock to our pride, self-satisfaction and self-confidence. Martin Lloyd Jones wrote 'God's great concern for us primarily is not our happiness but our holiness'.[5] (1 Thessalonians 4. 3, Ephesians 1. 4). So difficulties and suffering make us face up to wrong attitudes, values and goals in life. Times of loss or frustration, as we have seen, may be times of change and growth.

Sometimes there is a simple answer to depression but often there are several factors interwoven with each other. We have to be aware of these different strands and possible causes of depression but cannot expect to see the siutation as clearly as God sees it. But we can pray that we will more and more see things from His point of view.

Living in a fallen world—with hope

As we have seen, some Christian teaching leads us to believe that we can reach a plateau experience in the Christian life, when we really know what it means to walk in the Spirit and be broken before God. Then, we are told, everything will go smoothly and easily. But that is not the picture of the Christian life that Paul paints in 2 Corinthians 6. 4–10.

We commend ourselves in every way: in great

endurance, in troubles, hardships and distresses, in
beating, imprisonments and riots; in hard work,
sleepless nights and hunger, in purity, understanding,
patience and kindness; in the Holy Spirit and sincere
love; in truthful speech and in the power of God; with
weapons of righteousness in the right hand and in the
left; through glory and dishonour; bad report and
good report; genuine, yet regarded as imposters;
known, yet regarded as unknown; dying and yet we
live on; beaten and yet not killed; sorrowful, and yet
always rejoicing; poor, yet making many rich; having
nothing, and yet possessing everything.

The image is one of struggle and battle. Again and
again in the New Testament Paul emphasises our
relationship to Christ and that we are accepted, loved
and received by Him. Then he goes on to say what effect
this knowledge should have in our lives. 'Resisting the
devil', 'putting on the whole armour of God', 'putting off
the old self', 'reckoning ourselves dead to sin', these are
active words – we cannot sit back and expect it all to
happen automatically.

Paul elaborates on the true Christian hope in
Ephesians 1. 18–19:

I pray also that the eyes of your heart may be
enlightened in order that you may know the hope to
which He has called you, the riches of His glorious
inheritance in the saints and His uncomparably great
power to us who believe.

We experience the beginning or 'first fruits' of this
glorious inheritance now, but we will be given it
completely when we are with the Lord. Peter writes of
the same hope:

Praise be to the God and Father of our Lord Jesus
Christ! In His great mercy He has given us new birth
into a living hope through the resurrection of Jesus
Christ from the dead, and into an inheritance that can
never perish, spoil or fade – kept in heaven for you,
who through faith are shielded by God's power until
the coming of the salvation that is ready to be
revealed in the last time. In this you greatly rejoice,
though now for a little while you may have had to
suffer grief in all kinds of trials. These have come so
that your faith – of greater worth than gold, which
perishes even though refined by fire – may be proved
genuine and may result in praise, glory and honour
when Jesus Christ is revealed. Though you have not
seen Him, you love Him; and even though you do not
see Him now, you believe in Him and are filled with
an inexpressible and glorious joy, for you are
receiving the goal of your faith, the salvation of your
souls (1 Peter 1. 3-10).

The consequence of this hope is that it changes our
attitude to suffering so that we can rejoice *in* suffering –
not necessarily *for it*.

We are hard pressed on every side, but not crushed;
perplexed, but not in despair; persecuted, but not
abandoned; struck down, but not destroyed . . .
Therefore we do not lose heart. Though outwardly we
are wasting away, yet inwardly we are being renewed
day by day. For our light and momentary troubles are
achieving for us an eternal glory that far outweighs
them all (2 Corinthians 4. 8–9 and 16–17).

Changed into His likeness

God is actually transforming evil and suffering and
using it to bring about change in us. Paul says that

'We . . . are being transformed into His likeness with ever increasing glory,' 2 Corinthians 3. 18.

C. S. Lewis emphasises this theme in a simple and beautiful parable he borrows from George MacDonald:

> Imagine yourself as a living house. God comes in to rebuild that house. At first, perhaps, you can understand what He is doing. He is getting the drains right and stopping the leaks in the roof and so on. You knew that those jobs needed doing and so you are not surprised. But presently He starts knocking the house about in a way that hurts abominably and does not seem to make sense. What on earth is He up to? The explanation is that He is building quite a different house from the one you thought of – throwing out a new wing here, putting an extra floor there, running up towers, making courtyards. You thought you were going to be made into a decent little cottage: but He is building a palace.[6]

This is the perspective that gives hope – we are being changed. There is purpose in it all. God does bring good out of the apparent chaos of this fallen world. In us the image of God is being restored right now. This is the 'mystery, which is Christ in you, the hope of glory.' Without Christ in us, there would be no hope in or beyond this world.

Many of us may have to fight against particular weaknesses or 'thorns in the flesh' for many months or years, but we do so in the confidence that we are being changed. We long for the process of sanctification to be complete. We long to be free from all that holds us back. But we need patience, and that is why Paul so often talks of hope when he is encouraging the Christians in times of trouble. He speaks of 'endurance inspired by hope' (1 Thessalonians 1. 3) and of patience when struggling against our sinful nature.

A door, a helmet and an anchor

There are three beautiful images linked to the theme of hope in Scripture. Firstly, God says to His people 'I will make the Valley of Trouble a door of hope. Then she will sing as in the days of her youth' (Hosea 2.15). This is a prophecy of Christ's second coming when He will bring restoration and renewal to the earth. Hope here is seen as a door out of darkness. Secondly, Paul writes 'Let us put on faith and love as a breastplate, and the hope of salvation as a helmet' (1 Thessalonians 5. 8). A helmet, the hope of salvation, protects our minds from despair. Thirdly we read 'we have this hope as an anchor for the soul, firm and secure' (Hebrews 6. 19). Hope as an anchor, gives us a deep security and prevents us from drifting onto the rocks.

Paul himself finds he is unable to explain the full implications of this hope and writes 'God has chosen to make known among the Gentiles (you and me) the glorious riches of this mystery – which is Christ in you, the hope of glory' (Colossians 1. 27).

Because we have Christ in us by His Spirit, we have eternal life now and we are being changed and will go through death (if He does not come back before that time) into the glory of His presence. There we will be renewed and restored and there will be no more death, or mourning, or crying or pain. This is our 'living hope'.

Wonderful Counsellor

And, in the middle of suffering we know that Jesus promised that he would send a 'Comforter' or 'Counsellor', the Holy Spirit, to be with us to encourage, comfort and sometimes to challenge and change us (John 14. 16–26, 15.26). We can also take comfort in the knowledge that Christ himself has been through more suffering than we will ever know. On the cross, in some way that our finite minds cannot fully understand, He bore the agony of the consequences of our sin. He not only suffered an awful physical death but also experienced the judgement that we deserve for our self-centredness and sin. In deepest depression we can remember that He cried out from the cross, 'My God, my God, why have you forsaken me?' So when we walk through the valley of the shadow of depression and even death we know that He has been that way before us. 'For we do not have a high priest who is unable to sympathise with our weaknesses, but we have one who has been tempted in every way, just as we are – yet was without sin. Let us then approach the throne of grace with confidence, so that we may receive mercy and find grace to help us in our time of need' (Hebrews 4. 15–16). The cross and the resurrection are the turning points of history. They are God's gracious response to our rebellion and to a broken, suffering world, making it possible for us to have a relationship with Him and to be 'changed into His likeness'.

Minds and emotions renewed

So, in this broad perspective of what God is doing in the world and in us, as we are daily tempted to slip back into the world's 'way of seeing' we need to be 'transformed by the renewing of our minds,' Romans 12. 2. The beginning of this renewal is a whole new identity based on the significance, security, acceptance and hope that we receive in our relationship with God and with other Christians in the family of God. As we begin to see things from His point of view, we realise more and more that our self esteem cannot depend entirely on what other people think of us. It must be rooted in God's view of us. When we feel like saying 'I'm a useless failure' we have to remind ourselves that that is a lie – the reality is that we are loved and accepted with all our failings. As we expose ourselves to the truth of God's word, our thoughts and attitudes are continuously challenged and renewed. We begin to have a new understanding of our value, purpose and place in the universe. We know something of where we came from and where we are going to and of the fact that we are being changed and restored into the image of God.

We begin to have new attitudes to ourselves (a right self-acceptance) towards others and towards the details and difficulties of our lives. Emotions begin to be stabilised as we are not blown around by circumstances or by other peoples' attitudes towards us. We learn how to handle anger, guilt, fear, anxiety, and depression more appropriately and sensitively before God so that we are not ruled by our emotions.

Our consciences too are renewed as we are forgiven for sin. Consciences that have been made insensitive by constant abuse are renewed by the Holy Spirit and by a growing awareness of God's standards revealed in Scripture. Consciences that are 'weak' (1 Corinthians 8. 4), over-sensitive or undersensitive, are refined, strengthened and made more accurate. False shaping of consciences by parents and others is gradually undone as we come to see things more from God's point of view.

As we daily, hourly, minute by minute, affirm God's truth about ourselves and our situation, our emotions will become more truly sensitive and appropriate and less and less the dominating and controlling factor in our lives – mind and emotions will work together in harmony rather than in competition or at odds with each other. And our hope is that when we are with Him and see Him 'face to face' we will be made perfect.

Something to celebrate

Christians through the ages have, in the shadow of the suffering of the world and in the light of the hope of redemption celebrated the great historical moments of Christmas and Easter which stand for all time to remind us what God has done and is doing in the world and in us. Just as Moses often had to remind the doubting and grumbling Israelites to remember how God has delivered them, so we need to have feast days, not only to praise God but to remind ourselves and our children so that we do not lose hope. William Kilpatrick tells how

Auguste Comte, who is generally credited as the founder of the religion of humanism, wanted to establish new humanist feast days to replace the Christian ones, which he was sure would die out. G. K. Chesterton, the great English apologist, professed disappointment that none were forthcoming. He would be glad, he said, for an excuse for another celebration, and 'could easily imagine myself with the greatest enthusiasm lighting a bonfire on Darwin Day.' But, of course, Comte and his followers failed in their effort.

Were Chesterton alive today I think he might profess the same mock disappointment with the religion of psychology. Whatever its other virtues, and despite its claim to psychic liberation, psychology fails somehow to bring out our festive nature. We do not – if I might extend Chesterton's analogy – exchange presents or greeting cards on the birthday of Dr. Freud or dance in a circle on the anniversary of his cessions or sing hymns on Jung Day, though Jung would certainly have approved. The memory of Pavlov does not put a spring in our step, nor do we let loose streamers or set off firecrackers in commemoration of Stimulus-Response Day. We do not eat roast turkey or pass the punch bowl on the Feast Day of Araham Maslow, nor do we decorate eggs and hunt for them on Human Potential Day.

Despite our faith in the theology of psychology, we do

not find much cause for rejoicing in it. We do not do so today, and it seems safe to say that two thousand years hence we still will not.[7]

Valuable as some of their insights may be, the humanist psychologist's belief that man can save himself gives little cause for celebration and hope.

As I write this final chapter it is almost Christmas and my thoughts have been playing over some of the great promises of Christ's first coming. I was struck by how little difference there is between our culture with its faith in man, its fascination with the occult and its awesome potential for self-destruction, from the people to whom the prophet Isaiah spoke:

> When men tell you to consult mediums and spiritualists, who whisper and mutter, should not a people inquire of their God? . . . Distressed and hungry, they will roam through the land; when they are famished, they will become enraged and looking upward, will curse their king and their God. Then they will look toward the earth and see only distress and darkness and fearful gloom, and they will be thrust into utter darkness. *Nevertheless* there will be no more gloom for those who were in distress . . . The people walking in darkness have seen a great light; on those living in the land of the shadow of death a light has dawned . . . For to us a child is born, to us a son is given, and the government will be on his shoulders. And he will be called Wonderful Counsellor, Mighty God, Everlasting Father, Prince of Peace' (Isaiah 8. 19-9. 6).

These feast days not only remind us of what God has done but also of what He is going to do in the future. So Paul, while encouraging us to 'rejoice in all circumstances' also recognises that we 'groan inwardly':

> We know that the whole creation has been groaning as in the pains of childbirth right up to the present time. Not only so, but we ourselves, who have the firstfruits of the Spirit, groan inwardly as we wait eagerly for our adoption as sons, the redemption of our bodies. For in this hope we were saved.

What a great image of childbirth! What woman would endure a hard and difficult labour without the hope that it would end in rejoicing as the child is born. At times we are overwhelmed with the pain and 'groaning' of this broken world, at other times we can rise above it in the knowledge of our great hope. Sorrow without celebration leads to hopelessness. Celebration without sorrow is out of touch with reality. Groaning without the hope of glory leads to despair. From the roots of sorrow spring the shoots of hope.

> And we know that in all things God works for the good of those who love him, who have been called according to his purpose. For those God foreknew he also predestined to be conformed to the likeness of his Son, that he might be the firstborn among many brothers. And those he predestined, he also called; those he called, he also justified; those he justified, he also glorified.
> What, then, shall we say in response to this? If God is for us, who can be against us? He who did not spare his own Son, but gave Him up for us all – how will He not also, along with Him, graciously give us all things? Who will bring any charge against those whom God has chosen? It is God who justifies, Who is He that condemns? Christ Jesus, who died – more than that, who was raised to life – is at the right hand of God and is also interceding for us. Who shall separate us from the love of Christ? Shall trouble or hardship or